Incarnate Word College, 1979

Lou

FROM BROOKLYN
TO BROADWAY

The Chapel of the Incarnate Word, with its landmark steeple.

Lou
FROM BROOKLYN
TO BROADWAY

The University of the
Incarnate Word's
25 years with
Dr. Louis J. Agnese Jr.

PATRICIA A. WATKINS

Foreword by
William G. Moll

MAVERICK PUBLISHING COMPANY

Copyright © 2011
by the University of the Incarnate Word

MAVERICK PUBLISHING COMPANY
P.O. Box 6355, San Antonio, Texas 78209

Design by Brooks Art&Design, Austin, Texas

Library of Congress Cataloging-in-Publication Data

Watkins, Patricia A., Dr.
Lou : from Brooklyn to Broadway, the University of the Incarnate Word's 25 years with Dr.
Louis J. Agnese, Jr. / Patricia A. Watkins ; foreword by Wiliam G. Moll.
p. cm.
Includes index.
ISBN 978-1-893271-60-9 (alk. paper)
1. University of the Incarnate Word–History. 2. Agnese, Louis J.
3. University of the Incarnate Word–Presidents.
I. Title.
LD2475.W38 2011
378.764'351–dc23
2011022538

1 3 5 4 2

Front endsheets: In this aerial view looking northwest in 1979, the Incarnate Word College
campus nestled at the corner of Broadway, lower right, and Hildebrand Avenue, left. Its
centerpiece is the five-story Administration Building, at lower right of center, built in 1921.
   Adjoining the campus at the far right are buildings of the Sisters of Charity of the
Incarnate Word, including the Chapel of the Incarnate Word and its signature steeple, which
has become a symbol of the university. Off campus at lower left is the USAA Building, later
purchased by AT&T. Incarnate Word High School is at the top left and St. Joseph's Convent
below it. Olmos Dam stretches across the top right.

Back endsheets: By 2011, the campus had been transformed as the University of the Incarnate
Word. New buildings fill in the old campus and stretch up Hildebrand Avenue past the
McCombs Center—one of the largest buildings—beyond to Incarnate Word High School—
now incorporated into the university system—and to the Feik School of Pharmacy, at top
left. Athletic fields, Benson Stadium, Barshop Natatorium, McDermott Convocation Center,
nine residente halls and four covered parking garages, including the nine-story Ancira
Tower, help fill once vacant land.
   Off campus at upper right rises the 200 Patterson condominium tower, above the Village
at Incarnate Word, the retirement home complex of the Sisters of Charity of the Incarnate
Word. At top right, the reconfigured Olmos Dam is crossed by US 281, which near the upper
left is itself crossed by the Incarnate Word Sky Bridge, a footbridge linking Incarnate Word's
eastern and western campus areas.

CONTENTS

Foreword vi

Preface ix

Introduction xi

I. THE NEW VISION
A Welcoming Campus Is Stabilized

1: The Presidency – Job or Vision? 3

2: Let the Bartering Begin! 13

3: Selling the Plan 21

4: The Sign Painter and the Man in the Moon 29

5: Inauguration at "The College" 37

6: No Mafia – Just Lou 45

7: Fickle Fame and a Bowl of Chili 53

8: Déjà Vu in Waco 63

II. GROWTH AND CHANGE
"Somebody Stop That Man!"

9: The Brainpower Connection 73

10: A Slow Boat for Balance 81

11: Flak Jackets and Texas Rangers 89

12: From A to Zoo 97

13: All Dressed Up with No Place to Park 105

14: "The Rest of the Story" 115

15: Johnny's Bridge 121

16: The Year of the Tiger 129

17: Blind or Blind-sided? 137

18: The Other Shoe 141

III. RAISING ALL SHIPS
A Mature Campus; A Mature President

19: A Mouse in the House 149

20: Where were You When...? 157

21: The Right Prescription 165

22: Build It and They Will Come 173

23: Bad Year at Goodyear 181

24: Still Undefeated 187

25: To Be Continued 195

Epilogue 205

Index 212

FOREWORD

The first word I spoke to Lou Agnese was *"No."*

The first lesson I learned from Lou Agnese was that *"No"* is just the beginning of the negotiation.

Lou's a good teacher. We found a way to get to *"Yes."*

From that inauspicious beginning we fashioned a collaboration that has endured for twenty-five years.

Lionel Sosa made the introduction in 1986, saying he wanted to bring the new president of Incarnate Word College to KENS-TV, where I was president and general manager, to discuss the idea of a trade-out agreement: television advertising in exchange for scholarships for KENS employees.

My response: "There's no need to meet. Harte-Hanks has a firm policy against trade-outs."

"Well then, let's just meet so you can get acquainted with Lou. I'm sure you'll want to know him," said Lionel, persuasively.

Lou's timing was impeccable. There's a pattern to that good timing as you'll read in Dr. Pat Watkins' superb accounting of Lou's first twenty-five years at the helm of this remarkable university. The Sisters of Charity of the Incarnate Word must have had an inside track to that angel shadowing Lou at just about every turn in his tenure at UIW.

In 1986 the Texas economy was in the depths of a recession, largely as the result of the crisis that brought down large numbers of banks and savings and loans. The television economy was negatively impacted, compelling us to reduce expenses. One victim of that cost cutting was our tuition reimbursement plan. We had been encouraging staff members to continue their education by reimbursing them for the cost of tuition. I felt terrible that we had to cut the program.

Perhaps providentially, Lou and Lionel walked in at that moment with an idea: Trade free tuition for advertising on KENS. Propitious timing! It helped that my former Harte-Hanks colleague, Charlie Kilpatrick, publisher of the San Antonio *Express-News*, had already found a way to agree to the plan for the newspaper. I, too, found a creative way to manage within the boundaries of the Harte-Hanks policy. We agreed.

Lou now had the #1 newspaper and #1 television station in San Antonio on board as advertising partners. Incarnate Word College was on its way to becoming what it is today—the University of the Incarnate Word, the largest

Catholic institution of higher learning in Texas and the state's fourth largest private university. It was a win-win for each of us.

Always quick to say "Thanks," Lou and the board of trustees honored me with the prestigious Insigne Verbum award, and an invitation to join the board. The timing was not so propitious this time; we were moving to New York City and it would be impossible for me to attend quarterly board meetings in San Antonio.

It was 2002 when Lou and the board once again invited me to serve as a trustee. This time it was an easy "Yes." (By then, I'd learned—as had everyone else—that you just don't say "No" to Lou Agnese!)

There are other important lessons to be learned from Lou: vision, determination, focus, leadership. No one is better at networking, whether it is a community of interests, or a local, state, national or global community. Lou's reach and vision are vast. And they are inevitably focused on the benefits to UIW students, faculty and employees, as well as the Sisters of Charity of the Incarnate Word. Not for himself, but for the university!

The greatest lesson from Lou is how he has become the epitome of the servant leader. That is the story unveiled in this book. It is Lou's journey from Brooklyn in New York to Broadway in San Antonio, told with humor, insight and candor. It is a story of overcoming personal demons and near failures; a story of risks and rewards; and a story of the Sisters of Charity, who were willing to stand with the president of the university when there was little more than faith to support them.

The Sisters' faith has been rewarded. The University of the Incarnate Word is thriving. The students, faculty, board and community are one. Accolades to the university and to Lou continue to abound, in recognition of the accomplishments of so many: the Ila Faye Miller School of Nursing, the Gorman Business and Education Center, the H-E-B School of Business and Administration, the Feik School of Pharmacy, the Dreeben School of Education, the Rosenberg School of Optometry, the Ann Barshop Natatorium, the Gayle and Tom Benson Stadium, the McCombs Center, the Alonso Ancira Tower, the Cardinal athletic achievements. I don't know where to stop!

Any one of these accolades and accomplishments would be sufficient to fill President Lou Agnese with pride. And no doubt he feels that pride. However, it is humility that surfaces first in this servant leader.

It is Lou we celebrate here, and that is fitting. But he would be first to say that none of these accomplishments over the past twenty-five years—or those before—would have been possible without the support, advice and temperament of his wife of thirty-seven years, Mickey Agnese; his children, Louis III and Nancy; his late mother, Nancy; and, of course, "Papa" Agnese—Louis Sr.—who remains embedded in the spirit and culture that makes UIW the revered place it is today.

You will enjoy Pat's delightful work. She writes with affection and the certainty of one who was there with Lou almost from the beginning, experiencing most of these stories firsthand as an insider. When Lou had the vision, she—along with so many colleagues—was there to carry it out, whether acquiring St. Anthony Catholic High School, opening campuses in China and Mexico, building schools of pharmacy and optometry or fielding a football team. The stories resonate with charm, personality and character, and even a few "Lou-isms!"

The gentleman with the Brooklyn accent has made his mark in San Antonio. Lou has earned the respect and admiration of his peers and the community. He has gone from being among the country's youngest university presidents to being one of the most respected.

We are proud to call him friend.

WILLIAM G. MOLL

William G. Moll is President and CEO of KLRN,
San Antonio's public television station.

PREFACE

If anyone is looking for *The Canonization of Lou Agnese*, this is the wrong book. I have known and worked for Lou too long to make that mistake. It is the story of an outside-the-box thinker, the college he turned around and the impact both have had on San Antonio. I wish I had been at Incarnate Word when Lou arrived, but it took me another three years to get there. Since then I have been on a twenty-three year roller coaster ride named Lou Agnese.

While writing this book, I discovered people remember things the way they want them to have been, not necessarily the way they really happened. I felt a touch of panic at first. I would interview three people, get three different sets of facts and three different outcomes. The stories were colorful and would have made good reading, but I somehow felt compelled to get it right.

Then the library dean let me set up office in the archives room where I could nestle in with the musty minutes of almost every meeting ever held—of the board of trustees, the planning commission, the Faculty Senate and its precursor, the Faculty Association. All the planning documents were there, also. Mickey Agnese, Lou's wife, called with the offer of the family scrapbooks. There were about twenty of them, filled with pictures, newspaper clippings, notes from friends and notes from some not so friendly.

I was getting facts, but I could use some context. Lou offered to let me tape interviews with him for an hour every week. Those were golden. Dick McCracken and Vince Rodriguez joined us most of the time. It was often more of a free-for-all than an interview. My thanks go to Dick for his humor and endless anecdotes. The next problem was how much to leave out.

Many people helped make the book a reality. You will read about them in the acknowledgments. But there are two people without whose support I would have been lost. Bill Moll may be President and CEO of KLRN, but in real life he is a cheerleader. Bill read every word of this book, laughed at all the right places and encouraged me to keep it light. "Don't write a tome," he would say. "Just tell the story, it's enough by itself." It didn't hurt along the way that Bill was an English teacher in yet another life.

And then there is Vincent Rodriguez. Vince and I sat in the same booth at the same restaurant every Wednesday until people were starting to talk about us. He read every word of every draft. He sat across from me for months patiently moving my periods inside the quotation marks, and saying things like, "Is that really what you meant to say?" or "It sounds a little awkward to me, but it's your book!"

Pictures were almost as hard to locate as the facts had been. With help from all corners of the campus Vince and I unearthed pictures from personal collections, old boxes in storage and from slick power point presentations. We wrote captions together. Vince added pixel counting to the many hats he was already wearing—proofreader, frequent fact checker and overall sounding board.

My thanks go to Bill and Vince for their support and for the friendship that grew from the experience. My final thanks go to Lou Agnese for not only letting me live this crazy ride, but also for letting me write about it.

INTRODUCTION

The roots of the University of the Incarnate Word were firmly planted in 1869, when three French-born religious women arrived in San Antonio from Galveston to establish the first civilian hospital in the area—the Santa Rosa Infirmary, today known as CHRISTUS Santa Rosa Health Care.

The three had come to Texas at the invitation of Bishop Claude Dubuis to care for those suffering from cholera and yellow fever. Upon arriving, they started a religious congregation, the Sisters of Charity of the Incarnate Word, which now has health care and other ministries in the United States, Mexico, Peru, Zambia, Ireland and Guatemala.

Early ventures in health care and in the care of orphans, of which privately operated St. Peter–St. Joseph Children's Home is a legacy, led rapidly to the need for the education of those in their care and elsewhere, in addition to the continued education of their own Sisters. The ministries in health and education were formalized by State of Texas recognition in 1881, when Incarnate Word was chartered as a center of higher learning for women.

The education of children from the inner city led to the formation of the Academy of the Incarnate Word. By 1909 it was the College and Academy of the Incarnate Word and had relocated to the sprawling acreage some three miles from the center of the city that was once the estate of San Antonio banker-philanthropist George Washington Brackenridge. Incarnate Word now had a commitment to education from pre-school through graduate school.

That rich tradition continues in the twenty-first century through the elementary and secondary school outreach of the Brainpower Connection, the management of Incarnate Word High School and St. Anthony Catholic High School and of nearly eighty undergraduate and graduate programs, including doctoral degrees in education, pharmacy, optometry, nursing practice and physical therapy.

It was no accident of history that the first graduate of what had become Incarnate Word College was Antonia Mendoza of Durango, Mexico. From the beginning, international students have been an integral part of the educational community at Incarnate Word. By 2011, international students from nearly 70 countries represented approximately 14 percent of the overall enrollment of some 8,500 undergraduate, graduate and professional students. Incarnate Word also had more than 100 sister-school agreements for reciprocal education in over thirty countries.

Considering the school's early history and orientation, it's no small wonder that Incarnate Word has a national reputation for graduating Hispanic women with master's and doctoral degrees. Or that it is the only college or university nationally to have produced five nursing graduates who achieved the rank of brigadier general and headed the nurse corps of the U.S. Army and Air Force. Incarnate Word is also regularly rated as one of the nation's top universities graduating Hispanic students with bachelor's degrees, a category in which it ranked first in the nation in 2010 among faith-based universities and second among all private institutions.

In the early 1920s, the college and high school operations moved into a single, five-story building that still serves as the Administration Building. By 1925 collegiate offerings in all areas were fully accredited by what is now the Southern Association of Colleges and Schools. The nursing program was established in 1929, and the first nursing degrees were awarded to two Sisters the following year.

In the 1940s, Incarnate Word took a leadership role in Texas and the Southwest by transforming the study of nursing from a hospital-based diploma program to an accredited college degree program. In 1942 the nursing program was the state's first to receive full accreditation from the Association of Collegiate Schools of Nursing. Today, a majority of those in Bexar County who earn either a bachelor's or master's degree in nursing are Incarnate Word graduates.

In 1950, Incarnate Word High School moved to its present location at US Highway 281 and Hildebrand Avenue. In that year a coeducational graduate division was also established, offering master's degrees in several areas, notably education and science. By 1970 the College had become coeducational in all programs, and for the first time offered on-campus housing for men.

Key to Incarnate Word's success has been the support of community partnerships and brilliant, visionary academic leadership by its presidents, including Dr. Louis J. Agnese Jr., a native of Brooklyn, New York, who in 1986 was inaugurated as its eighth president. Lou, as he is widely known, is a firm believer that a successful president of a Catholic institution must blend academic expertise with business acumen and anchor both in strong spiritual beliefs. By mixing a keen business and marketing sense with a clear vision of UIW's mission and its past, Lou has led Incarnate Word from being a small college with an uncertain future into a financially robust institution that is one of the largest private universities in Texas. While some have said that Lou brought Incarnate Word into the twenty-first century, others have astutely observed that what he has actually accomplished is to bring UIW closer to the twenty-second century.

It's worth noting that despite the many changes at UIW during Lou's first twenty-five years as president, one constant has remained: Incarnate Word is the educational and spiritual conduit for people who value an affordable, global education that allows them to grow in their individual faiths.

RICHARD J. MCCRACKEN
VINCENT RODRIGUEZ

Richard J. McCracken retired in 2005 as Dean of Alumni after a 41-year career at Incarnate Word.

Vincent Rodriguez has served as Assistant to the President/Communications since 2000.

· I ·

THE NEW VISION

A Welcoming Campus is Stabilized

CHAPTER 1
THE PRESIDENCY—JOB OR VISION?

It gets cold in Iowa. Bone-chilling, thumb-numbing cold. March 1985 was no different. Snow had been falling on the Sioux City ranch house for hours and it wasn't expected to stop soon. In the den, Dr. Lou Agnese was stretched out in the oversized lounge chair while his wife, Mickey, huddled under a quilt on the sofa bed. They'd had this conversation so many times there was a slight edge creeping into their voices.

"You belong in private education, Lou. Besides, I'm tired of sloshing through snow!" Shivering under the quilt, Mickey was adamant.

Lou and Mickey Agnese were looking at a career change that had taken an unexpected turn. Several weeks earlier Lou had interviewed at the University of Michigan-Flint, where he was immediately offered the position of vice chancellor. The university invited Mickey to visit the campus before asking for a final decision. About that time Lou received an exciting but complicating call from Incarnate Word College in San Antonio, Texas. "Dr. Agnese," the voice on the phone said, "I have some good news. You are a finalist in our search for a new president."

Lou and Mickey visited both campuses before heading to St. Louis, Missouri. Their destination was the Provincial House of the Sisters of Charity of the Incarnate Word, the Congregation that sponsored Incarnate Word College. Agnese would be visiting Sister Margaret Patrice Slattery, the retiring president of Incarnate Word, as part of the interview process and to learn more about the college she had led for the past thirteen years.

There was now a definite but soon-to-expire offer from UM-Flint, and an agreement from Incarnate Word's search committee to call at 4 p.m. the following Monday with their decision. The committee could not move until the Board of Trustees met and that meeting was scheduled for Monday. To Lou and Mickey it seemed decisions were swirling around them like that night's snow, and they had no more control over them than they had over the Iowa weather.

Both knew Lou's vision for higher education could best become reality in private education, especially on a Catholic campus like the one they had just visited in South Texas. In addition, they were both practicing Catholics. "One's a job. The other is a vision," Lou told Mickey. "Joseph Campbell said, 'Follow your bliss,' but it's not always easy." Mickey agreed with Lou, but couldn't help thinking about San Antonio sunshine.

Lou and Mickey Agnese with their son, Louis III, and daughter, Nancy.

Tension was high, and Mickey was in bed with the flu when Dick McCracken, the search committee secretary, called. It wasn't what they wanted to hear. Incarnate Word's board had been unable to meet. There would be more delay. With Flint expecting an answer that day, Lou thanked McCracken but reluctantly withdrew his name from consideration. He was moments from calling in his acceptance to Flint when the phone rang again. This time it was the chair of Incarnate Word's board, Dr. Amy Freeman Lee. Dr. Lee insisted that it was her fault the meeting had not taken place as planned. She promised to convene the board the next day and asked Agnese for another twenty-four hours. He was willing to try, but it all hinged on whether Flint would also extend their deadline. Agnese called Michigan and explained his situation. He requested a twenty-four hour extension, but made it clear he was prepared to accept their offer if the extension was not a reasonable request. Flint understood that a presidency was at stake and graciously granted the extension. The promised call from Incarnate Word came the next day with the offer for Agnese to fly to San Antonio and negotiate a contract.

The flu bug had now made its way to Lou, and by the time he arrived to negotiate he was doing so with 101 fever. Dr. Lee had arranged a welcoming dinner at a favorite San Antonio restaurant, La Louisianne, where flu and rich French food combined for Agnese's first San Antonio challenge.

The next day they drove to a private home, where he and Lee negotiated the contract with the help of Ruben Escobedo, a local CPA, and George Mead, an executive with Frost Bank. Both men were members of Incarnate Word's board, and Mead was chair of the search committee. Dr. Louis J. Agnese Jr. accepted the negotiated offer that March day in 1985 and, at the age of thirty-three, flew back to Iowa as one of the youngest college presidents in the United States. The change that was about to take place in his life fulfilled a goal many would have thought impossible to attain—being a college president before the age of thirty-five. Agnese had already achieved another of his goals—to earn his Ph.D. before he was thirty. It was part of his makeup to continually set goals. That in itself was not unusual in a young person; what was unusual was that he almost always achieved those goals.

The coming changes would affect more than just Lou Agnese. The story of Incarnate Word College was linked to the story of the Congregation of Sisters who founded and sponsored it. The board, the Congregation, and the faculty all knew this was the beginning of a new era, and there were no assumptions it was going to be easy.

The Congregation had spent the past twenty years working their way through the Update and Renewal mandated by Vatican II. The Sisters' internal renewal had led them to accept the reality of this new era. That included strengthening the role of their boards and entrusting their charism to lay administrators. Since a congregation's charism is the distinct spirit that gives a unique and identifiable character to a specific religious community, a high level of trust was required to deliver it into the hands of others. Now the board, with an affirming nod from the Congregation, had just hired a business-oriented president. Higher education rarely did that in the mid-1980s. There would be many changes, and everyone knew the long-standing rule—"Change runs counter to the rhythm of higher ed."

Incarnate Word was not unlike many small Catholic colleges that existed primarily because the sponsoring congregation kept them alive. The contributed service of the Sisters of Charity of the Incarnate Word, a program that returned a percentage of their salaries to the college, not only kept the lights on in the buildings; it built the buildings. This Congregation was particularly mission-driven. There was nothing flamboyant about how they ran the college. Public relations simply meant courtesy and good manners. Fund raising and advertising were not in their culture. They had taken a small step into that world with a campaign to build the Coates Theatre in 1980. However the combined annual contributions of the college's board totaled just $5,000 in 1984, indicating that fund raising was not a priority with the board. The business model this new president brought with him was fearful to some and attractive to others. But many perceived the college was near a crisis, and that reality made it easier to accept the changes that would come from Agnese's dynamic and unorthodox approach.

Lou, as all of San Antonio soon came to know him, arrived on August 4, with a Brooklyn accent, a slight stutter, and not a pair of boots to his name.

Was this really going to work? Amy Freeman Lee had no doubts. Neither, apparently, did the students, faculty, and administrators who turned out to meet him at the airport on that August Sunday. With mariachi trumpets drowning out words, Dick McCracken came forward. That handshake was the start of a relationship with someone who could give Agnese a valuable understanding of all that had gone on before his arrival. It was also the beginning of a friendship that would last the next twenty-five years.

The son of an Italian immigrant father, Agnese was raised in Brooklyn, New York, and was just leaving Briar Cliff College in Sioux City, where he was vice president for student development. The self-confident man who was moving to San Antonio bore little resemblance to the younger Lou Agnese who had found early academic life uncomfortable. In a recent conversation, a well-seasoned President Agnese leaned back in his leather chair and reminisced about that boy. "I weighed over two hundred pounds when I entered college and was so shy I couldn't face an audience. Even when I did, I stuttered so hard I couldn't finish a sentence before losing them. I still carry a picture of that young man in my wallet," Agnese said, taking it out and laying it on the desk. "I never want to forget that kid; he helps me remember what these students might be going through today."

Dick McCracken, known as "Mr. Incarnate Word," guided Lou through the early challenges.

Early in his adult life, Agnese had begun to act on the tenacity and dedication he had been quietly internalizing from his Italian parents. He developed a work ethic based on a belief that you leave a place better than you found it. If you immigrate to a country, you help make it a better country. If you choose a career, you dedicate yourself to it. Agnese had chosen higher education, and his commitment guided everything he did. He knew what he thought a college should be, and he had the courage—some might say the brashness—to try to make it happen. Having turned thirty-four in April, he was an educator with fire in the belly and he was ready for the challenges of a college presidency. Most important, Agnese wanted his life and work to have a positive impact on people. A college presidency offered many opportunities for that positive impact.

Lou Agnese was taking the reins of a small Catholic college that, in some ways, would need the difficult metamorphosis he himself was making. Incarnate Word College would have to be reinvented if it were to survive.

The college had been formally recognized by the State of Texas in 1881 as a center of higher education for women. In 1909 it moved to the sprawling acreage that had been the estate of San Antonio banker-philanthropist George Brackenridge. That estate was located approximately three miles from the center of San Antonio and was the site of Brackenridge Villa, a three-story Victorian mansion Brackenridge had built for his mother and sister.

The college remained an all-woman institution until 1950, when it began to offer limited master's degrees to a small coeducational population. It wasn't until 1970 that it became fully coeducational in all programs and began offering on-campus housing for men. It was best known for nursing, education, and fine arts—and for being the school "across the street from Earl Abel's restaurant."

Lou Agnese would be the college's eighth president. Although Bishop Mariano Simon Garriga had a brief tenure as the first president, it was Sister Columkille Colbert, usually referred to as Mother Columkille, whose thirty-seven-year tenure defined the role of president. Agnese has often said that in times of indecision he asks himself, "What would Mother Columkille do?"

Columkille retired from the presidency in 1960, but in no way relinquished control of the college. She became chair of the board, while Dr. S. Thomas Greenburg assumed the title of president. Greenburg served until 1970, but always in the shadow of Mother Columkille. The lore passed down is that he did not even have keys to his own office, located in the library. He had to wait until the library officially opened each day before he could start work, and he had to be gone by closing time. This somewhat strained arrangement was followed by a two-year period during which the college experienced a swinging door presidency. Dr. Sterling Wheeler, Dr. Earl Jones, and Sister Alacoque Power each served brief stints from 1970 through 1972.

It was Sister Margaret Patrice Slattery's thirteen-year presidency that restored stability and confidence to Incarnate Word. Without Sister Margaret's steady hand, it is doubtful the school would have survived the problems it faced in the 1970s and early 1980s. Agnese remarked later,

(L-R) Sister Margaret Patrice Slattery, seventh president of IWC, the Rev. Theodore M. Hesburgh, president of the University of Notre Dame, and Amy Freeman Lee, chair of the IWC Board of Trustees.

"Sister Margaret provided the foundation of what Incarnate Word is today, in spite of those tumultuous times." He was grateful that she would become chancellor after she returned from a one-year sabbatical. Sister Margaret had established the position of chancellor and with her insight had insisted that it report directly to the president, rather than to the board as some had argued. She anticipated the potential conflict of two high-level positions reporting directly to the board. Experience had shown her the responsibilities of the presidency could not be housed in two different positions.

Agnese was bringing more than brilliance and vision to the job. He had three secret weapons in his arsenal. Michaeline (Mickey), college sweetheart and wife of eleven years, was confidant and advisor, while five-year-old Nancy and seven-year-old Louis III added warmth, humanity, and humor to the presidency. With school starting in August, Lou brought soon-to-be second grader Louis with him when he arrived on campus. Mickey stayed in Iowa with Nancy to handle the necessary business of relocating the family.

Father and son moved into one of the dormitories on the campus, immediately creating a coed dorm. Agnese rejected the idea of a hotel or an apartment. He wanted to experience the campus personally, and he needed the childcare resources available for young Louis during the times he would be busy as president. A seven-year-old on the first floor of their dorm delighted the forty-plus young women, who soon made little towheaded Louis the crown prince of Dubuis Hall.

As he settled into the president's office, Agnese quickly realized the value of other Incarnate Word administrators. Marge Draeger had been Sister Margaret's administrative assistant for nearly five years. Lou took Marge to lunch during one of his visits before moving to the campus permanently. They discussed whether she would stay on now that Sister Margaret had retired from the presidency. Lou, with the candor and self-knowledge folks soon learned to expect from him, warned Marge that he was hard to work for; his last three assistants had each lasted only a year. Marge, not easily intimidated by anyone, eyed this young president and responded that she had been here before he came and she would be here after he was gone. Humor and honesty brokered a long-standing relationship that Agnese valued.

He was right about being hard to work for, but his vision was compelling and his humor made his impatience and somewhat colorful speech not only tolerable but appreciated. Never obscene but frequently profane, Agnese could drop a malapropism that would make Yogi Berra proud. Over the years those became known as "Lou-isms." He would sometimes grin and remind the listener that English was his second language. That was technically true, but with his command of language and intense drive to make a difference, Lou proved himself a persuasive and charismatic leader.

Marge's institutional memory and clear, practical approach to daily life in the president's office was invaluable. She also became the stabilizing influence for the "crown prince." Lou would drop his son at school each morning, and he would be brought back to Lou's office in the afternoon. As the mother of three grown children, Marge brought reality back to the much sought-after seven-year-old when she set up a small school desk near her own. Each afternoon she saw to it that homework came first, regardless of the more entertaining offers he had.

Two other gifts that came into Agnese's life were Sister Ann Finn and Sister Antoninus Buckley. Sister Ann was in charge of all housekeeping at the college and consistently anticipated the day-to-day needs Lou and his son might have. She was a practical combination of Mary and Martha in that well-known bible story. Sister Antoninus, affectionately known as Sister

"The Crown Prince" getting some study help in dad's office.

Toni, was the registrar for Incarnate Word when Agnese arrived. As registrar she was the gatekeeper for academic records, transfers, and transcripts. But Sister Toni carried more than regulations and grades under her white hair and blue veil; she had been at Incarnate Word a long time, and had been the confidant of Mother Columkille. She reached out to this new president and shared his visions for the future of the campus she loved so dearly. She was able to convey to him the rationale for Columkille's early decisions and help develop many of his own.

Sister Toni had an abundance of stories, some serious and some on the light side. She delighted in the story of Mother Columkille and the chickens. With a generous heart and a practical sense of survival, Mother Columkille would often allow families that were pressed for cash to pay for their daughters' educations in unique ways. Payment by chicken was not unusual. The Sisters ran an almost self-sufficient operation at that time, raising chickens, cows, and vegetables in order to feed themselves and the students. Mother Columkille reasoned they all needed to eat as much as the students needed to study. The barter system worked well, a concept Agnese would take to new heights in his own presidency.

Sister Toni also reached out to the Agnese family as a whole. It was her hand that held little Louis's while Mom was in Iowa and Dad was studying his new responsibilities.

Agnese walked every square foot of the campus, sorting out the assets and the liabilities. He had known there were problems when he came for interviews, but now, opening every door and every ledger, he saw the challenges were even greater. Enrollment was on a downward spiral. In 1980 there were 1,500 students; in fall 1985 there were only 1,298, and the trend was not expected to reverse. The student-faculty ratio of 10 to 1 was an academic delight but a budgetary disaster. As enrollment kept dropping, no one wanted to let faculty go, but the tuition could barely pay salaries.

Buildings had slipped beyond benign neglect. The roads were potholed and overgrown, and in some places they just gradually came to an unfinished end. The campus, no longer visible from the street as the oaks closed in on one another, begged for a reprieve from troubles. Even the magnificent Brackenridge Villa had burned about eighteen months before Agnese arrived. In short, an aging order of Sisters, who had already accomplished miracles in education, nursing, and childcare, were in need of their own miracle for the college. They were hoping Brooklyn had just sent it via Iowa.

Where to start? Agnese explains today, "I patterned my first goals for the college on its past strength as an outstanding institution of higher education. I explained back in 1985 that the need for Incarnate Word College was as great then as it had been when it first started." He added, "I had to be careful not to lose the essence of Incarnate Word while bringing it into a modern reality. It was the old baby-and-the-bath-water issue."

In a 1986 interview with *Today's Catholic*, Agnese identified a major part of what would become Incarnate Word's long-standing image. "This is a first-generation college," he told reporters. "As such it has been dedicated to the first-generation immigrant; and I come, myself, as the first generation of a family of Italian Americans." He did not want to lose the college's image or forget his own roots. The demographics were going to change, but the needs of first-generation students would remain a thread woven through years to come of planning, advertising, and fund raising.

Agnese began outlining his plans with the help of individuals who knew the school and San Antonio. He postponed his formal inauguration until March 25, 1986, in order to present the board with his plans, many of which would require almost a blind trust in this new, dynamic president. He was about to embark on a series of transformations that would bring him face-to-face with many obstacles, and he would need the cooperation of the entire community. Externally there would be supporters and detractors he had yet to meet. Internally he had already identified many he knew he could rely on. He appreciated the institutional memory and support of Dick McCracken, Sister Ann, Sister Toni, Marge Draeger, and others, as well as Sister Toni's watchful motherly eye that was always on Louis III.

Meanwhile, little Louis was encountering his own challenges. He had just been visited by his first great tragedy since discovering he was no longer an only child. It seemed peanut butter was not part of the cafeteria culture at St. Peter Prince of the Apostles School. What was a seven-year-old supposed to do with fish sticks and green peas? Sister Toni listened sympathetically to the description of those little green peas and made a decision. She began sending Louis to school each day with a "Sister Toni Special"—a peanut butter sandwich, fruit, and two cookies.

CHAPTER 2
LET THE BARTERING BEGIN!

O n the first day of classes in mid-August, Lou stood on the steps of the Administration Building with now-assistant Dick McCracken and stared in amazement—not at students but at a lake of water pouring down Burr Road through the front of campus and straight into the Fine Arts Building. Lou made a beeline to the building and found faculty calmly bailing out the basement rooms with buckets and cans. "It looks like this isn't the first time you've done this," he said, standing in ankle-deep water. "Every time it rains," they responded. Lou cancelled classes for the day.

Back in his office, a wet and irritable Agnese assessed the situation. He was sitting in one of the few buildings on campus whose roofs were not leaking. In addition those leaky roofs were covering fewer than 1,300 students. He looked at the budget on his desk and reflected on what he had learned since accepting the job.

During his summer visits Lou had met with the vice presidents individually. He asked John Ray, vice president for business and finance, to bring the college budget for their first meeting. John arrived ready to share information and support, but with no budget. "It just disappeared, Lou. I was about to print it out, but when I hit the button, it vanished!" Both men knew there was more to the story. Budgets of the sort Lou's business-savvy mind expected simply did not exist on campus.

By the time Lou was back in August, John had prepared a detailed budget. It confirmed the picture Lou had begun to anticipate. There was very little available money; the entire budget was only $7.8 million. It was obvious why money

Mopping up the Fine Arts basement after a rainfall – again!

Dr. John Ray, vice president for business and finance.

had been diverted from grounds and buildings—payroll had to be first priority. Even the vehicles used by admissions and other offices were old and worn. The newest car in the "fleet" was a well-used 1978 Grand Torino that was losing its attempt to age gracefully.

Lou knew there was no tactful way to approach this, but looking at the budget raised some obvious questions about his own contract. That contract gave the Agnese family a residence and a car. In early interviews Lou had stated his strong preference to live on campus; he knew it was the best way to monitor the pulse of a college. But the campus had limited residence facilities, so he was given two options. Incarnate Word House was the residence of Sister Margaret Patrice, Sister Mary Daniel, and Sister Ann Dossmann. He could ask the Sisters to move or he could choose a house off campus that the university would purchase. As Lou explains it today, "My parents didn't raise a dumb enough kid for me to evict the former president and two other Sisters." So a search was under way for a suitable house near the university.

"John, where is the money to buy the house when they find it?" Lou suspected he was asking a rhetorical question.

"There isn't any," was John's simple answer.

"And the car?" he asked, realizing if there is no Santa Claus there is probably no Easter Bunny.

"Well, the car agreement is for $15,000, so we can handle that." John was clearly happy to have a positive answer for that one. Lou rejected the $15,000. "I couldn't drive around in a new car while everyone else was making do with the old ones," he explained. "We simply had to find a way to improve the situation."

He replayed those conversations in his head that wet morning when his first executive order had been, "Cancel classes!"

Neither the residence nor the car issue had been resolved when the semester's first meeting of the Higher Education Council of San Antonio was announced a few weeks later. Dr. Ron Calgaard, president of the neighboring and elegant Trinity University, was hosting the meeting of local presidents. Lou had no choice but to drive to the meeting in the not-so-Grand Torino. Conscious of the image of the college he now represented, he parked in a lot as far as possible from the other presidents. He participated in the meeting and was congratulating himself on dealing with an awkward situation pretty well when Calgaard approached and said, "Lou, let me walk you to your car." Lou bit back an expletive.

Calgaard really did have something to say that Lou appreciated. Walking past the Mercedes and Cadillacs, he talked directly about the challenge Lou faced but told him Incarnate Word had one great asset every college needed—location, location, location. "You've got it, Lou," he said, "and there is no reason you can't make that school a real success." Lou knew he was right. It had been location that first assured him Incarnate Word had the potential to blossom.

Lou's academic credentials were mostly in the field of psychology, but his tough, creative business sense had little to do with academic training. He learned it—rather, absorbed it—from the family produce business in New York City. His father started that business with a single pushcart shortly after arriving in the United States as a teenager in 1933. Insight, hard work, and a heavy dose of moxie helped Papa Agnese grow that business into the thriving produce company that both supported and absorbed the entire family. Lou had watched Papa and his older siblings solve everything from cash-flow problems to mafia shakedowns, and as soon as he could contribute he was thrust into the heart of the business.

This was the experience he was drawing on as he looked at the $15,000 car allowance. That would buy one decent car, but he needed a fleet. Well, if it worked with Brooklyn produce, why not with San Antonio cars? Lou walked into Red McCombs's office with a plan and Papa's moxie. He needed four cars and two fifteen-passenger vans. He outlined his plan to McCombs, a successful San Antonio businessman who was also a major sports supporter. McCombs was influential in bringing the Dallas Chaparrals—now the Spurs—to San Antonio and later became owner of the Minnesota Vikings. Agnese wanted a buyback plan that was a little like leasing, except the college would own the cars. Since it was already September, Lou reasoned that he could use the cars until the end of that fiscal

Papa Agnese—the tall one—in front of his produce business in the 1940s.

year and turn them back, thus paying for only nine months of ownership. Red listened and agreed to supply the fleet, charging 1.5 percent depreciation per month and taking back all except Lou's car at the end of the period. Lou would keep his for the entire year. With that arrangement, the $15,000 bought the college a fleet of new vehicles for recruiting and general use in the community. Lou gambled that enrollment would be up by the time Red replaced the fleet the following year. He would be able to pay the cost for more than nine months the next time.

Years later Lou remembers, "That was the first success. It helped me, and it helped bring a fresh sense of pride to the institution."

By then Lou and John Ray were working closely. "John Ray was a very intelligent man who really knew the finance business. On top of that he had been here since 1972 and was as much Incarnate Word as the Sisters themselves," Lou explained. "He became a loyal part of my administration and stayed on until he retired in 1993."

The new cars presented an improved image, but the college still had very little money. The good news was there were no debts except the dormitories; the bad news was the endowment was only about $3 million, and that was primarily derived from the contributed service of the Sisters employed at the college. Under that agreement, 50 percent of the Sisters' salaries were paid back to the college. Shortly after Lou arrived, the Congregation regretfully announced that even that source of revenue would be phased out over the next five years. The Congregation had given years of service to the various entities they sponsored, but now retirement costs and the Sisters' medical and basic living expenses had to be addressed. Lou saw the rationale for the decision and couldn't argue with the justice of it. The Congregation had fewer Sisters of working age at the college, and they needed 100 percent of those salaries. Still, it was one more unexpected blow to the budget.

Spurred on by the success of the vehicle fleet, Lou exhaled long enough to outline a plan for the house. The family was eager to be together. Lou suggested to John Ray that the college buy a home with funds from the endowment, making the property an asset of the endowment. John liked that solution, and the board's finance committee approved it. House hunting became a priority.

The search proved difficult. The house had to be near the college and had to serve two distinct purposes—a home where a young couple could safely and privately raise their children and an official residence for the entertaining that is part of every college president's life. If money had been no object, there were many beautiful homes in the Alamo Heights and Terrell Hills areas, but Lou knew the property had to be in keeping with the nature of the college. It had to reflect taste and provide pride to the college community while not being so grand as to set him apart from the faculty and students he was there to serve.

While the house search continued, Lou was busy meeting as many people as he could fit into one day. Dr. Lee hosted a cocktail party for board members at the upscale Plaza Club in late September. Mickey flew down to join Lou since this was the first time he would be meeting many of the board members. They included San Antonio mover and shaker Lionel Sosa, the owner of what would eventually become the largest Hispanic-owned public relations firm in the country. Gifted in his field and as determined as Agnese was to make a difference in the world, Sosa had been on the board since 1982. It was Sosa who had designed the steeple logo that became the identifying symbol of everything Incarnate Word did for the next twenty-five years. In fact, that logo influenced the first public relations move Agnese made, even before arriving in San Antonio the previous August. He had taken the logo to an artisan in Sioux City and had hundreds of lapel pins made from the design. Lou gave out the pins like candy as he introduced himself to the community. Today new board members still receive those same pins at their first meeting.

Lionel greeted Lou warmly, excited by what he had heard of his background and drive. Lionel sincerely wanted to help the college and had grown frustrated by its reluctance to enter into more aggressive marketing. Lou listened intently as Lionel shared his thoughts, recognizing the value of what he was hearing. He told Lionel he would get back to him as soon as things settled down. Lionel read that as a polite brush-off and feared things would not get much better after all. Little did Sosa know he and Lou Agnese would shortly become a team as close as family.

In mid-October Incarnate Word purchased a house at 117 Canterbury Hill in Terrell Hills. From the street it had a cozy cottage look. Inside was a large multilevel structure with two distinct areas, one that could be public and another just for family. Finally, on Halloween day, movers in Sioux City packed the rest of the Agnese family and headed to San Antonio. The family moved into the Canterbury Hill house on November 4, and Mickey once more took over the organization of family, entertainment, and the making of those beloved peanut butter sandwiches. Canterbury House was less crowded but just about as busy as Dubuis Hall. Within a short three weeks, furniture had been moved in, and Professor John Lodek of the college's interior design program had helped decorate the house as Mickey and Lou wanted it—a home first but also a welcoming venue for the social events that had already begun.

While the family settled in, Lou continued his second round of meetings with the vice presidents. Now that he was really aboard, he needed to get to know his executive team on a personal level. He invited them each to spend a weekend day with him socially. During his visit, Hugh McCabe, former Holy Cross Brother and Incarnate Word's vice president for institutional advancement, suggested that Lou and Mickey spend a day in Austin with Dr. Patricia Hayes, president of St. Edward's University and McCabe's good friend.

That meeting proved to be a watershed event. Dr. Hayes graciously received Lou into the circle of local presidents. If truth be known, she probably felt a little sorry for him because Incarnate Word was not up there with the big players like St. Mary's University and St. Edward's University.

Dr. Hayes hosted the small group for cocktails at her home on campus and then for dinner at an elegant Austin club. During dinner she spoke about her plans for St. Edward's and how she would be using not-for-profit bonds to fund construction projects. She described how the projects would enhance the campus, which was already serving 4,000 students. Lou listened politely, but his mind was racing. "Not-for-profit bonds!" He knew instantly that Dr. Hayes had just shown him the magic he needed.

Lou knew a municipality had to issue the bonds, but he was not an expert in that area. The next day he asked John Ray to begin researching how to float bonds in San Antonio. Lou knew if this idea were successful, they had all just taken the first big step toward much needed facilities repair and restoration. He had to recruit more students, but those students deserved a campus they could show off with pride.

The visit with Dr. Hayes had another unexpected outcome. Shortly before Thanksgiving, Hugh McCabe told Lou that St. Edward's had lost its vice president for institutional advancement and was opening a search. McCabe wanted to apply. Lou encouraged him to do so, knowing a person had to be happy with a job in order to do it well. Not surprisingly, McCabe emerged as the successful candidate, and a national search for his replacement was added to Lou's already long to-do list.

By now it was December and the Administration Building was filled with its usual Saturday morning emptiness. Lou was deep in thought while five-year-old Nancy played happily in the long empty hall that smelled of antique wood and years of polish. Lou couldn't stop thinking about Sister

Toni's story of the chickens. He had become a master of barter in earlier times when the currency of the day was seldom cash. However, right now he was into circular thinking—he needed to increase enrollment quickly, and that required heavy advertising. Advertising required money, and money was the other thing he needed and didn't have. To get it, he needed to increase enrollment. He wasn't dealing with fruits and vegetables anymore, nor were there any loose chickens hanging around. It didn't matter, because no one was going to give him ad space for a load of chickens anyway. He was a good pitchman, but not that good.

"All I have is a lot of empty space where there should be students," he said to himself. "Just empty space." Lou kept mulling that over in his mind. He thought about that empty space and had a sudden but absolute inspiration. That empty space was not just any space—it was space in classrooms, space where someone could get an education, could have life-changing experiences. He was excited now. Let the bartering begin!

Lou began to outline a plan. In exchange for advertising space, he would offer the newspapers and TV stations the opportunity to send employees to study at Incarnate Word at no cost. He would enlarge that to allow them to send needy students to Incarnate Word on scholarships named for the respective media partner. This could be big. He needed someone who knew the players and who was respected in the public relations community to help him break through the barriers he knew he would encounter. He thought immediately of Lionel Sosa.

The Christmas season was already approaching, with its spiritual and social obligations. He would continue to massage the plan and ask for a meeting with Sosa early in January. Exhilaration started to replace some of the stress. As he leaned back in his chair, a small familiar voice broke through his consciousness.

"Your hands are really wrinkled, Sister."

"That's because I'm old."

"How old are you, Sister?"

"I'm very old."

"Are you going to die soon?"

Sister Raphael Eccell looked down at her small guest and said earnestly, "I hope not."

Lou was out of his chair like a shot. Here was a conversation that needed intervention. As he got to the outer office they were just approaching the door. Nancy was still happily holding the wrinkled hand of her new friend.

"Does this belong to you?" Sister Raphael asked Lou with amusement.

"Yes, Sister, it does."

Seventy-six-year-old Raphael still worked in the library during the week and helped out with the switchboard on Saturdays. Lou watched the slightly stooped figure, in her long, black modified habit and veil, continue down the hall. He felt renewed determination to protect this place that had been carried for so long on shoulders like those of Sister Raphael Eccell.

Camera-shy
Sister Raphael Eccell.

CHAPTER 3
SELLING THE PLAN

I t had been a quiet Christmas. Sister Toni and Sister Ann had joined the Agnese family for Christmas Eve and a dinner with Lou's special fish sauce. The sauce was an all-day cooking adventure, following his mother's tradition and dating back to when some Catholics observed Christmas Eve as a meatless day.

After dinner the Sisters had a surprise of their own. They introduced Lou and the children to the Christmas lights of Windcrest, a San Antonio suburb known for its stunning and extravagant Christmas displays. Mickey chose to stay close to home "in case Santa might want some help" putting gifts under the family tree. The Windcrest lights brought back a wave of childhood memories for Lou—memories of his father and two older brothers decorating the family home in Brooklyn with their own spectacular array of Christmas lights.

After making their way through the slow traffic procession in Windcrest, the group headed back to the Canterbury Hill house, stopping just long enough for Mickey to jump in the car. Her elf tasks were finished, so the four adults and two sleepy children continued on to midnight Mass at the Motherhouse Chapel. Nancy and little Louis knew with a certainty that they would find Santa's presents when they got home from Mass.

The priest's homily struck another chord in Lou when he referred to Incarnate Word as the "Christmas college," a place dedicated to Christ whose birth was being celebrated that night. Lou had noticed the campus was dark and almost dreary when they arrived for Mass. He made a mental note to talk to his vice presidents about making it "just a little more festive" next year. Neither he nor anyone else was anticipating the annual Light the Way event that would grow from that first quiet Christmas.

But now he needed to focus on more pressing issues. This was the beginning of the busiest and most critical year of his life. Within the next few months Lou needed to finalize his promised five-year plan for the

Lou meeting with students shortly after he arrived.

college, implement the first stages, and guide the results. Those results could assure a different reality for the 1986–87 school year. The timetable he had set for announcing the plan included a February 14 presentation to the internal community and a public presentation at his inauguration on March 25.

Lou had been laying serious groundwork for the five-year plan, meeting with students, faculty, admissions personnel, and other administrators and staff. Dr. Pat Lonchar, a longtime employee and current assistant dean of the School of Humanities, Arts, and Social Sciences, recalled the early reactions and expectations of many who were part of those meetings. Lonchar remembers the anxiety of the admissions staff especially. Since Agnese had a strong student services background, they were certain he would bring ideas and positive energy to the declining enrollment issue. On the other hand, they were just as certain his experience would easily identify their own weaknesses. The declining enrollment and general state of affairs had already caused administrators to begin using the word "retrenchment," and to nervous employees that translated as loss of jobs. The wolf was at the door of this small college, and some of its warmth and solidarity was being replaced with blame-laying and finger-pointing.

Lonchar vividly remembers a meeting in what is now the McCreless Room of the Administration Building. The new president asked each person in student services what they thought should be done. One by one they respectfully answered with variations of "Whatever you want to do, sir." In retrospect, Lonchar ruefully acknowledges they were simply confirming the reality that no one in the room had any idea what to do.

Lou already had some personnel changes in mind. But he knew a new president could seal his own doom if he walked in and swept away the institutional memory and years of service represented by current employees. He would move slowly and hope that most would embrace his approach or that together they would find a good compromise. Hugh McCabe had already accepted the position at St. Edward's but would be staying on to complete the year. Dr. Peter O'Connor, the vice president for academic affairs, was interested in a presidency at a small college. In fact, O'Connor had applied for the Incarnate Word position during the early stage of the search. Lou understood the drive to serve in that capacity and was willing to assist O'Connor if possible. Things moved quickly, and the January 6, 1986 issue of "This Week at The Word," Incarnate Word's internal newsletter, announced that O'Connor had been named president of Aquinas College in Grand Rapids, Michigan, beginning July 1.

The search for these replacements would start soon. In the meantime Lou had to give his full attention to enrollment and to establishing a structure that would help restore confidence in the college. He had increased his meetings with key persons on campus and had begun what would be an annual occurrence—an out-of-town retreat for leaders in faculty and administrative positions. The first retreat had been held at the Benedictine monastery in the small town of Boerne, about forty-five minutes from the college. That leadership group formed the Committee on College Planning that would help develop and implement the five-year plan.

Lou already knew he would have to change the administrative structure of student development. He was sure that even the vice president of that area, Richard Nicholas, knew help was needed. Sister Ann Dossman, whom Lou had declined to evict from Incarnate Word House, was Nicholas's dean of admissions, but she had recently announced her retirement. Lou decided to take two steps: he would announce that he was changing Nicholas's title to dean of student affairs, and he would hire a dean of admissions to work with him and support the area. By having the workload divided between two deans he hoped to ease what was becoming an almost impossible burden for one person. Lou also planned to bring in a consultant for Nicholas—Sister Sally Mitchell, longtime colleague and a friend of the Agnese family.

Lou first met Sister Sally in June 1981. He had just accepted the vice president for student affairs position at Briar Cliff College in Sioux City and had driven there from his home in Erie, Pennsylvania. It was a Saturday morning when he pulled up to the campus building where he would live until the family joined him. As he started unpacking his car a Franciscan Sister came out of the building and asked if he needed some help. After driving all night, help sounded good. Sister Sally grabbed an armload from the car and said good-naturedly, "I just want you to know I wanted the job you got!"

Sister Sally had been at Briar Cliff for fifteen years, first on the speech and drama faculty and for the last four years as director of academic advising. She had applied for the vice presidency Lou had just accepted. That morning began a friendship that has included Sally as a family member for the last thirty years. Lou took Sally back to Erie when he went home, and she bonded immediately with Mickey and two-and-a-half-year-old Louis

Young Nancy Agnese with "second mom" Sister Sally Mitchell.

III. But perhaps the deepest bond was with nine-month-old Nancy Agnese. Sally became Nancy's second mother.

She worked for Lou in student affairs until he left Briar Cliff in 1985. He and the family were grateful that she had agreed to come to Texas and help grow Incarnate Word's student body.

As it turned out, Sister Sally was a consultant for just two months. An intelligent and sensitive man, Richard Nicholas talked with Lou and made the decision to enroll at the University of Texas at Austin in June 1986 to begin study for his Ph.D. Dr. Nicholas later became vice president for student life at Texas Woman's University. Sister Sally found herself as director of admissions in early March, weeks before Lou's scheduled inauguration, and Lou had one more search to add to his list. This was neither surprising nor distressing for Lou. With the exception of John Ray, he had not expected the vice presidents to stay long. His hopes were pinned on the hardworking faculty and middle managers on his team.

As Lou continued outlining the structure of his five-year plan, soon to be titled Target 90 since it would reach all the way to that year, he knew it hinged on the proposal he would bring Lionel Sosa in a few days. Lou had asked Dick McCracken to contact Lionel and try to arrange a solid two-hour meeting. That had not proven difficult. Lionel was more than ready for an in-depth talk about the college.

They met in Lionel's office. Lou explained that he wanted to launch a $1 million ad campaign in various media markets. Lionel was excited that Incarnate Word was getting serious about marketing. Doing a quick calculation, he realized the 15 percent commission would put $150,000 in his pocket. The businessman in Lionel was also getting excited.

Then Lou broke the news that there was no money involved. Lionel listened with amusement and admiration for this crazy guy from Brooklyn who thought the San Antonio media would buy into this notion of barter. "It's an interesting idea, Lou, but have you actually tried it before?"

"Sure," Lou replied. "I did it in Iowa and doubled the enrollment!"

Lionel was impressed. Maybe the guy wasn't crazy. "You really did that?" he asked. Lou was adamant. After all, he had tried it in Iowa, and he had doubled the enrollment. Why mention that he had also paid for those ads? Sioux City was a tiny media market and had been less expensive than the San Antonio market would be. There'd been no need to try bartering.

As Lionel listened, Lou went through the plan in detail. "The way it would work for you, Lionel, would be an eighty-twenty deal. Your agency would be our agency of record; you would do the work and we would pay you by giving 80 percent of the cost to deserving students as Sosa Scholarships. The other 20 percent would be reserved for your employees to take courses at Incarnate Word." Lou went on to explain that Lionel would represent Incarnate Word and would design all the ads. When it was time to go to a production company, their out-of-pocket costs, such as film, would be paid 100 percent in cash, but their time would be paid in scholarships.

Lou could afford to award those scholarships because he not only had space in most classes, but he also had a large supply of scholarships from grants and other sources. He just didn't have anyone taking advantage of them. He could put Sosa's name or the name of a media partner on any available scholarship without additional financial stress.

Lionel couldn't help himself; he was hooked. He still thought it was one of the more unusual approaches he had heard, but after all the man had done it before. He pointed out that the first thing they had to do was determine the message. Lou hadn't been in San Antonio long, but he had a clear picture of what people thought of Incarnate Word, if they thought of it at all. They "knew" it was a girls' school, though it was actually coed, and they had no idea where it was unless someone referenced Earl Abel's restaurant. The college simply had no image among the general public. But for the people who knew Incarnate Word—students, parents, relatives, and alumni—it was a different story altogether. Lionel summed it up recently: "People who knew us loved us. All we needed to do was get more people to know us!"

Lou had three major goals for the media project: double the enrollment in three years, approach a 60-40 female-to-male gender mix, and achieve a racial/ethnic composition that reflected San Antonio. At that time the San Antonio area was 47.39 percent Hispanic, 6.93 percent African American, 44.23 percent Anglo, and 1.45 percent other.

Lionel got straight to work. "He treated me like I was Anheuser-Busch," Lou said. "I didn't have a penny, but that didn't lessen the professionalism with which he handled every aspect of the project." Lionel's experience told him he had to have final print ads and TV commercials before going out to sell to the media. To do that he needed a production company; he chose Ashe/Bowie Productions, owned by Ken Ashe and Mike Bowie. Their share would be four full paid scholarships. Mike Bowie had a daughter about to go to college, and between the two partners there were enough nieces, nephews, and other relatives to use the four scholarships. With one day of shooting and three days of editing, all four family members had their college tuition paid. It was a win-win all around.

The next task was Lou's. Lionel suggested establishing seven focus groups—four for students, two for parents, and one for faculty. He urged Lou to pick people with outgoing personalities and to try for a mix of men and women. Dr. Sean Burke, a faculty member, became the voice-over for the first Incarnate Word commercials. Patsy Wesser, a student worker in Lou's office, made the first student commercial. To target opportunities for Hispanic students, they would also need English-speaking and Spanish-speaking Hispanics.

Lou with IWC faculty member Dr. Sean Burke – the voice of "The College" ads.

The purpose of the focus groups was to listen to those inside the Incarnate Word community. What did the college mean to them? Why did they love teaching or studying there? Why did parents feel so satisfied once their sons or daughters were part of the college? Lionel would tape these sessions, finding members of the focus groups he thought had good speaking voices and good camera presence. He wrote scripts for them using their exact words. There were no talent fees to be paid; these were volunteers who were eager to be part of a project that would showcase their college. Because the words were their own, the commercials were authentic. They sounded like students and parents. They sounded like proud faculty.

While the ads and commercials were being designed, Lou mentioned to Lionel that Incarnate Word was the only college in the area. "What do you mean?" Lionel asked. "There's St. Mary's, Our Lady of the Lake . . ." Lionel was puzzled by Lou's comment. Lou explained that the other institutions of higher learning had changed to universities while Incarnate Word was the only one that still used the designation "college." Sister Margaret Patrice had chosen to keep that term because she wanted to emphasize the teaching aspect of Incarnate Word; she felt that "university" implied a heavy emphasis on research. Lou couldn't argue with that logic. Incarnate Word had always been a place of good teaching, even when it was considered a girl's finishing school. Nevertheless, with graduate offerings expanding, Lou held a possible name change in the back of his mind. For now, Lionel knew they had invested time and energy in a plan that now had to be taken on the road. Would it fly? Lionel explains today, "I had not done so much as a penny of business with English-language stations, but I had lots of money in Spanish-language media."

"Start where you have the power base," Lou said. "Let's go to the Spanish-language stations first." They decided to tackle the Univision station, KWEX-TV. They scheduled an appointment with the president and part owner, taking with them the carefully crafted commercials.

"We made a great presentation," Lionel said. "And we got turned down flat!"

CHAPTER 4
THE SIGN PAINTER AND
THE MAN IN THE MOON

Neither Lionel Sosa nor Lou Agnese quit easily. They turned to the Spanish-language radio station KCOR, and as quickly as they had been rejected by KWEX, the radio station jumped aboard. They agreed to $150,000 worth of radio time.

Bolstered by one success, it was time to try one of the big English-language markets. They approached both San Antonio newspapers, the *Light* and the *Express-News*. They drew their first response from Charlie Kilpatrick, publisher of the *Express-News*. Kilpatrick was actually on the Incarnate Word board, but he and Lou had not yet met. Dick McCracken accompanied Lou and Lionel to the meeting on a Monday morning. Kilpatrick received them graciously, with a warm handshake and an open, relaxed manner.

Lionel then started to explain what they wanted to do. Kilpatrick's posture changed dramatically. His arms crossed in front of his chest. Lionel pretended not to notice. "We want $50,000 worth of space, and we need the ads placed on our schedule," he said.

"Lionel, it will cost me out-of-pocket money to print ads like that."

Lou jumped in like it was a tag match. "Well, here is how we pay out of pocket," he said. "We give you 50 percent of your payment in opportunities for your staff to attend classes, completely free, at Incarnate Word. And the other 50 percent will provide *Express-News* Scholarships for San Antonio students who would not otherwise have an opportunity for a college education."

Kilpatrick was quiet for a minute. It wasn't a slam dunk, but they had his attention. "Let me bring this to my executive team," he said. "I'll get you an answer."

This was Monday, February 10. Lou was due to present his five-year plan to the Incarnate Word community on Friday, February 14. "I need an answer by Friday, Charlie," he said.

"I can't guarantee that, but I'll try. Are you offering to do this with the *Light*, too?" Kilpatrick asked.

"Yes," Lou replied. "$50,000 worth there, too."

"Okay, I'll get back with you," he said.

There was nothing to do but wait. Meanwhile Lou needed to put the finishing touches on his Friday presentation and Lionel had to work on getting them in the door at KENS-TV.

The days ticked by with no response from the *Express-News*. February 14 came with Valentine decorations and the usual red roses to special teachers or special friends. But there was no Valentine call from Charlie Kilpatrick.

Moments before his address to the Incarnate Word community that afternoon, Lou was called to the telephone. The *Express-News* was on the line. At the time the only available phone in that building, even for the president, was the pay phone down the hall. He went to the phone, knowing it would be Charlie Kilpatrick. "This is either great timing or I'm about to punt," Lou thought.

Kilpatrick got straight to the point. "I have some news, but only if you agree to our terms," he said. Lou was thinking, "Here comes the cash part." Kilpatrick continued, "We're willing to do the barter on that fifty-fifty arrangement. The executive team is very excited about it—many would like to take the classes."

"And what's the problem here?" Lou was asking himself.

"We want an exclusive—all $100,000," Kilpatrick said. "We don't want you to give the *Light* any part of this."

"Charlie, for $100,000 I'll do it with the *Express-News* and only the *Express-News*," Lou said. "If the *Light* calls back I'll tell them they missed the deadline, which is today."

"Then we have a deal, Lou. Have Lionel put the contract together."

Lou swears that his heartbeat stayed normal as he headed back to the assembled group just in time to hear his introduction. But he admits the call gave him confidence.

The first thing he did was ask his new Committee on College Planning to stand and be recognized as the leaders who had helped craft the plan. It was actually 90 percent Lou's plan, but he wanted to project a solid leadership front. He then presented the six major components of Target 90—recruiting/admissions, retention/enrollment, facilities, finances, human resources, and the basic organizational structure. Lou explained there would be changes in the administrative structure in order to better support students and faculty. With Dr. O'Connor's pending departure for Grand Rapids, there would be a search for an executive vice president for academic and student affairs. The search would be from within the college and the Congregation. The new vice president would work closely with John Ray, vice president for business and finance, and with the person who would replace Hugh McCabe as vice president for institutional advancement. Lou also announced that the academic structure of five divisions would be changed to an arrangement still to be determined under three deans.

Lou then addressed the marketing plan, explaining that it would be aimed at changing the college's image in the San Antonio community. He discussed the focus groups that had been meeting and announced the ad campaign they would launch following his March 25 inauguration. He did not mention the bartering. He pointed out that they had existing sources for these scholarships, stressing no hard dollars would be used. He knew the last thing the internal community would want was for him to spend money on media and not on raises. No one had received a raise in three years.

The final part of the plan involved facilities and an estimated $30 million capital campaign to fund them. Among the more pressing projects would be road improvements and campus beautification, including expanded playing fields across the river and additional parking. The existing gym would be remodeled and expanded to include a complete fitness center. Lou described where additional living space would be developed to provide housing for the planned increase in enrollment. He closed with the statement, "The time has come to make IWC 'The College' in San Antonio."

The success they were having might have tempted Lou and Lionel to take a breath and ease their pace, but that was not how either of them worked. By Tuesday Lionel had secured an appointment with Bill Moll, president of KENS-TV. Lionel warned Lou that KENS didn't barter, but they had to try. He thought it was critical to get them on board somehow, and he would drop the suggestion that the Spanish-language media was committed. KCOR had said "Yes" even if KWEX had not.

They played the commercial for Moll and explained the trade arrangement, this time offering 80 percent for scholarships and 20 percent for KENS employees to attend the college. Lou was impressed with Bill's presence and obvious love for what he did. And Bill seemed clearly impressed with what they had just shown him, but he said, "Lou, KENS has a policy against barter."

"Well, this isn't barter. What you're going to be doing is a service for the San Antonio community. You're going to be helping students who can't afford a college education get a KENS Scholarship and come to Incarnate Word."

Bill was torn. "What if Our Lady of the Lake comes to the door with something like this?" he asked.

"Have they?" Lou asked, knowing the answer.

"No," Bill replied.

Lou had learned a quick public relations lesson four days earlier from Charlie Kilpatrick. "Well, you have an exclusive with Incarnate Word!" he said. "We came to you."

KENS was owned by Harte-Hanks, and they did have a firm policy about bartering. Bill was still trying to reconcile that. "Well, this is interesting and it is different," he said. "Give me a couple of days and let me get back to you."

Lionel knew it was important to close the deal. Leaving at that point could end it. He said, "Bill, you're either going to do it or not. Don't look at it as bartering—don't put that label on it. Think of it as just a different kind of public service announcement. Then you aren't breaking any policy."

"Between Lionel's salesmanship and Bill Moll's heart that was in San Antonio, we got it," Lou recalls. "Bill really saw this as a benefit to San Antonio." He told Lou, "I'll figure out how to place them like you want them, but I'm still going to call them public service announcements (PSAs) so I don't break any policies. But your PSAs will be played when you want them."

They left with a handshake deal. Lionel had to draw up the contracts, but they had a deal with Bill Moll for $250,000! KENS would be the only place anyone would see Incarnate Word's ads in English. Charlie Kilpatrick had given Lou insight into just how important competition was in San Antonio.

In a recent conversation, Bill recalled that early visit with Lou and Lionel. "I had a pretty good idea what they were going to ask me because Charlie Kilpatrick had called me right after they had been with him. You know, the *Express-News* was also owned by Harte-Hanks, and Charlie had been careful about how he handled that situation also."

Bill continued, "It's funny how things happen. I had an employee incentive program at KENS that encouraged my employees to take college courses. If they took one and passed it, I would reimburse them for the tuition. That was a popular program, but was becoming too expensive to continue. I hated having to end it, but I didn't have a choice. Then all of a sudden Lou and Lionel are presenting this plan."

Bill shook his head and laughed. "When Lou said, 'Your employees can take classes for free,' it gave me back my incentive program! I was motivated to help Lou as much for our employees' sake as for his." Today Bill and his wife, Marilyn, are good friends with the Agneses and Sosas.

Years later Bill Moll became a member of Incarnate Word's Board of Trustees and is the current chair of the board's Enrollment Management and Student Services Committee. He is also the current president and CEO of KLRN-TV, San Antonio's public television station. Actually Bill helped establish KLRN back in 1962 and had spoken that station's first words on the air. Prior to accepting his current responsibilities at KLRN, Bill served as chairman and CEO of Clear Channel Television.

Bill Moll at KLRN in 1962.

Later that week, Lou and Lionel decided to go back to the KWEX executive who had given them their first rejection. Once again the discussion returned to needing cash in order to make this work. Lionel had his bombshell ready. "Well, you know, KENS is doing it," he said.

"KENS is doing it? They don't barter!"

"They don't consider it barter. They're looking at it as a way to improve education in San Antonio."

"Well, if KENS is going to do it, we'll do it!"

Lionel already had the contract with him. It was signed before they left the office. It provided for 100 percent in scholarships to be targeted to students in San Antonio.

Although neither Lionel nor Lou realized it at the time, those commercials on the Spanish-language stations would be the first time a higher education institution had ever advertised in Spanish anywhere in the United States. It was a ground-breaking occurrence. Lionel's research confirmed later that it was also the first time a higher education institution had advertised on television, in any language, in the state of Texas.

Lou has always been quick to credit Lionel Sosa. "Lionel was crucial. If he had not been on the board or if I had not met him at that reception Amy Freeman Lee hosted or had not been able to convince him," Lou paused and added quietly, almost to himself, "Everything is in God's plan."

Lou then continued in his more public mode, revealing the depth of his feelings only by the amount of information he shared in the conversation. Normally a man of few words, Lou opened up and shared insight with Dick McCracken, his assistant in the beginning, and Vince Rodriguez, his communications assistant since 2000, as they and Dr. Pat Watkins enjoyed his reminiscences.

"When it comes to San Antonio, Lionel has been my mentor from day one. But I'm a good listener," he added, smiling. "Lionel knew the community

Lou and Lionel Sosa—"The Team."

and had become very influential—at that time with the Hispanic community, and now with it all. But he was like me in that he came from nothing, from scratch, like I did. We could relate to each other very, very well." He continued, "Lionel was a sign painter and I was a fruit peddler."

Both men knew it was illiteracy and poverty they were really addressing in this ad campaign, but to do that from the position of higher education was breaking new ground. Incarnate Word was the first school to talk about it so directly. Targeting the growing Hispanic population and striving for a student body that looked like the demographic of San Antonio was not just a challenge but a drive for them, and it reflected the long history of educational access the Congregation had maintained. But it would require increased community awareness.

"We weren't necessarily planning to reach students with the *Express-News* ads," Lou pointed out. "Those were not program ads; they were public appeal. They would be image building, us talking to the community, awakening them to the new Incarnate Word College that was building on all the old strengths, with new insights".

Lou continued, "The targets for the students would really come from the broadcast media—KENS, the radio, English and Spanish. That's where we were reaching the students. Our student ads spoke to the students and their parents. Mine spoke to the parents and grandparents. We were all saying, 'We welcome you.'

"I understood marketing from my years at Briar Cliff," Lou commented, "but Lionel shaped it all for me. Before I met him I was thinking English; I was not thinking English and Spanish. But after our first conversation, I definitely agreed we needed to blitz in Spanish, also.

"We needed to reach the parents and grandparents. Imagine the impact when they heard Hispanic students talking about their experiences at the college, or when I said in Spanish, 'Your daughter can come here; your son can come here. We want them at IWC. They're welcome.' Grandmothers watching their telenovelas realized their granddaughters could be the girl in the Incarnate Word commercial."

Lou remembered he took a lot of flak, even within the college community, because he appeared in all the print ads and many of the broadcast commercials: "People think I have a big ego and like being in public," he said. "I'm really a shy person. I had to constantly explain why 'Lou' was in everything. I had to let people know the reason was so I could get in the door of the community as a person worth someone's valuable calendar time."

He remembered how hard it had been to even get a return phone call the first few months he was in San Antonio. "I couldn't have gotten to first base with this media business without Lionel. The community respected Lionel Sosa; they didn't know Lou Agnese from the man in the friggin' moon."

So how did he end up on billboards and TV? "Lionel convinced me. He said, 'Lou, you know this—people give to people, not just to institutions. People need to see the face of Incarnate Word College, and the face has to be you.'"

Few think of Lou Agnese as shy. They see him constantly in the public eye and never realize that the demands of his position have turned a Brooklyn introvert into an extrovert. "You know," he said, "when I left Iowa, if you had told me I was going to be speaking Spanish on television, I'd have said you were nuts!"

Lou talked about the summers he spent in Cuernavaca, Mexico in 1987 and 1989 learning Spanish. "The Sisters have a retreat house there, and Mickey and I stayed with them while we were taking Spanish classes downtown," he recalled. "I didn't expect to be fluent, but it was important to learn the language. I wanted to do it out of respect for the Sisters and for the Hispanic community in San Antonio."

At the time, the Sisters of Charity of the Incarnate Word had two separate provinces—one in the United States and one in Mexico. Today they are all together in one.

"The Sisters in Mexico treated us like family. I think they were proud that Mickey and I wanted to learn more about their culture, and as much of their language as we could in that first summer of immersion. The retreat house was located in a beautiful area—more flowers than I had ever seen."

Lou explained that his and Mickey's wedding anniversary is July 27, and July 28 is little Louis's birthday. "We woke up on July 27, and as we looked out the window we saw that the Sisters had spelled out 'Happy Anniversary' in flowers across this huge lawn. By the next day they had rearranged the flowers to read 'Happy Birthday.'

"That's the warmth and acceptance we received in Mexico. I made close friends there and learned a lot from the Mexican Sisters. We are still very close, and I draw on their wisdom in many areas."

CHAPTER 5
INAUGURATION AT "THE COLLEGE"

It was now almost a year since Lou signed his contract. He had postponed the inauguration until spring 1986, wanting the board and everyone involved to know exactly what they would be getting before they took that formal step. As the inauguration neared, there were few doubts about how this man would handle the business of managing a college—with a clear emphasis on "business" and "managing" but never forgetting that the business was education.

Lou had chosen a significant date for his inauguration. March 25 is the feast of the Annunciation—the day, according to Catholic doctrine, that Christ was conceived in the womb of the Virgin Mary. The college's name, Incarnate Word, means Christ and derives from the biblical passage "and the Word was made flesh [incarnated] and dwelt among us." March 25, therefore, is also the feast day of the Sisters of Charity of the Incarnate Word.

Until now that feast day had been celebrated privately within the Congregation. Lou felt strongly that, as a lay president, he had an obligation to celebrate the Catholic sponsorship of the college more publicly. He instituted the annual campus-wide celebration of Incarnate Word Day by scheduling his inauguration for that special day in 1986.

This was Incarnate Word's first inauguration ceremony in over fifty years. Mother Columkille's appointment as president in 1923 was marked with some degree of ceremony, but there had been no formal inauguration for any subsequent president. Sister Margaret Patrice Slattery explained in her book, *Promises To Keep*, that she had requested the board set aside money for a President's Scholarship Fund in lieu of a traditional inauguration ceremony when she became president.

By unspoken agreement, this inauguration would be a public celebration of the college's new era. It was a big event, and everyone wanted it to be perfect. The excitement was palpable. Just how much effort went into it was clear when the planning committee showed up the day after the event wearing T-shirts declaring, "I survived Dr. Agnese's inauguration!"

Sister Toni makes her feelings known about Lou's inauguration.

The committee was co-chaired by Dr. Amy Freeman Lee and two dedicated alumnae, Brig. Gen. Lillian Dunlap and Barbara Condos. Committee members were recruited from every segment of the college—the board, Congregation, faculty, administration, students, and alumni—and also from the external community.

Registration, receptions, dinners, and entertainment were planned for delegates, presidents, and other representatives from more than thirty-five public and private colleges and universities in Texas, as well as those in other parts of the country. Delegates came from the local universities and from Texas A&M University, Rice University, Tulane University, Marquette University, Boston College, the University of Scranton, and St. Mary's of the Plains College, where Lou earned his bachelor's degree. Dr. Ron Calgaard, from the Grand Torino moment, represented Trinity University, while St. Edward's University was represented by Dr. Pat Hayes, who had given Lou the not-for-profit bonds tip. Mayor Henry Cisneros represented the City of San Antonio.

Members of the Congregation of the Sisters of Charity of the Incarnate Word were all invited, and special invitations were given to those Sisters who had served at Incarnate Word College. Sister Margaret Patrice Slattery had returned from sabbatical and was present in her new role as college chancellor.

The festivities began the night before with a special performance of the musical *Celebration* at the Maddux Theatre, followed by a reception on the patio for out-of-town delegates, guests, trustees, and spouses. Lou's former president from Briar Cliff College, Dr. Charles Bensman, had traveled to be with him and to serve as one of the deacons at Mass the next day.

The proudest guests for the next day's celebration had to be Lou's parents, Louis J. Agnese Sr., who is known simply as Papa, and Lou's mother, Nancy. Also present were his brother Mike and family, and his sister Susan. But it was Louis III and Nancy who watched wide-eyed as their father was the center of attention. One of the most memorable images of the inauguration was captured by both Philip Barr and Leonard Parness and published respectively in the *Express-News* and the *Light* on Wednesday, March 26, 1986. Their front-page photos both show young Louis sitting pressed against the shoulder of his dad's new academic gown, tired, proud, and happy.

The major event was the Celebration of the Eucharist, the liturgy during which Lou's actual inauguration took place. Shortly before 3 p.m. the procession left Centennial Hall, a facility normally used for congregational gatherings, for its long walk to the Administration Building. The setting for the Celebration of the Eucharist was the front of the building where Sister Eilish Ryan had prepared an altar for Archbishop

Lou with Dr. Charles Bensman, president of Briar Cliff College, and Sister Margaret Patrice. Lou had served as a vice president at Briar Cliff for the previous four years. This is also the last time anyone can recall Lou wearing his academic cap.

Patrick Flores, main celebrant of the Mass. The Archbishop gave the homily and brought greetings from the Archdiocese. Then, at the Offertory portion of the Mass, Dr. Agnese was inaugurated. George Mead, board vice chair, and Sister Juanita Albrecht, CCVI, board secretary, presented the president to the assembled body.

Dr. Amy Freeman Lee, board chair, was too ill to attend the inauguration of the man she had helped hire. In her place Sister Dorothy Ettling, CCVI, Superior General of the Congregation, presided as Agnese's academic regalia—a black cap and a gown in Incarnate Word's red and gray—was presented to him. He was also presented with the college mace, a symbol of Incarnate Word's then 105-year history and heritage. The mace was carried by Sister Helena Monahan and presented by Sister Margaret Patrice Slattery and Sister Dorothy Ettling. The official program for that day credits Dr. Donald McLain, professor of biology, with crafting the mace with an open orb of lacy silver and a Celtic cross set with sapphires. Representatives of the five academic divisions presented Eucharistic gifts symbolic of their disciplines. The gifts included a bound volume of the works of Shakespeare from the Humanities and Fine Arts and a microscope and live white orchid plant from the Natural Sciences.

Dr. Agnese gave his inaugural remarks after Communion. Plans had been made for inclement weather, but the event began calmly. The March winds blew in just as he began to speak. Floral arrangements, altar decorations, and loose programs took sail as he quipped, "It looks like the winds of Iowa have followed me." He then continued, "As Incarnate Word College approaches the 1990s, the community it serves has grown and changed dramatically, although many of the same nineteenth-century concerns—poverty,

A hat-less Lou speaking at his 1986 inauguration.

illiteracy, the needs of the disadvantaged—must be addressed and included in our present and future vision."

He focused on several areas that would improve the college and offer greater access to needy students. "We will raise our local profile by utilizing media," he said, with some degree of understatement in light of the media blitz about to occur. "We will increase financial aid to students." He announced Christian Leadership awards and Incarnate Word grants that would assure access for students even if federal aid sources decreased.

He went on to explain that with everyone's help they would improve and increase the number of programs at the college. Two of those, the Master of Science in Nursing and the Master of Arts in Peace and Justice, started in fall 1986. Lou also focused on building renovations and campus beautification, saying, "This is a beautiful campus, but after all these years things grow old. So we will start some building renovations in the summer." A priority was completing the Brackenridge Villa restoration, a project for which Sister Margaret Patrice had worked so hard.

Then Lou spoke directly from his heart. Watching video of that event twenty-five years later, one can see and hear the emotion he was experiencing. He talked about his own education with Sisters and priests and the profound effect it had on him. He referenced an article he had just read, saying, "The other day while reading, I realized for the first time that in the United States there are 117 colleges and universities like Incarnate Word that have been founded by Sisters of various religious congregations. And today more than ever the need for those types of institutions continues."

He continued, "My hope—my prayer—is to ensure that the process continues at those 117 institutions and at Incarnate Word College, so that the way I was touched as a youth, the way I and others were touched in college, the way I and my family continue to be touched today, will also be available for many, many generations to follow. That will only happen if we as a community in San Antonio, as a community in the United States—throughout the world—work hand in hand to ensure that mission is ongoing."

Lou turned to his parents and thanked them for their support: "It took me a long time to figure out why my dad kept saying, 'Education, education, education.'" Papa Agnese could see that his son had finally figured it out.

The Brackenridge Villa after restoration.

By 5 p.m., with the remarks and liturgy ended, Dr. Louis J. Agnese Jr. was officially president of Incarnate Word College. A reception followed outside the Fine Arts Building. The final inaugural event was a black-tie dinner in Marian Hall honoring the Agneses—by now, Lou and Mickey to all. The Incarnate Word Chorale provided the entertainment and Dr. Charles Bensman was the dinner speaker.

In August 2010 a shortened version of the inauguration video was shown at Incarnate Word's twenty-fifth annual leadership retreat, held that year in Fredericksburg, Texas. The original "Committee on College Planning" had grown much larger and had a new name—the University Planning Commission (UPC)—but it was still the president's working body. The video was shown as part of a surprise celebration for Lou as he began his twenty-fifth year in office. Only a handful of current faculty and administrators had been at the inauguration. Most of the UPC members knew an older and more polished president than they saw on the video. Some were amazed by the difference in Agnese's delivery.

"I've never seen him use notes," one said. That and the somewhat rougher delivery spoke to the growth that had occurred in Lou. It was much easier to see him as the shy man he always claimed to be.

"But he still doesn't like to wear that academic cap," said another, referring to the fact that Agnese doffed his new cap as soon as he began his inauguration speech. It is doubtful he has worn it since.

Lou spoke about the inauguration from his own perspective—clearly caught in a wave of retrospective thought and emotion. "It was a very important day because we would be showing the new face of the college; and it was very important for me personally, because it was a commitment. It

Proud parents Louis J. and Nancy Agnese with Lou and Mickey.

was like getting married. I was committing all my energies, my family's energies, to really making Incarnate Word *the* college in San Antonio."

He talked about why he had felt so comfortable with the Sisters of Charity of the Incarnate Word and their accomplishments. "What the Sisters had done and what they believed in just fit me. I could sell Incarnate Word because I was selling something I firmly believed in—then and now. Everything I did over those twenty-five years was just take what the Sisters did and highlight it. I always looked at the history and then accented it. That's why the Congregation, from day one, supported what I was doing, because it was exactly what they had been doing. But they never told anybody—that's not what nuns do, tell people. But I told the public what they were doing, and I built on it. Starting that very first year and continuing today."

Fighting illiteracy and bringing the demographic of Incarnate Word into a matching profile with that of the city of San Antonio were, in themselves, ways of accenting the school and Congregation's history.

The day after the inauguration, the first ad appeared in the *Express-News*. It was a full page with Lou Agnese's picture and an open letter to the community. It read, in part:

> San Antonio is a community that works. One that's together. Where there's growth. And Pride. But there's also 34% illiteracy. Here, new industry imports its talent, leaving too many of us on the outside looking in. The answer? Better education. Better opportunities. For all of us. That's where we come in. We're here to serve. We're The College.

The message "We're here to serve. We're The College" was Agnese/Sosa genius. Public reaction was simple and encouraging. The phones started ringing the next day and they didn't stop. Looking back, Lou commented, "You saw it in the numbers in the fall [1986]. We went from five years of enrollment decline to over 1,500 students. So it was real, and it took everyone by surprise."

The ads continued in English and Spanish, on radio and TV and in print. "The College" was joined by the word "Brainpower," another lucky moment in a conversation among friends. Lou, Lionel, and Dick McCracken were in

Lou's car when Dick casually mentioned that there was a lot of brainpower in the area. Lionel's practiced ear picked that up right away.

"Brainpower," he said. "What if we owned that word like we own 'The College'?" He copyrighted it immediately.

The ads continued until June. Bill Moll had kept his word and placed the public service announcements at peak times. The public even saw them as the 5 p.m. news was coming on. The blitz relaxed for about six weeks, following the major recruitment period, and then picked up again as August approached.

Until now other institutions like St. Mary's and St. Edward's had not taken Incarnate Word seriously. It simply was not in their league, and in fairness it seemed unlikely it ever would be. Lou knew that when the marketing plan started producing results, Incarnate Word would take the area by surprise. And that is exactly what happened. As the ads and the commercials continued to saturate the city, The College became serious competition. The publicity Agnese and the little college across from Earl Abel's were receiving met with sarcastic but humorous criticism from some quarters. Referencing the marketing blitz, one competitor dubbed Agnese "the Word made flash!" And he dwelt among them for the next twenty-five years.

CHAPTER 6

No Mafia—Just Lou

"**I** can't pay you, but you can stay at my house and we'll drink martinis."

That and a round trip ticket were the offer Lou made in 1986 to Herb Heidt, longtime friend and architect. The two had worked together at Gannon College, site of Lou's first administrative job in higher education. Incarnate Word was about to call for bids on the planned building and renovations, and Lou needed expertise he trusted to determine the bid specifications.

The renovations would be funded in part by the not-for-profit bonds John Ray had researched after Lou's meeting with Dr. Pat Hayes. John and Lou had just returned from New York, where they had hoped to obtain a Triple A rating for the bonds. "Texas banks were in deep trouble at that time. Bank names were changing faster than you could follow," Lou said. "The real estate bubble had burst, and we were seeing the first savings and loan crisis. John and I went to Moody and Standard & Poors and did a dog-and-pony show hoping for a good rating. We got a Triple B. We wanted an A so that we would have better bond interest.

"We came back to San Antonio and went to the one bank here that still had power to give us the higher rating, M-Bank, now Bank of America. They gave us a letter of credit. We paid half a point for that enhancement, but it was worth it. It changed our rating from a Triple B to a Triple A."

Heidt agreed to Lou's offer and flew in to help prepare the bid announcements. Either friendship or exceptional martinis brought him back a second time to help sort through the twelve bids that were submitted. Three were selected for interviews, and in the end the firm of Bradley-McChesney emerged as the successful bidder. The company later divided, and today Mike McChesney's firm—McChesney-Bianco—handles all architectural matters for Incarnate Word.

Shortly after his inauguration Lou had called another colleague from the past. In anticipation of the athletic opportunities that would be available

Steve Heying joined IWC in 1986 as assistant baseball coach.

once the convocation center and athletic fields were built, he hired Jim Ellwanger, head baseball coach at Briar Cliff, to be Incarnate Word's dean of students and athletic services as well as baseball coach starting June 1986.

"Here's where it gets crazy," Lou explains. "Ellwanger then insisted I had to meet this former major league player as his assistant coach. He told me the guy even had a master's degree in physical education. 'Jim,' I said, 'we don't even have a team yet. Why am I looking at an assistant coach?' The last thing I needed right then was a fancy ball player with a master's degree. Ellwanger kept pushing for me to meet him. I finally agreed to interview him while I was at a conference in Fort Worth.

"God was looking after me, I guess. I met Steve Heying, and the rest is history. Steve served as assistant baseball coach, and then when Jim left he served as head coach. But mainly Steve became my right arm as head of facilities management for the college."

The first task they tackled together was the Hildebrand beautification project. "The Hildebrand side of the campus looked like a parking lot," Lou said. "There were no trees, and the road needed substantial work. You never want to give up parking space, but we had to in order to plant the trees that now line that whole side of the campus."

Construction of a $4.7 million athletic complex would begin in fall 1986, just months after Lou's inauguration. The Sunday *Express-News* of April 20, 1986 gave full-page coverage with pictures and a story by Karl O'Quinn, whose headline read, "IWC taking big plunge into sports." O'Quinn reported not only on the new complex to be built but also on the sports program itself. He quoted Lou as saying, "At Incarnate Word, any program that exists need be of high quality or it need not exist."

That summed up Lou's approach to everything, including the sports program he was bringing. Lou wanted to balance athletics with the fine arts and other excellent programs at Incarnate Word. "We have fine drama, we have fine music. We want to have fine athletics. We will not have a program that is not competitive. I don't like to be second in anything," he said.

The athletic complex would include a new field house, a baseball diamond with grandstand, a softball diamond, a soccer field, a track, additional parking, and the renovated gymnasium. "Students need the spirit those athletic programs bring to a campus," Lou said. "Athletics also give us a better chance not only to increase the enrollment, but to target the gender mix we want." He confided to some of his executive team at the time, "I know football is the program we need, but it's not likely to happen."

Sports for the 1986–87 academic year would include men's and women's basketball, baseball, tennis, cross country, men's soccer, and women's volleyball. As Lou had recognized, football was not on the radar yet. The Incarnate Word Crusaders would move from the NCAA's Division III into NAIA District 4 as an independent team among schools like Southwestern, Schreiner, and Concordia Lutheran. The other teams in the circuit included St. Mary's and Texas Lutheran.

One major difference for Incarnate Word would be the availability of athletic scholarships, which are not offered in Division III. Lou was also clear that Incarnate Word wanted its athletes to reflect the total student body. He pointed out that 85 percent of the college's students are from Bexar County while the rest are mostly from South Texas. "We want athletes from this area," he told the *Express-News*.

While athletics were being covered in the news section, the last ad of the season addressed the literacy issue Lou and Lionel continued to attack. The May 20 ad featured the headline "We're breaking barriers at The College." The ad featured Lou's picture and text that read:

> 34 percent of our population is functionally illiterate. 40% are between the ages of 18 and 25. And 50% of our Hispanic youngsters drop out of high school—only 8% finish college. With your help we'll improve those numbers. With scholarships, with financial assistance, and with an attitude that says we care—that we recognize each student's worth, regardless of background or age. We're going to break the illiteracy barrier. We're working on it now. It's our mission. After all, we're The College.

A lot was happening at "The College," and Lou Agnese was calling the shots.

Through it all, Lou still had executive positions to fill. He decided to postpone the selection of a new academic vice president as Dr. Peter O'Connor's replacement in order to ensure a thorough and thoughtful search. Sister Audrey O'Mahony had been O'Connor's assistant and she now agreed to serve as interim vice president for 1986–87. Dr. Mary Lou Mueller accepted the interim position as dean of student development.

Lou felt comfortable with academic affairs in Sister Audrey's hands for the year, and he and John Ray had established a trust relationship in the

Paula and Tom Plofchan. Tom was vice president for institutional advancement, the first VP Lou hired.

business and finance area. However he was concerned about institutional advancement. With so many projects in various planning stages, fund raising would be critical. This was also a difficult economy in which to raise those funds. Lou needed a special person for the job.

In late May 1986 a national search yielded what Lou still talks about as "a great hire." Tom Plofchan had been vice president for institutional advancement at Mary Grove College in Detroit when he was asked to interview for the position at Incarnate Word. Tom's wife, Paula, still remembers the day he called and asked how she would feel about living in San Antonio. "You mean, Texas?" she asked, trying to keep the panic down. Tom told her about the small college and its very young president. He was intrigued by both.

After seven children, Paula was pretty sure she could handle anything, but Texas had just never entered her mind. She remembers telling Tom as the plane touched down, "Now, Tom, if this is all palm trees and cactus, we are not staying." Paula's concept of San Antonio as desert with the occasional cowboy riding by was quickly dispelled. She and Tom saw it as lush, green, and friendly.

Tom was exactly what Lou needed to help build the team. This was not the time to hire a shooting star that would use the job as just another resume item. Lou valued loyalty, and he saw in Tom both loyalty and stability. Tom had been at Mary Grove, a college not unlike Incarnate Word but in a very different setting, for seventeen years. Lou knew this was a good fit and knew Tom would bring a professional approach to the fundraising that was to play a major role in Incarnate Word's growth.

The two men could not have been more different. Tom's genteel side smoothed Lou's Brooklyn-bred, just-get-it-done style, and they balanced each other well.

Tom's elderly mother, on the other hand, was very concerned. She never completely lost her conviction that Tom was somehow in serious trouble with the Detroit mafia. That was the only reason he would have moved so far away—and to a place she saw as almost a foreign country. She would probably have worried more about a Texas mafia if she had ever met Lou Agnese.

One of Tom's first tasks was helping Sister Margaret Patrice Slattery complete the on-going campaign to fund the restoration of Brackenridge Villa. She had spearheaded the campaign and it was already 90 percent complete when Tom arrived. Shortly after Lou was hired the villa was restored and ready for office use and special events. Institutional advancement moved into the villa, and Tom had the opportunity to enjoy the setting with his staff.

A favorite Lou-ism, preserved and enjoyed by his good friends, was captured when Lou explained the cause of the destructive fire of April 19, 1983. Ironically, the villa was being renovated at the time of the blaze, and workmen had left oily rags in the building. As the hot sun bore down, the rags ignited. "It was just a case of spontaneous compulsion," Lou explained. "We've all had them," chuckled the friend, choosing anonymity for the time.

As the new school year approached, the executive team was in place, with a strong blend of old and new. The campus was responding to the attention Lou and Steve Heying were giving it, and the ads were about to start again. They emphasized the personal attention of a 13-to-1 student-teacher ratio, forty-one undergraduate fields, and fifteen graduate fields. They had the mandatory picture of Lou as the face of The College and, as always, ended with a phrase that would stick in readers' minds—"We're The College," or "This fall, go with the winner."

Unquestionably, the most appealing ad that August focused on the college's Katherine Ryan Development Center. It described the center as much more than a day care center, identifying it as a place where children experience their first formal learning environment and describing how that can make a difference in the first grade and beyond. As an ad for an early childhood development center there was nothing so special about it. But the headline read, "Send your four-year-old to The College," and this time instead of Lou's picture there was little Nancy Agnese, with a quote under her picture just like Dad always had: "Daddy is sending me to The College to prepare me for the first grade."

Now phones were ringing at both the Katherine Ryan Center and the college's admissions office. That August the final student count at the college was just under 1,600, and dormitories were at a record 97 percent occupancy.

By October the campus was vibrant. There was still much to be done, but the students could

Little Nancy as she appeared in an early ad.

Lou and Roger Staubach show off IWC's new athletic T-shirts.

see progress and the campus was alive with student energy as much as with fresh paint. October 27 was the groundbreaking for the sports complex. Mayor Henry Cisneros brought greetings from the community, Gov. Mark White sent a telegram of congratulations, and former Dallas quarterback, Heisman trophy winner, and Football Hall of Fame member Roger Staubach was the guest speaker. Staubach was interested in more than just sports at Incarnate Word College. His daughter, Jennifer, was a nursing student there at the time. The invitation to the groundbreaking featured Staubach on the front with the message, "Plan to join me and hear how The College produces winners—in and out of the classroom."

October was a busy month in more than sports. Major decisions were being made that would change roles for key persons at the college. Lou relied heavily on Dick McCracken as his assistant but knew he needed Dick's vast institutional memory in another position. If the college was to grow, someone with Dick's genius for names and events was needed to draw alumni home. Dick knew everyone and had a knack for keeping them involved in Incarnate Word. He agreed to become director of alumni for the following year and to help search for a new assistant to the president in the coming months.

The College Planning Committee had also been reviewing finalists in the extended search for an executive vice president. The parameters of the search stated that the successful candidate should come from current faculty or from the Congregation. At the October Board of Trustees meeting, Lou reported that the committee had recommended Sister Helena Monahan for the position. Sister Helena would be away on sabbatical during the spring semester, visiting colleges comparable to Incarnate Word. Sister Audrey would continue in her interim position as agreed, with Sister Helena's appointment effective June 1, 1987.

Thanksgiving was quickly approaching. Lou had two plans for the season. Back in January, he and his executive team had agreed it would be good to light some of the trees in celebration of the Christmas season. They had not planned anything big—just lights and extension cords like most folks use at their homes. Lou felt stronger about when the lights would go on than about how many there would be. "Alamo Plaza turns their lights on the Friday after Thanksgiving," he explained. "The City of San Antonio celebrates the lighting of the River Walk that same day. Since Incarnate Word is actually at the headwaters of the San Antonio River, I felt we should turn ours on first—the Saturday before Thanksgiving. That way there is a natural progression for the lighting ceremonies all the way to downtown San Antonio."

Only the trees on the Broadway side of the campus were lighted that year, but they amounted to almost 10,000 lights—a little more than the family extension cords could support. Southwestern Bell helped string the lights with their boom trucks. Mayor Cisneros and Archbishop Patrick Flores participated in the small ceremony that would soon have a name—Light the Way. Again, no one anticipated that by 2010 Light the Way would be a fairyland of over a million colored lights.

The second holiday idea was aimed directly at students. Lou didn't mind his hectic schedule; actually he thrived on it. But he was worried about the amount of contact he was having—or not having—with the students. He decided to tweak a tradition he helped start at Briar Cliff. When the budget at Briar Cliff caused the administration to cancel the annual faculty dinner, Lou had offered a less costly solution—one he had tried at Gannon University years before. He offered to cook spaghetti and Italian meatball sauce for the whole faculty. The event had been hugely successful.

This time he suggested cooking for the student body, with serving help from the faculty and administration. "Lou's sauce" was a well-kept secret as he took over the dining hall kitchen. Those who helped roll meatballs or carry supplies to and from the kitchen never got close enough to the huge pots Lou stirred to determine what he added as he tasted. Possibly the late Phil Bell, the energetic, self-appointed "marshal" of the spaghetti dinners over the years might have ferreted out the secret, but he never gave it away. The President's Spaghetti Dinner became a tradition that still finds Lou in the kitchen every fall. He stands at the serving table and dishes up hundreds of plates as students pour into the dining area. Faculty and staff help roll thousands of meatballs, bring desserts, and help serve the students. For Lou it is one more way to say to students, "We're glad you're here."

By early December Lou was saying those same words to Dr. Jim Van Straten, who had just been hired to fill the position Dick McCracken was leaving. Van Straten would officially become assistant to the president on January 1, 1987.

As the Christmas holidays neared, the December issue of *San Antonio Monthly* appeared, featuring a full-page article by well-known columnist

Lou as chef for the annual President's Spaghetti Dinner. The sauce is still a secret.

Rick Casey. The color photo was of Roger Staubach, but the article told the story of Lou and Lionel's ad campaign. The article was positively written and showed Lou Agnese as a true professional who had worked hard to get where he was. Casey described the "scholarships for trade" with humor, sensitivity, and obvious admiration. The most amazing part of the article was the ad count he had pulled together, presumably with help from Lionel or Lou. Not many people actually knew how many ads had been part of the blitz, but Casey reported there had been more than 300 television spots, 1,200 radio spots, and scores of newspaper ads that year. "During the months of January, March, and April of next year, a total of 40 thirty-second spots a week will run on Channel 5 and on Spanish-language Channel 41," he wrote. "Up to 70 radio spots weekly on three San Antonio stations and up to 65 in Corpus Christi and the Rio Grande Valley will be running in a similar time period. Meanwhile, newspaper ads will run continuously."

The article was public affirmation for Lou and Lionel—and a nice Christmas present. Lou didn't know that another present would arrive in January.

CHAPTER 7

FICKLE FAME AND A BOWL OF CHILI

The January 1987 issues of the *Express-News* carried the ads Rick Casey said would be forthcoming, each with Lou's picture. But the January 14 *Express-News* and *Light* carried Lou's picture for another reason. The *Express-News* announced it this way: "The San Antonio Jaycees organization has narrowed its search for the Outstanding Young Person of 1986 to five final candidates." The *Light* led with this paragraph: "The Outstanding Young Person of San Antonio for 1986 will be either a college president, an Air Force captain, a television anchorwoman, a supply systems analyst, or a counselor with the Bexar County Sheriff's Department."

On January 20 the suspense ended as Dr. Louis J. Agnese Jr. received the award. A panel of judges selected him "based on a number of qualifications, including overall education, career accomplishments, and contributions to the community," the *Light* reported.

Lou's parents, who were visiting the younger Agneses, also attended the awards banquet at the Gunter Hotel. As he did at his inauguration, Lou thanked them for his education when he acknowledged his award. "One thing I was really thinking about was how gratified I was that my mother and father were here. It kind of tells the story of what we're all about," he was quoted by the *Express-News*. Everyone who knew the story of the immigrant parents and their "fruit peddler" son understood.

Lou joined Henry Cisneros, Porter Loring Jr., Judge Tom Vickers, and other previous honorees dating back to 1945. The next level of the competition was Outstanding Young Person of the State, but Lou had a college to run and was not daydreaming about that.

With the growth in student population, it was time for the promised new dormitories. Ground was broken for the Village of Avoca apartment-style housing on February 2. The event was combined with an academic convocation during which an honorary Doctor of Humane Letters was awarded to Bishop Thomas J. Drury, a native of County Sligo, Ireland, and retired bishop of Corpus Christi. The Irish connection was appropriate for a project named Avoca. Dick McCracken, Incarnate Word's unofficial historian and favorite storyteller, explained the name Avoca in the dedication program:

> Shortly after the fall of the Alamo a group of Irish settlers in San Antonio, led by a Mr. William Howth, established and platted a new city called Avoca two and a half miles north of downtown San Antonio at the headwaters of the San Antonio River. Until 1842 lots were sold, streets named, and some homes partially or completely built. When San Antonio city leaders realized that whoever owned the land at the head of the river virtually controlled the river, a Spanish land grant was used as the basis for the city's expansion of its limits to include Avoca. This effectively put an end to Mr. Howth's dream city, which probably would have been to the Irish what New Braunfels is to the German community. Avoca is listed in the Texas almanac as one of 40 famous Texas ghost towns.

McCracken further wrote "The word 'Avoca' comes from a place in County Wicklow, Ireland, where two rivers meet called the vale of Avoca, made famous in a poem by Thomas Moore. It is likely that the meeting place of the Olmos Creek and the San Antonio headwaters on the [Incarnate Word] campus, more active and wider then than now, might have reminded these Irish settlers of the place not far from Dublin known as Avoca."

The Hon. Peter Gunning, consul general of Ireland, served as guest speaker, and Incarnate Word Artist-in-Residence Maureen Halligan arranged for soil from Ireland's Avoca to be sprinkled on the ground dedicated for the new apartments. Incarnate Word's Avoca was completed in August 1987 and now houses approximately eighty students.

As the first anniversary of his inauguration approached, it was Lou's turn to bestow some special honors. He invited Sister Joseph Marie Armer, Monsignor Thomas A. French, Sister Theophane Power, and Sister Margaret Patrice

(L-R) Sister Alocoque, Sister Toni and Maureen Halligan.

Slattery to a small luncheon. None of them knew what was coming. It was not a secret that four endowed professorial chairs in natural science, religious studies, education, and English would be in place for the 1988–89 school year. What was unknown until that luncheon was that Lou had decided to name the chairs for religious persons who had made significant contributions to the college.

The natural science chair was named for Sister Joseph Marie Armer, science faculty member and founder of the Alamo Regional Science Fair. Sister Joseph Marie had started teaching at Incarnate Word in 1929, after graduating from the University of Texas at Austin. She was twenty-two years old and known as Annie Armer. Annie converted to Catholicism and then joined the Sisters of Charity of the Incarnate Word. Though legally blind in her later years, Sister Joseph Marie continued to teach until retirement and then tutored until her death in 2000.

The chair in religious studies honored Monsignor Thomas French, who had been part of the religious studies faculty for thirty-five years. Sister Theophane Power was honored with the chair in education. Sister Theophane, a native of Ireland, began teaching education courses at the college in 1950. Her specialties were research and philosophy of education. The chair in English carried the name of Sister Margaret Patrice Slattery, former president and at that time chancellor of the college.

All four honorees were shocked and protested the honor. "In religious life Sisters are not singled out," Lou explained. "They are part of a congregation. But I singled them out because they deserved that recognition. And Father French was as much a part of the Congregation as the Sisters." French protested the strongest. "I had to pull rank on him and tell him this was the way it would be, period," Lou laughed.

Funding for the endowed chairs was almost complete. It came primarily from a delayed grant by the Kenedy Foundation, a Catholic entity. Although the money had been granted during Sister Margaret Patrice's presidency, a lawsuit against the foundation froze all awards for several years. When the money was finally released, the silver lining was an additional $600,000 in accumulated interest. Raising the rest of the money, approximately 20 percent, was another fund-raising responsibility for Tom Plofchan.

Lou was not finished giving awards. That year he also asked the board to approve a special recognition for individuals who gave meritorious service to the college and to the San Antonio community. The Insigne Verbum (Sign of the Word) award was to become a prestigious award that Incarnate Word would bestow on a small number of individuals over the next twenty-four years of Lou's presidency. The first recipients were Charles Kilpatrick, Bill Moll, Emilio Nicolas, and Bernard Waterman. Roger Staubach and Lionel Sosa received the award in 1988, while later honorees included Archbishop Patrick Flores, Tom Benson, and Larry Walker. In addition to the honor, recipients receive a handcrafted porcelain representation of the university logo, created by Incarnate Word artist Nancy Pawel and mounted by Steve Heying in a carefully handcrafted frame.

Success and a high profile are often lightening rods, and Lou Agnese's rising profile was no exception. Less than a week after the newspapers carried the story of the endowed chairs and about two months after praising San Antonio's Outstanding Young Person for 1986, the headlines had a different tone. "Sports complex is called threat to river headwaters," read a March 31 headline in the *Light*. The excitement that was shared in the media when Roger Staubach helped break ground for the complex now turned into a feeding frenzy played out in the newspapers.

The controversy centered on the fact that the San Antonio River headwaters, called by many the "Blue Hole," are located on land then owned by the Sisters of Charity of the Incarnate Word. That land is immediately adjacent to land the Sisters leased to Incarnate Word College and on which the sports complex was being built. During an exceptionally heavy rain in December 1986, numerous hidden springs began bubbling up, leading critics to conclude they were the river's source.

"In my opinion, this is a criminal act," the *Light* quoted the chairman of the Brackenridge Park Advisory Committee chair as saying. "They've destroyed the headwaters of the San Antonio River. Those springs are what start the San Antonio River." By April 9 a popular columnist had joined the fray

Lou with the first four Insigne Verbum award recipients
(L-R) Charlie Kilpatrick, Emilio Nicolas,
Bernard Waterman and Bill Moll.

San Antonio *Express-News* cartoon faults IWC development (cartoon courtesy of the San Antonio *Express-News*).

with a long, scathing opinion piece that attacked Agnese to the extent of calling his public explanation "insulting nonsense." The next day an *Express-News* editorial cartoon added visual impact to the controversy.

Jim Van Straten had been Lou's assistant for three months when the storm broke. He, Lou, and Dick McCracken spoke to media representatives and answered the constantly ringing phones. On April 13 architect Mike McChesney spoke with *Express-News* writer Tom Bower, and Incarnate Word's conscientious protection of the headwaters began to reach the public. McChesney said, "To my way of thinking, we are not destroying anything at all. We are enhancing the river." He explained how Incarnate Word was improving the flow of the springs. An engineering firm had been hired to re-engineer them and provide better drainage during wet years. The firm laid 6,000 feet of eight-inch perforated plastic pipes, wrapped in fabric to filter the silt. McChesney described the pipes as "French drains" and explained that fourteen of them were being set in gravel two feet underground.

Letters to the editor began to swing in the college's favor. Finally, on May 17, after back-and-forth accusations and explanations, *Express-News* columnist Maury Maverick Jr. wrote a column as colorful as his name. In it he posed questions to Dick

Architect Mike McChesney has translated Lou's brainstorms into buildings since 1986.

McCracken and printed Dick's answers. But it was Maverick's summation that was the bottom line to the controversy: "Finally, what do I think about all this? Are the folks at IWC the good guys or the bad guys? Before you read my answer you should know I'd rather criticize Catholics than eat a bowl of chili."

He addressed the question of environmental damage. "Here I think a judge with a lick of common sense would, to use a lawyer term, 'balance the equities.' IWC is not some cold-blooded developer constructing half-a-million-dollar homes over the aquifer for fat cats. It is a small college reaching out to all parts of Bexar County, including the ghettos, trying to help young people have a chance in life, and in the process is giving you and me a hiking trail to the 'Blue Hole.' That, sweet readers, is balancing the equities. That is when the fat lady begins to sing, and don't think for a minute IWC's lawyer, Pat Maloney, who can be meaner than h---, doesn't understand this."

The last word printed on the subject appears to be an article in the June 20 *Light* with the small tongue-in-cheek headline, "Drainage system at IWC site dries up controversy." The headline was subsumed under a larger, equally pun-ny one: "With no springs attached." Few know that Lou also worked with the Congregation over the years to protect the headwaters as the Sisters formed what is now known as the Headwaters Coalition.

With the attack over, the college resumed its normal activity, which was always intense. Enrollment numbers again soared, new faculty were hired, and Sister Helena Monahan settled into her role as executive vice president for academic affairs. The academic structure Lou had mentioned earlier was now in place with three academic divisions and deans. Dr. Mary Beth Swofford was dean of the humanities and fine arts division, Dr. Ann Hillestad was dean of natural and behavioral sciences and nursing, and Dr. Jim Van Straten moved from assisting Lou to being dean

New academic deans (L-R)
Dr. Mary Beth Swofford, Dr. Jim Van Straten and Dr. Ann Hillestad.

of professional studies, which included business, teacher education, and applied arts and sciences.

Enrollment for fall 1987 was 1,885. To accommodate the growth and maintain the student-faculty ratio, thirty-two faculty members and twenty-five support staff were hired. Jerry McCarthy replaced Van Straten as assistant to the president. McCarthy was now Lou's third assistant in three years, but this time it was not because Lou was "hard to work for," as he had warned Marge. McCracken and Van Straten just happened to be exactly what Lou needed in the two dean positions he created.

As the weeks went on, Lou received two other honors. First, he was one of four San Antonio business leaders honored by the International Association of Business Communicators. That award was particularly significant for someone who had conquered the earlier communication problems of shyness and a severe stutter. Lou's openness about these early challenges has been valuable for students who see what he accomplished as he overcame them. "A weakness is just an unidentified strength," he tells them. "Once you identify the weakness, you work at it until it becomes an asset, a strength for you."

The other honor was equally important to Lou. Gannon University in Erie, Pennsylvania, named him one of their Distinguished Alumni for 1987. He was selected "in recognition of his lifelong commitment to Catholic education in America, and for his service to and support of Gannon University." Lou had received his master's of education from Gannon in 1974 and his education specialist degree in counseling services in 1976. He had previously completed his B.A. in history and psychology from St. Mary of the Plains College in Kansas and went on to receive a Ph.D. in counselor education with an emphasis in administrative development and supervision from the University of Pittsburgh in 1981.

Lou financed all that education in as creative a fashion as he still finances endeavors today. He worked as a crop duster both in the air and on ground ("inhaled DDT all the damn day"); briefly loaded live turkeys ("nasty birds, really nasty"); and then "got my first decent job as bartender at the Dodge City Country Club. Besides feeding my personal habits of smoking and drinking, that job was the first opportunity I ever had to interact with successful people of means. I learned a lot as their bartender."

Back at Incarnate Word, campus improvements continued as did the new traditions of the President's Spaghetti Dinner and Light the Way. The Christmas lighting had gotten a boost during the bond-funded work on the campus infrastructure. Steve Heying pointed out to Lou that it would be a good time and a simple matter to lay new cable for the trees on Broadway and those that had just been planted along the Hildebrand side. Actually, Steve was remembering how hard it had been to rig the earlier 10,000 lights, and he now knew Lou well enough to know 10,000 was only the beginning.

Ever the entrepreneur, Lou sought a sponsor for the heavy costs of the 1987 event. He went back to media partners and others who had been supportive of earlier projects. Red McCombs, Sosa and Associates, and KTSA-KTFM sponsored the lighting, while Southwestern Bell and Rogers Cable helped with bucket trucks and manpower. Steve Heying had been right—10,000 was only the beginning. Two hundred volunteers helped place 30,000 feet of wire and almost 20,000 lights. Archbishop Flores was again present, this time for a Mass and a procession to the site near the San Antonio River where a switch turned on the magic of the lights.

While reminiscing about how Light the Way had grown, Lou shared the story of the 1988 event. It started as most of Lou's stories start, with how to get it funded. This time the event would have over 50,000 lights, so he needed

The Administration Building during an early
Light the Way ceremony. By 2010, the lights had
increased from 10,000 to more than a million.

a strong sponsor. Earlier Dick Mc-Cracken had arranged for Lou to meet Bill Crain, the region's Budweiser distributor and a member of the board of St. Peter-St. Joseph Children's Home that Dick chaired.

Bill Crain was leery of friendships with college presidents, according to Dick, so it took a little time to arrange the meeting. But it took place, and Bill and Lou hit it off immediately. Over the years Bill and Pat Crain became close friends of Lou and Mickey, and Bill eventually joined the Incarnate Word board, becoming one of its most involved and generous members.

Spuds McKenzie, object of Lou and Bill Crain's mischief during the Budweiser "puppy" issue. (photo courtesy of the San Antonio *Express-News*)

Crain already sponsored the downtown San Antonio lighting, so it was not hard to convince him to sponsor Incarnate Word's. The event was now publicized as Bud Lights the Way. A giant blow-up of Spuds, the Budweiser canine logo, was hauled to campus and sat happily facing Broadway—and Earl Abel's restaurant, where Dr. Amy Freeman Lee was having breakfast.

Marge warned Lou as soon as she hung up the phone: "Amy's on her way, and she's hot about Budweiser." Amy arrived quickly and closed Lou's door as she entered his office. Lou recalls, "She was livid. 'Dr. Agnese, this time you've gone too far! Promoting beer!'" Lou still laughs as he tells the story. "We're not promoting beer, Amy. That's a puppy. Everyone loves puppies," he said with exaggerated innocence. To her credit, Amy didn't settle for the puppy story. Lou talked to Bill Crain, and Spuds was moved closer to the auditorium, out of the limelight. "Bill wanted it out in front, but he was always a very reasonable man and he understood my problem," Lou said.

Bill Crain and Budweiser continued to sponsor Light the Way until Bill sold the distributorship. After that, Dennis O'Malley and his Miller beer distributorship sponsored the event until O'Malley sold his distributorship in 1998. Since then, H-E-B has been sponsor for the event, which has grown to over a million lights, life-sized nativity figures, toy drives, and local and international participation.

The international participation grew from an event that Lou actually had to miss. Earlier Mayor Henry Cisneros had invited Lou to accompany him to Kumamoto City in Japan, representing the educational component of San Antonio's new sister city relationship with Kumamoto. Lou was unable to arrange his calendar and had reluctantly foregone the trip, but in 1988 dignitaries from Kumamoto traveled to San Antonio.

As the two cities strengthened their sister city bond, Kumamoto Gakuen University became Incarnate Word's first sister school. More than 100 others would follow.

Incarnate Word is now known for its international strength and Lou Agnese is one of the most traveled and cross-culturally skilled college presidents in the country. Yet with the exception of trips to the Congregation's schools and retreat houses in Mexico, Lou had been out of the United States only once, when Cisneros gave him a rain check to travel to Kumamoto the next year. That experience changed Lou and Incarnate Word for the next twenty-plus years.

CHAPTER 8
DÉJÀ VU IN WACO

As the spring 1988 semester began, there was more evidence that the ad campaign was working. Spring enrollment totaled 1,905 students — a 57 percent increase over spring 1986. The number was even more significant since spring enrollments are usually lower than fall ones. In addition, there were over 400 graduate students that spring, the largest number in the school's history.

However, *Express-News* columnist Paul Thompson was either feeling particularly grumpy when he wrote his February 19 column, or he really was sick of Incarnate Word ads. Under the headline "Infuriating," Thompson wrote, "Why can't The College understand that it is very easy to run a good thing into the ground by overexposing its content and mercilessly pounding it into the human ear?" Thompson ended his tirade with boldface type: ". . . look guys, the time has come to lighten up." He suggested there would be an enraged outcry from people of "We've had it with The College."

The ads didn't stop, the outcry was a whimper, Thompson received some negative letters to which he responded negatively, and the band played on!

In fairness to Paul Thompson, the ads were everywhere. Even Marge, Lou's faithful administrative assistant, was occasionally overwhelmed by them. One Saturday Marge was called to the office to solve a problem for Lou, who was out of town at the time. She returned home late and somewhat out of sorts, only to hear Lou talking in her living room. She went in to find her husband, Ralph, watching an Incarnate Word commercial on TV. "Good Lord, I can't get away from that man even in my own house," she complained.

The use of "The College" as a branding term reached further than Lou Agnese or Lionel Sosa had expected. It was apparently being noted internationally. Dr. Merry Saegert, a faculty member in the home economics department, received a letter from a hospital in mainland China addressed to her at Incarnate Word; the second line of the address was "The College". No one knew at that time just how involved The College would become with the People's Republic of China in another ten years.

That same spring *Express-News* columnist Maury Maverick Jr. was in his usual good form. He was not writing about ad campaigns or the earlier San Antonio River controversy; he was simply having a good time publicly sharing humor with Lou Agnese. Maverick was an advocate for purple martins and used his February 7 column to tell readers where to buy purple martin houses. He also told readers that Amy Freeman Lee and some professors and students at Incarnate Word had raised money for a huge purple martin house to be located on campus near the headwaters of the river. When the money was sent to Agnese, Maverick stated, "I wrote him a letter and accused him and all Italian-Americans of being anti–purple martin. I knew that Agnese was good at cooking pasta for the nuns over there, but had no idea he had such a delightful sense of humor. Let me share his letter with you for it's more fun than a barrel of monkeys. Watch!

> Dear Maury: It is not true that Italian-Americans are prejudiced against purple martins. About the only *Martin* Italian-Americans know about is Dean Martin . . . We are, however, prejudiced against purple *martinis* and perhaps that is what you heard. In fact it is well known that Italian-American Catholics love birds. Look at all the cardinals we have! Why in the Vatican they even have a college just for cardinals. We'll let the Lutherans have a college for purple martins. Please be assured that the money raised for the purple-martin condominium will be matched by the college, and [the house] will be installed on a pleasant spot overlooking the recreation areas. We won't even ask the purple martins for proof of baptism before moving in.

That lighthearted exchange—even though really written by Dick Mc-Cracken, not Lou—showed the comfort zone developing between San Antonio and Lou Agnese. Lou needed the acceptance it implied in order to deepen public perception of him as more than just a marketing dynamo. He was about to take on an issue with local and national ramifications—the critical civilian and military nursing shortage. This would lead him into a philosophical debate between the nursing profession and the American Medical Association (AMA) a few months later. In order to succeed, he needed to be trusted not only for how his views affected the academic world but also for the impact they could have on the nursing profession.

He organized a four-point program aimed first at access into Incarnate Word's school of nursing, one of the oldest accredited west of the Mississippi. He told the *Express-News*, "We've been working on ways to improve access to health care [education] through The College, SAC [San Antonio College], and the three hospitals in the program." The three hospitals—Santa Rosa Hospitals in San Antonio, Corpus Christi, and Fort Worth—were sponsored by the Sisters of Charity of the Incarnate Word.

The first part of the plan involved an articulation agreement offered to and signed by San Antonio College allowing students from its two-year nursing program to move seamlessly into Incarnate Word's bachelor's and later master's degree programs. Such agreements are commonplace now but were unusual twenty years ago. The second part involved unprecedented loan forgiveness. This opportunity was provided by a cooperative program between Incarnate Word College and the three hospitals of the Incarnate Word Health System. The hospitals agreed to underwrite nursing education costs in return for employment agreements. The third part involved an Incarnate Word program to secure grant money for nursing education. According to the May 7, 1988, *Express-News*, "That effort was kicked off by the announcement that the Clayton Fund of Houston had provided an initial gift of $25,000, providing scholarships for 20 students." Finally, the fourth part was a new graduate degree combining a Master of Science and a Master of Business Administration. "Nurses are no longer the hospital employees of earlier times; today's nurses are valuable health care professionals who will continue to take on more responsibilities in the medical field," Lou explained. The *Express-News* touted the degree as the first of its kind in the southwestern United States and one of only a half dozen in the country.

Not surprisingly, Lou and Lionel worked the nursing focus into the new ads. "1 + 3 = Brainpower" headlined an ad announcing, "The College is building a network of partners to prepare you for the future. We've signed three historic agreements with our sister colleges of the Alamo Community College District. These agreements mean access. Access to college. Access to financial aid. Access to jobs."

The three agreements included one with Palo Alto College in banking, one with St. Philip's College in hotel and restaurant management, fashion design, and interior design, and an agreement with San Antonio College targeting nursing. In a break from the usual format, Lou's picture did not appear in that ad. Instead the logos of the three community colleges and Incarnate Word were prominently displayed, along with statements like "Four colleges working together to make education accessible and affordable" and "Four colleges working together to provide access to an exciting future in South Texas."

Those who know Lou well can guess right away that another reason there were four logos instead of his picture was because the ad cost was divided among the four institutions. Lou might not be tight, but as they would have said back in Papa Agnese's day, "he could squeeze a nickel 'til the buffalo hollered." Lou would not have paid — even scholarships — to publicize another institution.

It was a mark of Sosa and Agnese that they chose just the right day to announce the nursing focus. The project was announced at a press conference on May 6, National Nurse's Day. The *Light* carried the story and reported that "the nursing shortage has resulted in at least 544 current vacancies for registered nurses in San Antonio." The ad announcing the MSN/MBA reflected Lou's position on the role of nurses, a position that would lead him to take on the AMA later that year. The ad, with the subhead "Business Brainpower for Nurse Professionals," explained why the college had instituted the degree: "At the heart of the health care mission are today's nurses who administer approximately 45% of the total budget of a large hospital and as much as 60% of the work force."

Lou continued focusing on ways to help provide access for prospective nursing students. He addressed the shortage of military nurses by directing that an unsolicited proposal be drafted and sent first to the Department of Defense and then to U.S. Rep. Albert Bustamante. The proposal called for the DOD to pay half of students' nursing education while the college would raise funds for the other half. To merit this assistance nurses would have to agree to serve either four years in the military reserves or two years of active duty.

The *Express-News* carried this item from its Washington Bureau, "A proposal born at Incarnate Word College took a big step forward when a House subcommittee voted to direct the Pentagon to launch an experimental cooperative effort with college nursing programs." The story quoted Bustamante as saying, "The nursing shortage within the military services remains particularly acute . . . currently a 1,700 shortfall in the active components and a 31,000 shortfall in the reserves' wartime requirement." He continued, "Not only does this situation pose immediate problems during peacetime, it would represent a war-stopper during wartime since critical specialties like medical surgical nurses and nurse anesthetists comprise a large part of the overall shortfall."

The nursing profession and new degrees were not the only things occupying Lou Agnese the spring and summer of 1988. On March 17, St. Patrick's Day, ground was broken for the Incarnate Word Convocation Center. Mayor Henry Cisneros hailed the structure as another facility that could be used by the city. He told *Express-News* reporter Tim Price, "IWC has made it official that it is going to open this facility to everyone. This gives us another open space, another backyard. It also helps organized collegiate sports to be

Lou with (L-R) Dolores Mitchell, Sister Margaret Patrice Slattery,
Brig. General Robert McDermott and Bishop Edmond Carmody.

developed in San Antonio." Archbishop Patrick Flores blessed the site and,
according to Price, used the moment to encourage Cisneros in his push for the
Alamodome. (It became a reality in 1993.)

The convocation center was later named for Alice McDermott, the late wife
of Brig. Gen. Robert McDermott. Alice McDermott was an active member of
Incarnate Word's Development Board and had been especially good to young
Agnese. He and "Grandma," as he affectionately called her, developed a warm
relationship. "She gave me good advice," he said. "And I usually took it."

The convocation center did become the site for many civic activities, and
the San Antonio Spurs basketball team used it as their practice facility. Like
many sports or multi-use facilities, the center had a glassed-in room on the
second floor overlooking the main event area. That room served as the first
boardroom for Board of Trustees meetings.

Several years after the center was built Incarnate Word hosted a group of
mathematics professors from out of state and used the room for a breakout
session. The Spurs were practicing downstairs, but Incarnate Word faculty
and students had grown accustomed to that and granted the Spurs their pri-
vacy. No one even mentioned the Spurs to the visitors. The session modera-
tor noticed that one professor rose several times and stood looking down at
the basketball court. Finally, after his third trip to the window, the visitor
couldn't help but comment, "You know, this is a small college, but they have
a hell of a basketball team!"

By June Lou and Sister Helena Monahan were hiring faculty and administrators for the coming year, a year that would bring over 2,200 students
to the campus. Among those hired for the 1988-89 academic year were five
people Lou would eventually choose as vice presidents — Frank Ayala, Dr.
Pat Burr, Dr. Denise Doyle, David Jurenovich, and Dr. Pat Watkins. Burr,

Lou (far left) and Dr. David Jurenovich in their student days at Gannon University.

Doyle, and Watkins were new faculty in business, religious studies, and education respectively. Watkins was hired on a one-year contract to replace Sister Mona Smiley while she was on sabbatical. Ayala was hired as dean of student advising, and Jurenovich was dean of student affairs and services.

Lou had known David Jurenovich from their days at Gannon and had reached out to him the year before as a visiting consultant for campus development and student services. Lou had been a first-year graduate student and assistant dorm director at Gannon when David was a freshman. Lou eventually became director of student living, and David became associate director. When Lou left Gannon in 1981 to move to Briar Cliff, David replaced him as director. The two men had built a strong base of trust by the time he rejoined Lou at Incarnate Word.

Lou came up with many creative ideas while jogging.

The year started with the excitement new students always bring to a campus. This time they had another reason to be proud they were at Incarnate Word. Their president had just been named one of the Five Outstanding Young Texans in the second round of the Junior Chamber of Commerce competition. The award ceremony, held in Waco on August 13, honored Lou, Jack M. Fields Jr., a U.S. congressman; Dr. Glenna G. Harris, a pediatrician specializing in children's infectious diseases; Jeff B. Love, an attorney and partner in a Houston law firm; and Robert A. Mosbacher Jr., president of Mosbacher Energy Company and commissioner of the Texas Department of Human Services.

Lou, whose favorite exercise was jogging ("until my hip gave out"), recounts a déjà vu experience he had during his morning run in Waco. "My hotel was near a bridge, so I took that route and jogged across the bridge. I had a weird feeling I had seen that bridge before, but I had never been in Waco. I wasn't even sure how to pronounce it—Way-co or Wack-o. I kept running, and then on the way back I had the same sensation as I neared the bridge. This time I saw a plaque at the base of one of the supports. I stopped to read it and discovered why it was so familiar. It was built by the same man who designed the Brooklyn Bridge and was a smaller copy of the bridge I grew up with. It really is a small world."

Lou went on to be named one of the Ten Outstanding Young Persons in the United States and then to be chosen one of the Ten Outstanding Young Persons in the World. He was singled out for those honors because of his efforts to provide access to higher education for underserved populations, especially the Hispanic population of South Texas. In addition, he had not only restored a small college to stability, but while doing so had also achieved a racial and ethnic mix reflecting the city's demographics. That translated into an unprecedented number of young Hispanics enrolling in college and successfully completing bachelor's and master's degrees.

The award ceremony for the world competition took place in Birmingham, England, in 1989. The ceremony was held as an historic and moving event was about to take place. Television monitors were strategically set up around the room to provide optimum viewing of the award ceremony. But before the awards were given, the monitors switched to live broadcasts, and the assembled guests watched in awe as the Berlin wall was knocked down. Lou adjusted the speech he had prepared in order to share his emotions and address the earth-shaking event just witnessed.

Lou was appreciative of the recognition he received, but when he looked back at the series of awards beginning with the Five Outstanding Young Persons of San Antonio, he shared a story that only a father would remember in the midst of such acclaim. "Louis was eleven at the time and he said, 'Dad, first it was outstanding in San Antonio; then in Texas; then the United States. Now it's the world. What's next? Outstanding on the moon?' I assured him this was the last part," he said, with a laugh and then the quiet smile of a parent remembering.

Lou with President George H.W. Bush during the reception for Outstanding Young Americans.

· II ·
GROWTH AND CHANGE
"Somebody Stop That Man!"

CHAPTER 9
THE BRAINPOWER CONNECTION

N ot everything works. The nursing proposal that passed the House subcommittee never made it further. Lou and others who were committed to improving the nursing shortage worked without the help of the proposed bill.

Incarnate Word's close relationship with the military did not falter, however. Lou and Col. W. N. Gower, director of personnel at Kelly Air Force Base, signed a memorandum of understanding that allowed the college to increase the number of on-base degree programs it offered. Business-related degrees began immediately and were offered in five eight-week terms at reduced rates for Kelly personnel. Retired Brig. Gen. Lillian Dunlap, a graduate of Incarnate Word's nursing program and an active alumna, kept military nursing in the forefront as students chose careers.

The Incarnate Word ads included the message, "We go where today's professionals need education. We offer programs at military bases, at corporate headquarters, at the South Texas Medical Complex, and at Downtown Santa Rosa Hospital."

In late September 1988 Lou wrote a full-page opinion article for the *Light* refuting the AMA's answer to the nursing shortage, which called for "the creation of a new class of health provider, the registered care technician." He argued, "It is necessary to remember that the shortage of nurses is caused by increasing demand rather than shrinking supply." He quoted the figures for entry into nursing programs and the number of nurses currently working. "The problem of a shortage," he continued, "has come precisely because of the growing importance of the RN [Registered Nurse], and the growing importance of the RN is directly related to the fact that the profession has become more and more sophisticated in delivering health care as it has increased its professional standards." Lou explained that the AMA plan "would, in effect, reduce the bedside health provider to a technician qualified only to administer care prescribed by a physician who is not around to witness changes in the patient's condition."

Lou also stressed that in Texas alone 81 percent of 1988's RNs were Anglo. He quoted the Interim Report of the Commission on Nursing, established by the Department of Health and Human Services, which concluded, "Attracting minorities into the profession of nursing is the one certain way to ensure a sound supply." He ended by emphasizing the inconsistency of the AMA's position since minorities were the very market they planned to target for the new program. Lou argued the program "would offer them a dead-end career path, a guaranteed low-paying job and an education which would not put them on the success ladder."

Response was immediate. One letter to the *Light* read, "Our profession should applaud one who is so knowledgeable and can articulate the profession's problems. It seems Agnese has found the pulse of nursing, and he's not even a nurse." Another stated, "The San Antonio chapter of the American Association of Critical-Care Nurses would like to thank the *Light* for printing Dr. Louis Agnese's article on the nursing shortage . . . It was an extremely factual and insightful view on the registered care technician issue."

Incarnate Word continued to implement the four-point program Lou had outlined. Nursing classrooms filled as students, many of them minorities, took advantage of the loan forgiveness program and other financial assistance made available to them at that time.

Like every semester, this one went quickly. In December the college awarded retired Brig. Gen. Robert McDermott an honorary Doctor of Humane Letters at the winter commencement ceremony. McDermott, the chairman and CEO of USAA and an outstanding community leader, also gave the commencement address. Lou conferred 158 degrees that day, 61 of them graduate degrees. He also helped install three community leaders as charter members of Incarnate Word College Emeritus Board. The board functions as an advisory council and is composed of retired members of the Board of Trustees and the Development Board. The honorees were Charlie Cheever, chairman of the Greater San Antonio Chamber of Commerce and senior chairman of the board of Broadway National Bank; Sister Alacoque Power, retired IWC English professor, former board chair, and briefly president of Incarnate Word College; and Charles O. Kilpatrick, president, editor, and publisher of the *Express-News*.

Shortly after the spring semester began, Lou was apprised of a decision the Congregation was struggling to reach. Incarnate Word High School, an all-girls high school begun in 1881 and located directly across the highway from the college, was steadily losing students. The high school and college had originally been together until the construction of Highway 281 sepa-

Incarnate Word High School.

rated them. In fact, after much discussion and dissention, the Texas Department of Transportation built a pedestrian bridge over the highway to keep the two campuses and their respective staffs of Sisters connected.

Both institutions were sponsored by the Sisters of Charity of the Incarnate Word, and both had grown from the Sisters' original mission in 1869 when they came to nurse cholera victims. The Sisters had first built Santa Rosa Hospital; then, as the disease decimated families, it was necessary to build an orphanage, the St. Peter–St. Joseph's Children's Home, on whose board Dick McCracken and Bill Crain served. Teaching then joined nursing as part of the Sisters' mission. Incarnate Word High School and Incarnate Word College are just two of the schools the Congregation built in the United States and Mexico.

Now faced with declining enrollment and fewer Sisters choosing to teach at the high school level, the Congregation was seriously considering closing Incarnate Word High School. Lou approached the Congregation with the proposal that Incarnate Word College take over management of the high school and return it to its honored place in the Incarnate Word structure. Lou had always felt strongly that colleges had an obligation to care what happened in K-12 education. "If those of us in higher education stand by and wait for students to complete those formative years, or drop out before finishing, we have lost the opportunity to provide any guidance or have any influence in the education of our future students and the country's future leaders," he said.

Lou knew he had to walk a careful fiscal line as he outlined the proposal. The college was more secure now, but there was no room for error or miscalculation. As much as he wanted to reunite the high school and college, Lou had to be sure he was not taking on an additional responsibility that could be fiscally unsound. In addition, the high school had several problems that were caused by declining enrollment, but at the same time were contributing to that decline. As enrollment dropped, the high school administration had reluctantly reduced curriculum offerings. That resulted in even more students looking elsewhere for advanced foreign language courses, higher-level science courses, and other electives. The most recent problem was that word on the street talked of the school closing. Parents were reluctant to enroll their daughters if the school would not be there for their entire high school education. As had happened earlier at the college, the decline was also affecting faculty morale.

Lou knew what he wanted to do, but he decided to appoint a task force to study the issues and make a recommendation he could take to the board and to the Congregation. He appointed Dr. Pat Watkins, recently hired IWC faculty member who had experience in secondary teaching and administration, to chair the task force. What the task force found was a jewel tucked away on the slight hill called Mount Erin. The students were outstanding, as was the approach to educating them. The task force report concluded that "it would be a travesty to let this exceptional institution close." Lou Agnese already knew that.

With their responsibility completed, the task force members returned to their busy college schedule. Pat had just been selected for a tenure track position in the education department and was looking forward to the fall semester, but things would get a little complicated first. She explains, "I came home and found sticky notes all over the house telling me Lou Agnese was trying to reach me, but my husband had added, 'Call Jim Van Straten before you talk to Lou!'" Jim knew what was coming and wanted to avoid the train wreck. Unfortunately, Jim had already left for the evening. It was after 8 p.m. and Pat needed to return the president's call.

Lou had two pieces of information to share—one expected and one definitely not. "We have decided to take over the management of the high school," he said. Then the unexpected: "We have created a new position, combining principal of the high school with dean of college preparatory programs at the college." He was calling to offer her that dual position.

"I hadn't reached the point where I was comfortable calling him Lou. He was definitely 'Dr. Agnese' to me," Pat explains. "So I said, 'Dr. Agnese, I can't do that. I've already accepted the other position.'" Lou assured her there was no problem; she would still be on tenure track at the college. But hearing the distress in her voice, Lou said, "Listen, I'm sorry. They tell me I do this all the time. I get in a rush. You need time to think about it. Talk it over with your family. Call me at ten. I'll still be up."

The decision took more than the suggested hour and a half, but with Jim Van Straten's support the deal was struck. Van Straten had one piece of advice about working with Lou. "You're about to get on the fastest moving train you've ever been on." He was right. The Agnese train is so fast you can't get off—the fall would kill you. But the ride would be worth it.

The public reacted positively to news that the college was now managing the high school. Knowing the school was safe from closing, the bleeding stopped and enrollment increased. By the time the doors opened in August 1989 enrollment had increased by over 100 students.

The Sisters teaching at the high school could have made the transition hard or easy. Fortunately, they chose to make it easy. Incarnate Word High School had only had one lay principal in its history, and that had been a man. The Sisters who chose to stay once the transition was announced were the strongest supporters Watkins and Agnese could have had. Sister Clarita Burke who ran the testing center like a general, and the Keaveney sisters, Sister Agnes and Sister Ailbe, made themselves available twenty-four hours a day. No task was too menial or too tiring if it helped the high school or the college.

One of the first hires Watkins made was Roger Labat, a retired army officer recommended by Van Straten. Labat was originally hired as school manager, with the physical plant as his major responsibility. He later became vice principal and in 1995 replaced Watkins as principal when she returned to full-time duties at the college.

Not everyone was pleased with the idea of the high school being part of the college. It was impossible to argue with the rightness of reuniting the two.

(L-R) Mickey, Sister Ailbe Keaveney, Sister Clarita
Burke, Lou and Sister Agnes Keaveney.

It had been the Sisters' vision from the beginning. But turf issues and egos caused a degree of resentment in some quarters. At the high school there were mixed feelings—gratitude that things were stable and a concern about autonomy. At the college some faculty, and probably some administrators, were uncomfortable with high school students participating in activities like the opening Mass of the school year. "There are too many of them," "They're noisy," and "They chewed gum in church" were a few of the comments. Actually, noise and gum had little to do with it. The college community was changing. It had been changing for several years, but this was a change you could point to. Even the Incarnate Word Christmas party almost doubled in size when the high school faculty and spouses were included. Some college faculty felt invaded and resented the fact that they had lost the intimacy of "their party." The resentment was not strong enough or widespread enough to be serious, but the high school was a suggestion of things to come, and that made some people anxious.

Lou had a vision for more than just a high school and a college working together. He saw the potential for a continuum from pre-K through graduate school. The Katherine Ryan Center, the developmental preschool Nancy Agnese helped her father promote, was already on the college campus. The college had close ties with two elementary schools in the area—St. Anthony's, a private school in the Monte Vista neighborhood that had been purchased by parents when the sponsoring congregation of Sisters decided to close it, and St. Peter Prince of the Apostles, an Archdiocesan school in Alamo Heights.

Lou shares his meatball-rolling technique with then Incarnate Word High School Principal Dr. Pat Watkins (photo courtesy of the San Antonio *Express-News*).

Lou envisioned a consortium arrangement that would benefit all the schools, especially the K-12 ones. With the college's mantel spread over them, the schools could join together for both financial and academic advantage. He reasoned that one large entity ordering supplies, paper for example, could command a much better purchasing price than one small elementary school could. Carrying the idea further, if a school needed a plumber or an air conditioning specialist, they would have to call someone to come to the campus, assess the problem, and give a quote on the work. Each call incurred a service charge. Lou knew he could arrange a system whereby a small charge would cover hiring one person to add to the college physical plant staff. Then when a school needed help, the college could send a plumber, an electrician, a security officer, or whatever service person was needed. By helping pay for one worker, the schools would receive access to the entire array of specialists at the college.

Academically, the consortium would bring together faculty in various disciplines and help develop a seamless curriculum from grade one through a bachelor's degree. Articulation points would be established to help eighth graders move into high schools and twelfth graders move into college. Lou described his vision to Pat, and she, Lou, Lionel, and his staff discussed what to call this arrangement.

"Well, we're really trying to connect all the brainpower in the five schools," someone at the table commented. Lou and Lionel jumped on "The Brainpower Connection" as the name. Pat thought it sounded a little anatomical, like something at the base of the skull that might explode if you had a stroke, but she was overruled and The Brainpower Connection was born.

Lou and former Mayor Henry Cisneros
display the first Brainpower Connection ad.

CHAPTER 10
A SLOW BOAT FOR BALANCE

While the Brainpower Connection was gaining momentum, so was the first formal student exchange program. Kumamoto, Japan, was eager to send college and high school students to San Antonio, its new sister city. San Antonio was also courting international trade at that time and any positive engagement with Japan was important.

College exchange didn't present any real challenge—most strong college programs favored international exchange. But convincing high school officials and parents to send sophomores or juniors all the way to Japan was another issue. Incarnate Word parent Henry Cisneros urged Lou to launch an international exchange program at Incarnate Word High School. There wasn't time for many serious Japanese language classes, but intense culture study did begin once students were selected. The Kumamoto program continued for twenty years, and Japanese became a standard language offering for both Incarnate Word College and Incarnate Word High School students.

The Brainpower Connection helped those classes become reality. Part of Lou's vision included allowing students from the high school to participate in classes and other activities at the college. It began with the Senior Connection, a program in which selected high school seniors could take courses such as English at the college and receive credit for both senior English at the high school level and English I at the college level. Students could take four to six courses in this manner throughout their senior year, and upon graduation they received transcripts from both Incarnate Word High School and Incarnate Word College.

Later many other high schools and colleges offered dual credit, sometimes at the expense of quality, but the arrangement between Incarnate Word College and Incarnate Word High School maintained the highest level of academic integrity. All of the courses were taught by full-time Incarnate Word faculty, including Dr. Pat Lonchar and Dr. Mary Beeman. At first they were offered at the high school, but soon that arrangement was changed to allow the students to be enrolled with their undergraduate cohorts on the college campus.

Carol Mengden and other qualified high school faculty who normally would have taught the high school courses were given the opportunity to teach as adjunct professors at the college. But they did not teach the Senior Connection classes. All were in agreement that in order for students to experience the full impact of college courses, they needed to leave their comfort zone, including the faculty members they had known since their freshman year. High school students received credit in English, foreign languages, political science, mathematics, chemistry, and other sciences. The demand for Japanese was not yet great enough to offer it at both institutions so classes were combined, a break from the original design for seniors only. All reasoned that whether students were high school or college freshmen, they were starting Japanese at the same point—entry level.

The reasoning continued into eighth grade also. If high school seniors could study with college students, why couldn't eighth grade students study with high school freshmen? Algebra classes were the first for this experiment. Years later the Senior Connection was offered to neighboring Alamo Heights High School and to North East Independent School District's International School of the Americas. It was no secret why Alamo Heights was included; young Louis III, who had been growing up under the scrutiny of an entire college community, was by that time attending Alamo Heights High School.

As the first year of managing the high school was winding down, Lou was gearing up. He was already on a schedule that should have killed him, but it was growing more intense. He was everywhere and in everything. Each day brought a new idea, and each idea had a suspense date of yesterday. Tom Plofchan told his wife, Paula, "I don't know when he sleeps. He must get up at four in the morning to think of all this." Lou knew what had to be done if the college were to stay on course. He knew it was not enough to have caught up; the college had to pull away from the crowd in order to be secure in the coming years

Lou was now a fascinating mixture of parental figure and demanding taskmaster. He had established the President's Advisory Council (PAC), which brought together deans and vice presidents and several members appointed by the faculty. He also insisted on student representation. As the campus grew, the PAC meetings were more important to Lou. They became his way of staying in touch with everything that was happening. Occasionally some of the happenings were not what he wanted or were not moving as quickly as he knew they should. Never accused of being a patient man, Lou's irritation would sometimes flare. That did not upset those who knew him well. But others were nervous and uncomfortable when the expected quiet of higher education discussions were peppered with irritation and the vocabulary Lou had honed to perfection.

He decided to address that issue at a PAC meeting one morning. "Look," he said, "I'm Italian. We get excited sometimes. Grant me that. I'm not yelling at you—I'm just yelling!" The yelling and the impatience were balanced by a caring that was sometimes touching. Lou knew and cared about everyone at the college. It was not unusual for him to ask about a family member or offer a personal comment during meetings. One of those caring times occurred at Christmas when Lou arrived with individually selected presents for each PAC member. One former member recently pointed to the bookends in her office. They carried the message, "Continue to Search for New Horizons," something Lou himself always did. "They probably aren't expensive, but they're valuable to me," she said.

Lou was even playful with PAC at times. That Christmas he reached into the box of gifts and pulled out a teddy bear. Confronting a long table of very grown up administrators, he chuckled and said, "Santa left this at my house by mistake. It was supposed to go to the high school." He passed it down to the principal. The teddy bear gift was Lou's way of being part of a trend that had started at the high school. Its mascot is really a shamrock, but some of the students pointed out, "You can't hug a shamrock," and the teddy bear became the unofficial mascot. Bears popped up around campus like mushrooms—in the principal's office, tucked in backpacks, on posters, and now in the middle of a PAC meeting.

The 1989–90 school year was also a time that Lou once again changed assistants. Jerry McCarthy moved on, and Lou hired Jim Tilton, who would become one of Lou's serious go-to persons. It was Jim to whom Lou now turned for writing and later for help with his budding international program. Jim was almost as energetic as Lou, but he had one nervous habit that drove Lou crazy. Jim would sit in meetings and click his ballpoint pen back and forth, in and out. "Stop it—you're driving me nuts!" Lou would tell him. But the clicking would resume in a few minutes. Jim was Lou's assistant for the next nine years. He and Lou clicked as well as Jim's pen and he helped Lou with many difficult issues during those nine years.

This same year Lou made the decision to move the Katherine Ryan Center to St. Anthony's, one of the Brainpower elementary schools. Actually, his original decision was to close the center, but the outcry from parents and the general public was too great. Lou, who always claimes problems are just disguised opportunities, applied his own philosophy to the situation and negotiated the move. But even that decision received mixed reviews. It made sense for a developmental preschool to be at St. Anthony's, but it was another change and changes were growing more worrisome to parts of the community. Many wanted the center to stay on the college campus, but the education department was growing and the space was badly needed. The move also strengthened the connection with St. Anthony's since college staff continued to manage the center and share expertise with the elementary and preschool staff. Most folks had to grudgingly admit that Lou had hit a home run—even if accidentally.

Yet another change occurred on April 6, 1990. Amy Freeman Lee announced her resignation as longtime chair of the Board of Trustees, effective at the end of May. Amy had served on the board for twenty years and as chair for eighteen. It did not come as a surprise to Lou or to those who knew Amy well. She had just celebrated her seventy-fifth birthday, and the president she had helped select was proving successful. In a prepared statement, she said, "I am grateful to have had an opportunity to serve a liberal arts college like Incarnate Word because ideally I am convinced that in order for each person to reach his or her maximum potential he or she must learn to live on the human level." Sister Dorothy Ettling, superior general of the Congregation, thanked Dr. Lee, stating that "Amy has led the board with wisdom and grace, and her numerous commitments to Incarnate Word have been an invaluable service to the college."

In anticipation of Amy's decision, Lou and Sister Ettling had been examining lists of potential successors. They knew they needed someone who could open new doors. Dolores Mitchell, who had joined the board in 1987 and was serving her second three-year term, accepted the position. A graduate of Incarnate Word High School, Dolores had also briefly attended Incarnate Word College. She received her bachelor's degree in English literature and history from the University of Texas at Austin. The trustees chose Lionel Sosa as vice chair, Sister Carol Ann Jokerst as secretary, and Bill Crain as treasurer. There were other changes occurring in the board itself; Lou and the Congregation had agreed to term limits for the trustees and board officers. Lou brought a business-like approach to the meetings and was conscious of the value of time, not just his own but that of the busy, executive-level men and women on the board. He and Dolores Mitchell proved to be a good team.

By now efforts to increase the athletic program were bearing fruit. The men's soccer team won the Heart of Texas championship, the Crusader softball field opened, and Ruth Eileen and Daniel Sullivan, onetime owners of the San Antonio Missions baseball team, made Sullivan Baseball Field a reality. In addition, the Run for Brainpower was begun as a scholarship fundraiser. The endowment fund was twice what it had been in 1986, and enrollment numbers for the 1990–91 school year set an all-time high. The college enrolled 2,616 college students and the high school 445 students.

Under Sister Helena's direction and with the insight of faculty leader Dr. Bob Connelly, the faculty had established its new core curriculum, the rank and tenure process had been formalized, and the new faculty handbook was completed. Jim Van Straten had left the college in 1990 to become dean of allied health at the University of Texas Health Science Center, and Dr. Bill Platzer was now dean of professional studies.

In September 1991 *Money* magazine named Incarnate Word one of the 100 colleges and universities rated as "best buys." The *Light's* headline for the story read "IWC, Trinity listed among nation's 'best buys' for college education." This was the second year in a row the two schools were named to the list. Selection was based on a survey analyzing 1,011 colleges and universities for quality of students, faculty and facilities, and tuition. "All of the factors that are involved in having a good value for your dollar are here," Lou told the *Light*. "And at the same time, we're a very unique campus."

Homecoming events that April included the dedication of the Sister Antoninus Buckley Alumni Courtyard. Directly behind the Administration Building, it featured a fountain flowing from green marble reused from the college chapel. It was Lou's opportunity to honor his beloved Sister Toni.

The close ties Incarnate Word had maintained with the military were once again in the spotlight when the Nursing Building was rededicated that year. Retired Brig. Gen. Lillian Dunlap had participated in the original dedication in 1971 when she was chief of the Army Nurse Corps. She returned now to serve as mistress of ceremonies as the building was named for Sister

(L-R) Mickey and Lou, Ruth Eileen and
Dan Sullivan enjoying a Fiesta dinner.

Charles Marie Frank, who was once dean of nursing at Catholic University of America.

Sister Charles Marie helped develop Incarnate Word's nursing curriculum when that program was accredited in 1942. Board chair Dolores Mitchell and Col. Sue Ellen Turner unveiled the dedication plaque. Col. Turner had graduated from the nursing school in 1973 and had just been selected for promotion to brigadier general. She would assume the office of Air Force chief of nursing later that year.

The gymnasium was redesigned and reopened as the Richard and Janet Cervera Wellness Center. Considering the wildest dream the faculty had for technology in 1985 was "a telephone of my own—on my own desk," it was a triumph for all when the Paul Daher Computing Center opened in 1991.

The college was just where it needed to be, but it was getting there at a high cost to Lou Agnese. "Things were getting crazy—out of balance," he recalls. "My whole life revolved around the college. Mickey was keeping the family connected, but I knew I was nearing burnout.

"Nancy brought it all into focus as only a child can do. One night she looked at me and said, 'Daddy, I don't even know you.' That hit hard." Lou paused and shook his head. "I knew I needed to get away and try to put a personal plan in place, a way to restore my connection with family, to restore balance in our lives."

Lou decided to use October and November 1991 for a sabbatical. He needed to get away in order to get close. To some that might seem contradictory, but "I needed time to regroup; to find myself again," he explains. Lou chose a cruise to Latin America. "I deliberately chose that cruise. The average age of the other passengers was over sixty, so I wasn't surrounded with people my age. I read fourteen books on that cruise—things I would never have gotten around to." He left the cruise in Rio de Janeiro so he could fly home for Thanksgiving.

Lou had worked out a plan he shared with Mickey. He knew he would never be able to have a large quantity of family time, so he opted for quality time. The "family plan," as he and Mickey called it, included three family vacations a year—Christmas and New Year's, spring break, and summer. They were good times to be away because, except for summer, the major activity of the campus was closed down.

With Mickey's blessing, another part of the plan evolved. In order for Lou to have time with the children, he would take them on a trip of their choice to mark special occasions. "When Louis finished elementary school he wanted to go to Cancún, so he and I went with Club Med for a week," Lou explained. This continued all the way through their young adulthood—to Louis's graduation from law school and Nancy's graduation from veterinary school. Just before her wedding, Nancy and Lou traveled to Korea and China, Nancy's choice of destinations.

Lou became acutely aware of the gift of time. He frequently points out that since no one knows how much or how little time is left, it must never be wasted.

Talent is the other thing Lou can't stand seeing wasted. He never misses talent. He spots it on the street, in the classroom, in meetings, or when traveling the world. Sometimes it is in young people who need a mentor and a break; sometimes in powerful executives or gifted men and women whose presence or involvement with Incarnate Word enhances the college. The young people who are drifting, or whose talents are not being used, find a mentor for life if they are willing to work. And Lou and Mickey's home is always open to the young people they mentor. They have "adopted" a daughter in Mexico and a family from China.

·····················Part of Lou's "Valued Collection"·····················

 Dr. James Creagan, former U.S. Ambassador to Honduras and former president of John Cabot University in Rome, is now Distinguished Professor and Ambassador-in-Residence.

 Raul Rodriguez, former president of the North American Development Bank, is now Distinguished Professor in Banking and Finance and holder of the Benson Chair in Banking.

 Lou Fox, former City Manager of San Antonio and Lubbock, is now Assistant to the President and Instructor in Management.

 James Rangel, retired Vice President of Anheuser-Busch and a founding member of the National Association of Hispanic Journalists, is now Interdisciplinary Faculty-in-Residence.

Lou urges many of the powerful or gifted men and women he meets to share themselves with Incarnate Word students and faculty. They sometimes join the faculty or administration where they have direct impact on the entire community. "Lou doesn't collect stamps or coins," one person observed. "He collects people."

CHAPTER 11
FLAK JACKETS AND TEXAS RANGERS

The annual planning retreats had grown a little more sophisticated, and benefactors were generous in providing transportation and lodging for them. In 1989 administrators and faculty representatives had traveled to Puerto Vallarta. True to his concern for families, Lou allowed spouses to attend. Only the airfare had to be paid by the couple; all other expenses were absorbed by the college and its benefactors, who saw these getaways as bonding opportunities for campus leaders.

Puerto Vallarta was beautiful. It was easy to picture Ava Gardner on one of the balconies during the film *Night of the Iguana*. In fact, the little and not-so-little iguanas were everywhere. You could even have your picture taken with a not-so-little iguana if you were willing to pay the price—and willing to hold a scaly reptile in your arms.

Another Mexico retreat was held in Mazatlán. But this time it was a totally different situation. The beach was lovely; Sister Helena Monahan, who couldn't reach five feet in high heels, landed a marlin on a deep sea fishing trip in rough waters with the help of Steve Heying and others; and even the meetings were productive. But somewhere in one of the off-site kitchens, the shrimp became contaminated and almost all of Lou's planning team fell ill. Tom Plofchan missed most of the later meetings, and there was debate about flying him home early. Dick McCracken, whose illness also hit hard, managed to keep his sense of humor. Dick had made a trek up in the hills while Sister Helena and others were out fishing. One of the administrators had seen a great terra cotta cooking pot earlier and asked him to look for one on his trip to the little hillside village. He returned successfully with the pot under his arm, but with all the symptoms of food poisoning. Back home, the administrator approached Dick to pay for the pot. Dick's tongue-in-cheek response was, "I don't want your money. I just want you to be as sick as I was!" In spite of the illness and the occasional inconvenience, the retreats proved to be times to get away from telephones and offices and concentrate on two things—planning for the next five years and having the opportunity to learn more about colleagues. Not everyone supported the retreats. Some who did not understand that donated funds were earmarked for the retreats made comments about a better use for the money. Others expressed embarrassment when they returned because colleagues had not had the same vacation. But overall, the retreats were appreciated for the closeness they offered administration and faculty representatives. And the negative remarks were just part of the growing resentment against the growth and change all over campus. Life was not seen as simple any longer and the retreats added fuel to the fire that would eventually blaze.

Renovation was everywhere and in 1992 Marian Hall was renovated to provide a spacious eating facility for students and employees. The student center was dedicated at the same time and provided office space for administrators and staff working in student affairs.

Academics and athletics were learning to coexist. In 1991 and 1992 the college received the Heart of Texas Academic All-Conference Award, an honor for athletes maintaining high academic standing. The men's and women's soccer teams won Heart of Texas Conference championships again in 1992, as did the men's and women's tennis teams. Though it was a good year for athletics, it was also a year that saw the loss of a good friend. Dan Sullivan, a well-known San Antonio figure and Incarnate Word benefactor, died in June. He had given the college Sullivan Field in 1986. "He was a very good friend of mine and of the college," Lou told the *Light*. "He really was the patriarch of the baseball

team. He worked closely with the team and knew the individual members." The *Express-News* reported that Billy Williams, batting coach for the Chicago Cubs, had extended his sympathies through legendary announcer Harry Carey on WGN-TV during a Cubs game. Williams had been a member of Sullivan's 1959 San Antonio Missions, and the two had become friends.

There were new undergraduate majors in music therapy and environmental science that year, and the Tom Benson Chair in Banking and Finance was filled. Benson had donated a large sum of money during Sister Margaret Patrice's presidency to help establish a banking Chair, which Lou later named in honor of Benson.

Lionel Sosa, who served as El Rey Feo (The Ugly King) XLIII in the early 1990s, with Sister Walter Maher and Lou, his self-proclaimed "Prince Charming."

Dr. Richard Rose was the college registrar from 1990 through 1993. He survived food poisoning and a lost passport during the Mazatlán retreat to leave a legacy that has become a hallmark for Incarnate Word. It was Richard's idea that the graduation processional be led by the drone and beat of the San Antonio Pipes and Drums. The tradition continues today as the much larger procession marches from the Administration Building to the convocation center. That necessitates crossing a bridge built to unite the two parts of the campus. In 1998 Dr. Bobbye Fry, the current registrar, added another touch to what Dr. Rose had designed. Today faculty line both sides of the bridge and applaud the graduates as they process across. "Whenever I ask stu-

Tom Benson and Sister Margaret Patrice at the establishment of the Banking Chair in the 1980s; the Chair was later named for Benson.

dents about their favorite part of the commencement ceremony, without fail they tell me they loved having their faculty greet and applaud them as they crossed the bridge," Bobbye says. "Many may never see their faculty again, and this is a final tribute between students and faculty. It is an emotional time for all." She also points out that it is hard to keep everyone in line before the processional begins. "They get in line as directed and then at almost the same time they get out of line to greet friends they know are going separate ways. But when that first note is played by the San Antonio Pipes and Drums

Registrar Dr. Bobbye Fry leads the graduation procession
that includes the country flags of all graduates.

the students fall into line, straighten their backs and focus on the processional." The bagpipes, which were often used to lead soldiers into battle, bring excitement and pageantry to the long procession.

In September 1992, Lou and Sam Barshop, chairman and founder of La Quinta Motor Inns Inc., struck a deal almost as unique as Lou's earlier trade of scholarships for advertising. Barshop installed twenty-five computer terminals and all the trimmings at Incarnate Word High School. They became the school's computer lab and La Quinta's remote reservation site. During the day the students used the computers for lab work, word-processing classes, and computer math classes. In the evening, a master switch was turned and the lab became the reservation center where students from the high school and the college took reservations for La Quinta's motels. "It's a win-win," Barshop told Chuck McCollough, business writer for the *Express-News*, adding that he and Lou worked it out at a party.

"We were talking about business-education partnerships," Barshop said. "The discussion turned to La Quinta's reservation needs and the availability of space and students at the high school. From there it just developed into the program." Barshop explained that the budget was $500,000, of which "we invested $150,000 for the equipment and training." La Quinta's telephone system allowed calls to be switched to the remote site at the high school with no delay to the customer. As many as seventy high school and college students could be employed over the course of a year. "This gives the students a sense of pride in earning a salary and valuable job experience," Barshop said. "It helps La Quinta by giving us excess capacity and redundancy in case of a main system shutdown."

The computers were a much-needed gift, but not everyone was ready to accept the concept of business and education establishing a partnership, and some questioned out loud, "When will he stop?"

By now Frank Ayala had been promoted to vice president for student affairs, and David Jurenovich had been promoted to vice president for planning and marketing. David, who had completed his Ph.D. and was teaching as an adjunct, would soon be named a Distinguished Professor, an honor for certain non-tenure track faculty. In his role as vice president, David was responsible for the departments of athletics, financial assistance, recruitment and enrollment, public relations and marketing, institutional technology and research, and international initiatives. He also planned the retreats and helped build the college's five-year plan. Since David and Lou had been friends in their earlier days at Gannon, he was the perfect traveling colleague when Lou began his visits to various international sites.

A large part of Lou's vision was the internationalization of the college campus. "The world can be a frightening place to young people if they are not given the opportunity to learn how small it really is," Lou explains. "The beauty of the San Antonio and South Texas area lies in its people, and the majority of them are Hispanic. It is important to understand that the Hispanic culture is a close-knit, family-oriented culture. As beautiful as that is, it also causes families to be more reluctant to send their sons and daughters—especially their daughters—abroad for educational experiences."

Lou wanted Incarnate Word students to be exposed to the cultures and insights of other countries, but he knew the only way to do that was to bring those cultures and insights to the campus. He set out on a plan to visit almost every country on the globe and encourage international attendance at the college. He acknowledged that "Incarnate Word" was not exactly a household term around the world, and understanding the name required some knowledge of Christian beliefs. Even in later years, after the school became the University of the Incarnate Word, Lou and others received mail addressed to "University of the Incarnate Work," "University of the Incarnate World," and everyone's all-time favorite, "University of the Internet World." Incarnate Word was The College until 1996, and Lou had a lot of explaining to do in order to introduce it to the rest of the world. "I traveled to other universities and just knocked on doors. Sometimes I had a letter of introduction and a formal appointment, but a lot of times it was just cold calls. I was back in the selling business," he said.

Lou's approach was the same he and Lionel used in the ad campaigns: "People will respond to people, not just to letters and impersonal ads." He eventually traveled to almost every country with his message about Incarnate Word and the education it offered. His message was the same it had been for South Texas Hispanics: "You are welcome here." Schools in Korea, Turkey, Japan, Brazil—in fact, most of Asia and South America—began sending students to Incarnate Word. Actually they were sending students to "Lou's school" where they believed the students would be well received. They felt they knew Lou. How many other presidents sat with them over tea, or kimchi, or fish heads and rice? How many other presidents wanted the heat of habanero chilies with their tacos and enchiladas or had matched toast for toast with Turkish raki? Lou and David were a great team, and Lou continued on to more and more countries after David settled in to other duties and Jim Tilton began overseeing international issues. Not surprisingly, the emphasis being placed on international recruitment was viewed as more change and brought mixed feelings from some parts of the campus community.

Except for the excitement of La Quinta, things at the high school were fairly quiet, and that should have been a warning about the calm before the storm. The Ursuline Sisters, who had befriended the Sisters of Charity over a hundred years ago when the Incarnate Word Sisters' new home burned to the ground, now decided it was time to close Ursuline Academy, their all-girls high school. They had worked through the same dilemma the Incarnate Word Sisters had faced in 1988.

Lou immediately offered any help the college or the high school could give. Ursuline Academy was not an Archdiocesan school. Like Incarnate Word High School, Ursuline Academy was an independent, private high school under the sponsorship of a religious congregation. Nevertheless, Ursuline's future soon became the question of the day in many venues. Lou offered to take in the school's students and as many of their faculty and staff as wanted to join the Incarnate Word family. This was not going to be the easiest task, but it seemed the right course. Lou and Pat, still the high school principal, remembered everyone's angst back in 1988. Lou's offer was received with gratitude by Sister Anne Therese Mayol, OSU, Ursuline principal, but the decision was up to parents as to where their daughters would complete their high school studies. The offer was seen as empire building by some competing high schools and was even an issue for the Catholic Schools Office. They were caught in the awkward position of knowing the Ursuline students needed a home, while not wanting to favor one high school over the others.

This was one decision Lou did not push. He made the offer, explained what it would entail, and graciously sat back while the decision was made. What the offer entailed was amazing. Incarnate Word High School would operate a school-within-a-school for the first year, accommodating curriculum needs for students already launched on certain pathways and allowing Ursuline students to choose a diploma from either school upon graduation—a special concession for those who had only their senior year to complete. Ursuline agreed to provide the seal for the Ursuline diplomas for those choosing that route. Students who had been in attendance at Ursuline for one or two years would be handled as regular transfer students.

Running a school-within-a-school was a challenge. Lou and the principal explained to Incarnate Word faculty, parents, and students that even the uniforms would be changed so that all students started with the same ones. There could be no room for "we's" and "they's" when the new school year began.

In the end, most of the Ursuline students moved to Incarnate Word, and the school added some of the city's finest faculty to their already exemplary teaching staff. Even Sister Anne Therese's secretary, Itza Casanova, became secretary to Incarnate Word's principal when Yolanda Lomas left that position.

Graduation at the end of the 1992–93 year was more than an exercise in togetherness for Incarnate Word and Ursuline students. That was also the year Henry Cisneros's younger daughter, Mercedes, was graduating from Incarnate Word. Cisneros, former San Antonio mayor, was now U.S. secretary of housing and urban development. As a special honor to him and his daughter, Texas Gov. Ann

Henry Cisneros, former U.S. Secretary of Housing and Urban Development, congratulates daughter Mercedes at her graduation from Incarnate Word High School. Master of Ceremonies Dick McCracken looks on.

Richards agreed to be the graduation speaker. The arrangement grew out of an impromptu and informal conversation with the Cisneros family, but it was an honor not to be declined by the high school.

Almost at once there were explosive reactions. Gov. Richards, only the second woman governor in the state's history, had campaigned on a wide platform, but one of the planks was pro-choice. And this was a Catholic high school.

If where Ursuline students should attend school had become a citywide point of conversation, this new issue brought an almost violent response from some who were sure the governor would use the graduation address as a bully pulpit to push abortion. The high school phone was disconnected as the calls grew more unpleasant. Most parents were supportive, but some worried about their daughters participating in graduation. Radio talk-show hosts had a field day. The question of the day was "Should a Catholic school allow the governor to speak at graduation?" Listeners were invited to call in with their opinions. At one point a host asked the Incarnate Word principal to call in and participate in the conversations. Lou's gentle words of advice ran something like, "You do and I'll kill you."

Since the high school was part of the college's academic division, it and its dean reported to Sister Helena Monahan. She received so many threats she had to wear a flak jacket to the baccalaureate dinner the night before graduation as well as to the commencement ceremony the next day. As small as she is, those who knew she was wearing a flak jacket hoped she wouldn't trip. "She'll never be able to get up wearing that thing" was the general opinion.

Texas Gov. Ann Richards addresses the 1993 graduates of IWHS.

Graduation day dawned and the long walk to the college convocation center began. A small but vocal group of about fifty was waving placards and shouting as the procession formed. The roof of a neighboring business was lined with Texas Rangers standing guard. The governor had been taken directly into the convocation center through a side entrance, with Lou and Sister Helena escorting her. The rector of the Oblate School of Theology was scheduled to give the invocation at the ceremony. He added class and dignity to the occasion when he chose to join Watkins and others who were walking at the end of the procession. Incarnate Word police closed in behind, and Texas Rangers kept a close watch. A gracious Gov. Richards delivered a motivating address to young women about to enter the next phase of their lives. No word of politics or abortion was spoken that afternoon.

Later several people speculated who the charming young man was sitting between Sister Helena and the principal at the baccalaureate dinner. No one ever knew he was a well-armed Texas Ranger.

CHAPTER 12
FROM A TO ZOO

I t had nothing to do with governors or rangers, Sister Helena insisted, but she had decided to apply to law school. Her acceptance arrived in time for her to start with the fall 1993 class. Everyone congratulated her, but what was going to happen at the college? Who would be the next academic vice president? Speculation was rampant. Every possible person was viewed as the new VP, and some of the possibilities were scary.

Lou might not be the most patient man you will ever meet, but he is surely one of the luckiest. In 1990 Dr. D. Reginald Traylor had decided to return to higher education after a brief venture in business. Looking for all the world like "Tex" instead of "Reginald," with boots, a white Stetson, and a heavy drawl, Reg wanted to get back to teaching mathematics. Incarnate Word hired him to do just that, and he kept a fairly low profile. Few people knew he was the founding president of the University of Houston-Victoria. But Lou knew! After some discussion that Reg called "horse trading," he agreed to one year and only one year as academic vice president. He would serve just long enough for a search committee to find the new vice president. Then he wanted to get back to mathematics.

The year started quietly, but it didn't stay that way. It didn't take long for Reg's administrative juices to start flowing again. His was a 180 degree turn from Sister Helena's approach. Where Helena would calmly reason and allow second, third, and even more chances, Reg could just as calmly fire you. Helena was conscious of the changes already being absorbed by the college while Reg, new to private education, saw change as "getting with the program." Quite a few personnel issues were decided that year, and it was pretty clear they had been thoroughly discussed

Dr. D. Reginald Traylor and his ever-present Stetson.

with Lou first. Reg was nicknamed Chainsaw Traylor for a while, and he loved it. Actually, most of the campus grew to respect and like him. "What you see is what you get" was most folks' opinion of Reg and it was his own opinion, too.

It was during Chainsaw's first year that Professor Bernadette O'Connor proposed the CCVI Spirit Award. She wanted to create an award that would be given to employees who best reflected the charism of the CCVI's—Sisters of Charity of the Incarnate Word. Whether she was trying to bring back the calm of earlier days or just trying to promote the values of the Congregation doesn't matter. The award was embraced and is given annually to this day. Recipients have included Lorraine Ewers, administrative secretary in the humanities, arts, and social sciences; Dr. Bob Connelly, current dean of that area; his wife, Dr. Kathi Light, dean of nursing and health professions; and Dr. Denise Doyle, current provost.

To the delight of longtime library director Mendell Morgan, 1993 saw the start of a huge campaign to build a new library. Tom Plofchan launched the $6.2 million campaign that would span three years and result in the J.E. and L.E. Mabee Library, named for the Mabee Charitable Foundation. Tom and Lou had also worked to triple the endowment fund from its 1986 figure. The nursing program had gone through a grueling reaccreditation process and emerged successfully. The soccer and tennis teams continued to win Heart of Texas Conference championships, and the men's basketball team joined the winners' circle that year.

With all the athletic activity, it was not hard for faculty to develop and approve a master's of education degree in physical education under Dr. Bill Carlton's direction. Meanwhile the arts were celebrating the opening of the Douglas and Donna Semmes Art Gallery. The School of Humanities, Arts, and Social Sciences had just hired Dr. Gilberto Hinojosa as dean; he would serve in more than one administrative position during his years at Incarnate Word. Gil, a respected historian, wrote a standing column for the *Express-News* and was occasionally a featured expert on the PBS series *History Detectives*.

John Ray retired at the end of 1993, and Doug Endsley was selected following an extensive search. Doug, with the quick mind Lou continued to need in a chief financial officer, brought a dry sense of humor that delivered lines with a straight face and understatement. He would be part of Lou's team through the intricate growth of the next fifteen years and beyond.

Toward the end of the second semester it was clear that the search for Sister Helena's replacement had been unsuccessful. No one had satisfied the search committee, and truth be told Reg, like Sister Helena, turned out to be a hard act to follow. Lou negotiated one more year with Reg, who made it clear this was his absolute limit. By now everyone knew that when Reg said, "This is it, folks," there was no compromise. The search would have to be successful the next time.

Having temporarily solved that problem, Lou was ready to turn his attention to the future, where he usually focused. It was Fiesta's Battle of Flowers parade day when he called Dr. Denise Doyle to his office. It was obvious to Denise that Lou was in serious planning mode, and this could easily turn into one of those "Why me, Lord?" moments.

Lou wanted to start a degree for working adults who had to leave school for job or family reasons. It was the right thing to do, but it would also be a major benefit to the college. "He knew we had the potential for attracting a sizable number of these adults who had not completed an undergraduate degree," Denise said, "but it couldn't be done with a traditional program."

The program would have to move fast. Working adults would be going to school for classes, not social activities. They needed to know they could finish their degree in less time than in a traditional program. This meant eight-week semesters instead of the sixteen weeks typical at Incarnate Word and most other semester-based schools. Earlier, the college had offered a limited number of business courses in an eight-week format at Kelly Air Force Base, in a concession to military personnel who faced frequent transfers. "I knew the format he was proposing would be very attractive to these folks, if we could only figure out how to do it on this campus and in this climate," Denise recalled.

As a faculty member she knew there was growing tension about change, and this would be a big one. It struck at the heart of those who were convinced that, with few exceptions, any good course lasted sixteen weeks. There would certainly be the belief that if the number of weeks were going to change, the faculty should decide that, not the administration. She asked almost the same question Lionel Sosa had asked in 1986: "Have you ever done this before?" Lou acknowledged that he had not, but a good friend had. Dr. Jim Rocheleau, then president of Upper Iowa University in Fayette, had started successful adult learning centers there and knew how an adult degree completion program should operate. When Jim retired Lou invited him to campus on several occasions, hoping to find the right person or persons to begin a program at Incarnate Word. This time Lou made sure Jim met Denise.

"Lou knew this was not going to be an easy sell to the campus," she explains. "He talked about the need to secure faculty support for the program and his belief that my connections in the faculty would increase confidence in an accelerated program." Denise became as intrigued as Lionel had years earlier. "It was a chance to reach out to an underserved population in San Antonio. I also had recently heard someone say that San Antonio will be the same old San Antonio until more people get a university degree."

With that thought and Lou's full support, Denise began work as director of the Adult Degree Completion Program. The acronym would be ADCP—pretty hard to pronounce. Denise added a small "a" in the middle to make it ADCaP.

Jim Rocheleau was a good mentor. He was on campus frequently over the next several years to guide ADCaP's development, but it was Denise who would be doing the work. The program was planned for off site and would be offered in business, education, and nursing. In addition, all core courses would have to be offered in order for students to complete their degrees. ADCaP tuition would be lower than that on the main campus, with the rationale that students were not using the entire campus infrastructure. There would be six eight-week semesters a year, and students could finish a degree in two or three years depending on the number of credits they brought into the program.

For the first few months after agreeing to shepherd this program, Denise worked to get the needed faculty support. Even as well liked and trusted as she was, she hit the barriers she and Lou anticipated. "There were so many obstacles to confront, it's hard to say which were the most difficult," she said. "Probably the greatest concern came from the business faculty, who feared their night classes would move en masse to ADCaP. That was a fair concern because it did happen."

Lou had anticipated that, but was not overly concerned. He wanted the undergraduate emphasis to be on daytime classes for the main campus and on evening ones for ADCaP. He also knew the business program was too strong to suffer any serious setback. Undergraduate evening classes never ended on the main campus, and today there are quite a few in business and other disciplines. The immediate effect of offering the ADCaP option, however, was that many working students did leave the main campus evening program.

Then there were the inevitable turf questions: "Who is going to teach the classes?" or "That course is mine; I always teach it—but I have no intention of teaching in that format." Format was a huge issue. Denise had a difficult time explaining how to convert sixteen-week courses into eight-week ones. What would have to go untaught? "It is not a case of just going into fast forward or whacking off half of the content," she would explain. The courses needed to be revised for this type of program. That started the slippery slide down the curriculum path. "Who is going to be in charge of curriculum in this program?" "It's off site, so how will we know what is going on?" "Who will hire the faculty?" Some decided Denise and Lou would be running an entirely new Incarnate Word without any controls from faculty.

While Denise was struggling with her new program, Lou had another idea—this time for the high school. Pat explains, "Lou wanted to talk about bringing the boarding program back. All I could think of was the expression 'insurmountable opportunities.' This could be one." The last boarding student had left Incarnate Word High School in the 1970s, so it would be hard to find the institutional memory to guide the effort. With Lou's intent to always share innovations with the high school, there were increased opportunities to enroll international students. The Kumamoto students had been the first ones, but now there were other high school students eager to study in San Antonio. The high school had tried home-stay arrangements that year and the year before but had decided not to continue them. Boarding would certainly bring things full circle in terms of how the Sisters had originally operated Incarnate Word High School, but it would be a major logistical operation.

While Denise talked to faculty about ADCaP, Pat began working with student affairs at the college. The boarding program would be a shared responsibility, and the dormitory would be managed by the college's residence life office. Dr. Jeannie Ortiz, dean of student life, and her staff worked hard with Pat and Vice Principal Roger Labat. A building previously used as living quarters for Sisters was converted to a dorm. Steve Heying and his staff handled the conversion and installed kitchen facilities, doors, and windows to code requirements. Security was everyone's biggest concern, and additional security staff were hired. Five students would occupy the dormitory when the fall semester began.

Steve Heying, Director of Facilities Management, caught in a rare moment at his desk. Steve is usually roaming the campus, checking out the facilities first-hand.

The planning retreat that August was in Long Beach, California, aboard the permanently docked Queen Mary. There was a lot to talk about. Denise was given a large part of one day to explain ADCaP, answer questions, and hopefully increase her support base. The program would not start until January, so there was still time for prayerful conversions. Lou had been correct in giving this program to Denise. With humor and passion she began to win over many of the naysayers. She had immediate support from the nursing faculty, whose RN to BSN program was popular and needed a good evening home. The program allowed registered nurses without college degrees to earn their Bachelor of Science degree in Nursing. The education department wanted to cooperate, but they had a major concern; by state mandate they could not offer teacher certification classes in two locations. Fortunately, once it was determined where the program would be housed, there was no problem. By the end of the retreat Denise had gained ground, or certainly not lost any.

The high school began its fall 1994 semester as a boarding school. It was not easy, but it was not impossible. The persons who laid the groundwork for that program had no idea how much it would grow over the next fifteen years. Dr. Renee Moore later became dean of student life and shouldered much of the program's future responsibilities. Meanwhile, one thing had not yet been announced—where would the Adult Degree Completion Program be located? Lou and Denise carefully explained to Pat that ADCaP needed the high school buildings at night. Surely they were joking

There were still some at the high school trying to get used to Lou making decisions about them. It was difficult to accept that even their principal was one of "Lou's deans." Pat had her hands full trying to walk the fine lines that were being drawn. Clearly the high school would no longer exist were it not for Lou Agnese and the college, and this fact needed to be recognized. In addition, the high school was becoming an example of innovation and opportunity. But with all that said, there were still concerns about who was making the decisions. It wasn't that anyone regretted the Ursuline arrangement or objected to the international flavor when exchange opportunities arose. And it was great to have college staff restore the gym floors and solve air-conditioning problems. Even the plumbing worked again. But somewhere along the way there was the nagging thought that someone else had decided it was time to redo the gym floors and someone else was deciding to put the beautiful Christmas lights on the high school campus. Even if Pat and the administrators she appointed made the decisions, some still reminded one another that Pat was a college dean. Although the majority of high school faculty and parents were supportive and excited to be part of the college/high school family, no amount of communication could change the mindset held by some. It was not all that different from what was happening at the college. Change was the issue, and change involved control and trust. One had to be relinquished and the other had to be granted—and earned.

The first time the campus had been used at night was for the La Quinta Reservation Center, and teachers worried about having others, even college students, in "their" building after hours. That was how the stage was set when Lou and Denise broke the ADCaP news.

ADCaP started in January 1995. As a new program it didn't yet have infrastructure support. It was an experiment that was expected to work, but no one was going to invest too heavily until they were sure. Denise recently shared some of the adventures. "ADCaP was advertised as one-stop shopping. You could get your textbooks, pay your tuition, attend class, whatever, all at one stop. But I was the 'one stop'". She continued, looking back with both humor and amazement that it had worked. "I was running around dragging textbooks over to the high school, writing out signs about where to go for what, taking money for books and tuition, and teaching two classes. It was a zoo, and I was the keeper."

Denise would take the money at night and stand in line at the business office the next day like everyone else to turn in fifteen different registrations and tuitions. "One night I was taking money and stuffing it and the students' names in my pockets like crazy while trying to do three other things when Jim Rocheleau said, 'Are you just stuffing that money in your pocket? Don't you have a receipt book?' He was horrified. I wanted to say, 'Look, I used to be a nun. My Ph.D. is in canon law. What the hell do I know about receipt books?' "

Denise recalls how crazy it was for the high school and ADCaP at times. "Pat kept explaining to me that for high school teachers the classrooms were their offices. They didn't have offices like college professors did, so they kept important and often personal things in and on their desks. She was right. ADCaP teachers and students would grab pencils and pens and whatever from the desks and usually forget to put them back. And then there were the chalkboards. The high school teachers would leave notes asking that something not be erased, and it would be erased anyway."

Pat shared the other side. "Here were these adults coming in from work, tired and trying to concentrate on class and all the halls and bulletin boards had happy faces or little lacy valentines—all really cute, but really high school stuff. The two sets of faculty wanted to cooperate, but they were coming from two entirely different approaches. The high school faculty got more possessive and the ADCaP faculty got more demanding. Denise is right—it was a zoo at times."

Fortunately the two deans had worked together before, even sharing offices and a secretary. They had hired Zurich native Martin Klingbacher in 1993 when Pat was commuting between the high school and the college and Denise was director of the Pastoral Institute. Martin was now Tom Plofchan's administrative assistant. "I could have used Martin and his Swiss precision to help make this work," Denise said with a laugh.

Dr. Denise Doyle (right) with first ADCaP graduate Kate Crosby.

ADCaP did work, becoming one of the college's most successful programs. It began with 29 students and grew to 242 in just one year. The program continued to build and saw 1,000 adults complete their degrees during its first ten years.

CHAPTER 13

ALL DRESSED UP WITH NO PLACE TO PARK

While those Sosa ads were bringing in students, the students were bringing in cars. Parking had become a major challenge. Dick McCracken still tells the story of the remains of a prehistoric bison one faculty member spotted on campus. As archeologists worked to identify and date it, students were quick to claim that the poor thing had died looking for a parking place.

The parking crisis peaked just as the college was dealing with tax issues on the Canterbury Hill house where the Agnese family lived. There was a back-and-forth legal battle about the tax-exempt status of that residence since it was owned by Incarnate Word. Lou had always wanted to live on campus, but would not use the valuable land required for a home. But now, if the Canterbury Hill house was to be taxed, he was ready to look for another option.

Lou and the board were already working with architect Mike McChesney, who donated his services to design a six-story parking garage. The building would include four floors of parking, two floors of dormitory space, and additional space for future classrooms and meeting rooms. Lou now suggested adding a seventh-floor residence for him and the family, and for future presidents. He told the *Express-News*, "We have had tremendous growth and there was no more room for surface parking. And we were also out of space for housing."

McChesney made creative use of every bit of space for the land-locked, rapidly growing college. In addition to 200 parking spaces and apartment-style housing for eighty-plus students, he also designed offices and aerobic exercise rooms under the garage ramps. The seven-story building was named for the Agnese and Sosa families. On October 6, 1994, Archbishop Patrick Flores blessed the Agnese-Sosa Living and Learning Center. Lou, Mickey, and their children moved into the 5,000 square-foot penthouse apartment that November.

The word "children" was no longer quite accurate. Louis III was now sixteen and a sophomore at Alamo Heights High School. Nancy, the little girl who advertised the Katherine Ryan Preschool Center, was now fourteen and would soon enter Incarnate Word High School. In addition to watching the college grow and mature, Lou and Mickey were living those bittersweet sunrise/sunset moments all parents experience.

Lou has always loved to show off the college, especially to his family. His parents were frequent visitors and his twin sisters, Susan and Nancy, along with brother Mike, dropped in from time to time, especially for special events. But John had never seen the college, nor ever been to San Antonio. Johnny, as he was called, was the oldest of the siblings. "He was more of a father than a brother to me," said Lou. Shortly after moving into their new house on top of the parking garage, Lou had the opportunity to show Johnny the campus.

"Johnny never missed a detail in his life," Lou said. "He wandered all around the campus, looking at buildings, checking out the grounds, everything. That evening we were standing on the balcony looking out over the campus and Johnny said, 'You've really done something good here. It's really good.' I have to admit that was a thrill for me. I think it was the first time Johnny ever gave me a flat-out compliment." Lou laughed as he added, "But he couldn't leave it there. He had to be big brother and point out at least one thing. 'But that bridge down there by the river. You gotta do something about that. It's a piece of shit. The wood's all rotten; it's rickety. Somebody's goin' get hurt on that. You better fix it.' I brushed it aside and said something like, 'Yeah, I'm goin' take care of it.'

"I got busy and completely forgot about the damn bridge. Months later I saw Johnny back in New York, and the first thing he asked was if I had fixed that bridge. I said 'Yeah, it's all done.' I didn't want to go through all the stuff I would hear if I said it hadn't been done. I would get to it, but there were really big things coming up and I needed to work on them first." Neverthe-

St. Anthony Catholic High School.

less, Lou acknowledged it was a good feeling to know Johnny cared about what he was doing in San Antonio. Even when you are the president of a college, it is still good to have a big brother.

One day in the middle of ADCaP and boarding's first-year excitement, a courier arrived with confidential information that would change another piece of San Antonio history.

The message requested preliminary discussion with the Oblates of Mary Immaculate. The Oblates had operated St. Anthony High School Seminary since 1903 as a minor seminary for the formation of young men preparing for the priesthood. The Church was moving away from the minor seminary model, and the Oblates were making a difficult decision to convert St. Anthony to a Catholic high school. They knew their expertise was the formation of young men for the priesthood, not the operation of a high school. The Oblates eventually handed the management of St. Anthony to Incarnate Word. This was a difficult and painful decision for the priests and for St. Anthony parents and alumni.

On the plus side this completed the Brainpower Connection, which until now had been able to provide education from preschool through college only for young women; for young men there was a break between eighth grade and college. The Brainpower Connection now had a complete educational program from preschool through graduate school for all students.

The management of St. Anthony Catholic High School, as it was renamed, brought with it personnel changes. Dr. Gary Short was hired as principal, Roger Labat was promoted to principal of Incarnate Word High School, and Pat Watkins, as dean of college preparatory programs, became the chief administrative officer to whom both principals reported.

Dr. Renee Moore had a second high school dormitory to supervise when UIW assumed management of St. Anthony Catholic High School in 1995. Dr. Moore is shown receiving the CCVI Spirit Award from Lou in 2007.

As part of his Vision statement disseminated on August 17, 1995, Lou stated the Brainpower Connection was unique in the country. "It is a powerful concept that is beginning to make its presence known nationally," he said. "Because it is unique, its structure and staffing patterns are unlike those in other schools. The daily operation of the schools is the responsibility of the named Principals, while the Dean represents the interests of the schools in interface with college planning and policy-making bodies.

"In the Brainpower Connection model," he added, "I am in the Superintendent position, in that I am the final reporting level before the Board. (In the Catholic School Office, Brother Peter Pontililo serves as the Superintendent with oversight responsibility for the religious instruction of all Catholic schools, including private schools such as ours.) The Dean of College Preparatory Programs is the rest of our 'Central Office' and, while working directly with the other college deans, is supported by the established college offices."

Lou also used the document to express thanks to Incarnate Word High School for sharing their campus with ADCaP: "That sharing by you, has provided space and support to a program that now allows us to talk about K–Life rather than just K–12 or K–16."

In May 1995, as ADCaP finished its second eight-week semester and St. Anthony prepared to join the Incarnate Word family, Lou received an honor that had nothing to do with advertising or academics. But it was one he was thrilled to bring back to the board of trustees. Fashion Group International of San Antonio named him Best Dressed Man in the professional category. Lou loved it. He talked good naturedly about it in a recent interview. "Ever since I arrived in Texas I had been kidded about my clothes. I only wear Italian suits—good Italian suits—and shoes. Friends would make joking references to my 'mafia' look. I also wear colored shirts, and board members would joke that someone needed to give me a white shirt. It was great fun to bring that award to the next board meeting."

The Italian shoes had caught the eye of Amy Freeman Lee almost eleven years earlier when Lou was being interviewed. "I like his shoes," Amy had said. She thought a man who paid attention to how he looked would pay attention to professional details as well. Lou learned how to present himself professionally from Dr. Charles Bensman, his former president at Briar Cliff.

The Brainpower Connection principals in 1995, from left: Mary Ann Leopold, St. Peter Prince of the Apostles Elementary School; Carol Mengden, St. Anthony's Elementary School; Roger Labat, Incarnate Word High School; and Dr. Gary Short, St. Anthony Catholic High School. The Brainpower Connection suffered a great loss later that year with the untimely death of Carol Mengden.

"I watched Charlie and learned a lot about how professional people dressed and handled themselves in social situations," he said. "When I was growing up I had one suit and I wore it if somebody died. We didn't have the money to think about fashion." He explained that Dr. Bensman knew he aspired to a college presidency and made sure he had the opportunity to observe those important, sometimes subtle details.

As agreed a year before, Reg Traylor would leave the vice presidency on May 31, 1995. This time the search committee had found a candidate they liked. Dr. Eduardo Paderon, a soft-spoken man with a Ph.D. in philosophy, was recommended and hired. Ed was another personality change for that office. He was introduced to the College Planning Commission at the August retreat held that year in Las Vegas. After two years with Reg, the assembled group was somewhat taken aback when Ed decided to lead them in a sing-along after his introduction. It had taken time for the community to feel comfortable with Chainsaw, and it was going to take time for them to communicate well with Ed.

Reg returned to mathematics, but not in the way he expected. Lou was not about to lose that kind of administrative expertise. He appointed Reg acting dean of what was then the School of Nursing, Mathematics, and Science until a permanent dean could be found.

In September 1995 San Antonio's best-dressed man was shoveling dirt. But it was with a gold shovel. Saturday, September 16 was the long-awaited groundbreaking for the new library. The colorful and somewhat wordy invitations read, "Come help us celebrate the turning of the first shovel of earth that begins the capstone project of a 10-year building program at Incarnate Word College—the $6.2 million renovation and expansion of the Library." When completed, the library would more than double in size and be equipped with the most advanced technology for research.

This was a time for celebration, and the invitation mentioned almost every possible kind. "Come join us as we take one giant step into the 21st century with food and drinks, booths, strolling mariachis, piñatas, computer demonstrations, music and an outdoor Mass." Only the pony rides were missing.

On this occasion Lou would not forget Sister Raphael Eccell whose wrinkled hands had delivered little Nancy to his office ten years earlier. Sister Raphael had died in 1995. The invitation to the groundbreaking celebration included these words: "Ground breaking ceremonies dedicated to the memory of Librarian Emeritus Sister Raphael Eccell, CCVI."

Joy Ann Walker helped Incarnate Word say one more good-bye in December. This time it was a joyful one filled with anticipation of what was to

Lou looks on as Joy Ann Walker crosses the stage as the final graduate of Incarnate Word College after being awarded a Master of Science in Nursing and a Master of Business Administration on December 16, 1995. IWC became UIW—the University of the Incarnate Word—the following year (San Antonio *Express-News* photo).

come. Joy, who received two master's degrees that day, was the last student who would ever graduate from Incarnate Word College. The decision had been made for Incarnate Word—The College to become University of the Incarnate Word on March 25 of the next year. Lionel had his work cut out for him.

But this was December, and March was three months away. In Lou Agnese's world that was an eternity in which almost anything could happen. Already 1995 had seen the completion of the Clarence Mabry Tennis Center, the full accreditation of the nuclear medicine and music therapy programs, and complete reaffirmation of the college's accreditation by the Southern Association of Colleges and Schools. These achievements were the result of hard work by faculty and deans—the kind of hard work that is behind the scenes and often over midnight oil. John Newman had brought the tennis center to reality, Dr. Bob Connelly had chaired the working committee for college reaccreditation, Pam King had led the nuclear medicine program and Teresa Lesiuk the music therapy program. Students were also making names for themselves. Thirteen student-athletes were named All-Americans that year and four were named Academic All-Americans.

Before breaking for the Christmas holidays, Lou and the board released plans to renovate the old St. Joseph's Convent at the corner of Hildebrand and Highway 281. That building had served the Congregation for years as a convent and retirement center for older Sisters. In 1986 the Congregation had decided to sell the building and the large wooded corner on which it sat. Clearly prime real estate, its sale would have helped the Sisters plan additional care facilities for their members.

Sister Rosita Hyland, congregation treasurer at the time, recalled, "We had a contract for $17.5 million. The first installment of $1 million was paid, but the buyer could not get further financing due to the collapse of the banking system in Texas, which had followed the real estate speculation boom."

The Sisters then found themselves with a sizable amount of money while still holding the deed to the property. Lou Agnese will continue thanking the Lord for that turn of events for the rest of his life.

The renovation would begin March 1, and by August the convent would start its new life as the University International Conference Center and Residence Facility. The first-floor chapel would be converted to a meeting room with retractable seating for 163 persons, three translation booths, and a priest's sacristy so that religious services could be conducted. The dining facilities and kitchen would be updated for conference use, and the second floor would provide twenty-nine rooms dedicated to the conference function. The third and fourth floors would have fifty-six single and five double rooms dedicated to housing sixty-six resident students during the school year but available for conference use in the summer. Each floor would be fitted with a lounge, laundry and kitchen facilities, and private and common shower areas.

This was a major step for Incarnate Word. Although adjacent to the current campus, with no streets dividing them, the grounds were roughly the equivalent of two blocks from its heart. Connecting roads and footpaths would be built and 150 additional parking spaces would be added. This was the expansion needed to allow the college, soon to be the university, to grow. Building the International Conference Center also emphasized the growing international aspect of the college. Lou's travels were resulting in more sister school agreements and other international collaborations.

 Some awards seem to touch just the right spot. On January 23 Lou received one such award. Lou, former San Antonio Mayor Lila Cockrell, and investment broker Oscar Ehrenberg were the recipients of the 1996 National Conference Brotherhood/Sisterhood Humanitarian Awards. *Express-News* religion writer J. Michael Parker explained their significance. "Previously known as the National Conference of Christians and Jews, the group is dedicated to fighting bias, bigotry and racism in America by promoting understanding and respect among races, religions and cultures." Lou was the Catholic recipient, Cockrell the Protestant recipient, and Ehrenberg, president of the San Antonio Holocaust Commission, the Jewish recipient. Close to 650 guests attended the awards banquet at the Hyatt Regency Hill Country Resort. Committee member Shirley Wills explained that proceeds from the dinner would provide funding for programs such as diversity awareness.

This was clearly where Lou belonged. Only five months before he had written an opinion piece for the *Express-News* feature, "Your Turn," in which he stressed the difference in the "melting pot" his father had worked to be part of and the "cup of stew" metaphor Lou uses when he talks with his own children about diversity. He explained that people did not want to be "melted down" into one crucible. "The fact is that people want to maintain their roots, preserving their unique cultural habits and lifestyles." He continued, "If you want to know about diversity . . . look into the stew pot. America's unique identity comes from our differences, which in turn shape our community values and dreams."

Incarnate Word had always been a safe and welcoming place for diverse groups and people of other faiths, and Lou continued to stress that after he arrived. "We are a faith community," he would say. "We are proud to be a Catholic college, but we honor and respect all faiths. What we want is for each person to grow in his or her faith because they have been in a nurturing environment."

Just a few years before, the Rev. Buckner Fanning, longtime pastor of Trinity Baptist Church, attested to the climate at Incarnate Word. In 1992 both Buckner and his daughter, Lisa, received Incarnate Word degrees. Lisa's was in child psychology while her father's was an honorary doctorate. Lou told the *Express-News*, "Buckner has been an outstanding ecumenical leader and open to all faith traditions. He's always out front on important issues and he represents all of us in an outstanding way." The paper quoted Fanning as saying the honor came as a complete surprise to him. "I can't think of any honor I've ever received," he said, "for which I've been more gratified than for this one. It says a lot about the spirit of ecumenism in this community."

The Rev. Buckner Fanning was awarded an honorary doctorate from IWC in 1992.

Buckner added that he was even more grateful to Incarnate Word for what it had done for his daughter. "It has broadened her horizons both academically and spiritually," he said. Referring to her plan to work with emotionally disturbed children or those in the criminal justice system, he added, "The college has given her confidence and experience to do this and made her more spiritually sensitive to the needs of people."

Lou explained recently that one of the reasons Incarnate Word is a comfortable place for non-Catholics and especially for Jewish students is that there is no proselytizing. "The Sisters understand prejudice." Lou said. "They have experienced it." He related the story of Mother Columkille Colbert when she went to Washington, D.C., to study for her Ph.D. at the Catholic University of America. "Mother Columkille had to sit out in the hall and peer into the classroom taking notes," he said. "Because she was not a man, she could not participate in the classes." He added, "Mother Columkille was the first Sister in Texas to receive a Ph.D., and she did it the hard way. These women understand the insidiousness of prejudice."

The Jewish community had begun to rally around Incarnate Word during Sister

Incarnate Word has long been able to count on the support of members of San Antonio's Jewish community, including Sam and Ann Barshop.

Margaret Patrice Slattery's presidency. Several Jewish businessmen had generously given their time to serve on the board. That generosity has continued over the years. Lou had already experienced the computer gifts from Sam Barshop, but even Lou would have been shocked if he could have seen the future and what Barshop and other members of the local Jewish community would do for Incarnate Word.

CHAPTER 14

THE REST OF THE STORY

It is true Incarnate Word College became the University of the Incarnate Word on March 25, 1996, but the planning for that change began long before. As early as 1990 Lou knew that for the college to continue its growth, not just in size, but in scope and influence, it would have to develop doctoral programs. That would require the change to university status. The idea was mentioned, but the time was not yet right. As impatient as Lou is once a project is launched, he has remarkable restraint when it comes to timing. He may rush everyone else, but he cannot be rushed. More than once when prodded to move on an issue before he thought the time was right, Lou would quote Papa: "One day at a time, sweet Jesus." And then he would credit Papa with the line.

Sometimes events, even historical ones, are taken for granted—especially if one is not there when they happen. Unfortunately many of the players in this important part of Incarnate Word history are deceased or retired. Archived documents and the collective memories of Drs. David Jurenovich and Denise Doyle, among others, made it possible to reconstruct events, some rather dramatic, that unfolded in August 1995 when Lou decided the time was right. So with a nod to Paul Harvey, here is "the rest of the story."

There had been increasing but quiet discussion about the possible change. There was certainly no consensus, but there had not yet been an opportunity to seek it. On August 17, as the College Planning Commission left for the 1995 summer retreat, large brown envelopes were carried aboard the plane with strict instructions that they not be distributed or opened until the plane was airborne.

Somewhere over Texas, on the way to Las Vegas and Ed Paderon's sing-along, envelopes were opened and Lou's "Vision for the Millennium 2000" was shared. At first glance there were no major surprises, except perhaps the timeline he was envisioning and maybe the intensity of his international focus. Those involved in planning generally knew what was on Lou's mind, but that didn't mean they always agreed. Nor did they have the same detailed knowledge as his Executive Council. That body, comprised of the vice presidents and chancellor, met regularly with Lou and functioned as the president's cabinet. In 1996 Sister Helena would return from law school and rejoin it as Incarnate Word's legal counsel. The earlier President's Advisory Council had been replaced by two bodies, an Academic and an Administrative Council.

Two major documents were now shared—the *Millennium 2000 Vision* and another, *Reaching for the Global Perspective.* Both carried Lou Agnese bylines, but you could see Vice President Jim Tilton's words smoothing Lou's Brooklyn phrasing. Regardless of the phrasing, the message was unmistakably Lou's. In some ways he was taking a big gamble on this trip. It was probably appropriate they were heading to Las Vegas.

Lou with Jim Tilton and Marge Draeger, his assistants during the 1990s.

The Millennium Vision document was the major one. It was a carefully crafted account of the last ten years, with frequent references to how those years had retained the original vision of the Sisters who founded the college. Lou addressed the current image of Incarnate Word:

"In order to achieve success over the past decade we positioned ourselves in recruiting campaigns as Incarnate Word: The College . . . This has created a perception of our institution as having a unique teaching emphasis in an intimate learning environment . . . a perception we continually strive to fulfill. This distinctive identity has set us apart from the other institutions of higher learning in the area. We have used the considerable power and influence of the mass media to create this perception . . . The result has been the doubling of enrollment to current levels and dramatic growth in the annual operating budget. Other effects have been substantial growth in our endowment, expansion and enhancement of the physical plant, and campus beautification efforts."

The document went on to discuss the continued commitment to liberal arts studies, within a context of career or professional preparation, and pointed out that this dual emphasis has historically been articulated as the focal point of the Mission. Lou acknowledged that the new initiatives in professional studies accounted for the largest growth in graduate programs over the past ten years. He added, "It is time to align our public perception with our new vision. Our positioning at the moment does not match our current needs and expectations, our aspirations for the future, nor our evolving capabilities and resources."

Then came the words everyone was scanning the pages for. "At this point in our development we should consider formally recognizing the type of institution we are now—and are becoming—by changing our name from Incarnate Word College to University of the Incarnate Word. Our emerging institutional character has outdistanced the image 'The College' provided."

Lou knew he had to give reassurances, not just to his team but to the people who would go to them for explanations. And then there were the media. The Vision document would have to be released to them and they would surely look for changes that might creep into the Incarnate Word teaching philosophy. "The College" had been too strong an identifier to just quietly go away.

Lou wrote, "This name change does not diminish but rather reinforces our commitment to be a teaching institution. Our commitment to mission, values and priorities should leave no doubt about preserving our primary emphasis on the personal interaction of the professor and student, conducted in an intimate atmosphere of learning with focus on education of the whole person."

Once the airborne readers had found the college-to-university paragraphs, they began searching for how the change would affect them individually. They wondered, "What will the change look like?" They didn't have to scan too quickly nor skip many lines to find out.

"How would we be structured as a university?" continued the document. "Quite basically, we will reflect where we are right now, with modified administrative responsibilities. However, the University will have its graduate programs separated from the undergraduate programs to enable us to focus and concentrate our efforts on our academic offerings that have shown the most dramatic growth in the past decade and hold the largest potential growth for the future."

Some wondered aloud, across the aisles to one another, "Does that mean some majors will be cut if they aren't large or aren't growing?" They also wondered about those "modified administrative responsibilities." Would any of the deans be changed? What about the vice presidents? Some who had been at the college when Lou first arrived reminded others that John Ray was the only vice president who was there the second year. Reading on, they found more information. "We are proposing four academic units within the university, headed by Deans reporting to the Vice President for Academic

Affairs: The College of Liberal Arts and Sciences, The School of Professional Studies, The School of Graduate and Evening Studies, and University Preparatory Programs."

"Where is nursing? Where is mathematics? Are they in with Liberal Arts and Sciences?" they murmured. Dr. Hinojosa was the dean of humanities, arts, and social sciences, and Dr. Traylor had just been named acting dean of science, mathematics, and nursing. It already looked like trouble. There was no dean of graduate studies, but Dr. Doyle was the director of ADCaP.

Did that mean she would take over all graduate programs? Dr. Platzer was dean of professional studies and Dr. Watkins was dean of preparatory programs. But that could change, too. Everyone was prepared for a complete fruit basket turnover, even speculating on whether Dr. Paderon would be academic vice president for more than just that year.

Lou had two more important points to make in the document. He stated there was another, external reason to change to a university. As Incarnate Word moved more into the international arena the name change would avoid the confusion of international students and educators, in whose culture the word "college" applied to secondary school rather than to institutions of higher learning. But Lou did not want anyone to be able to say the change was thrust upon them because of what other cultures expected. He added, ". . . the university appellation is more descriptive of a comprehensive learning institution harboring several different colleges, schools and divisions, capable not only of extending knowledge through teaching, but also of expanding knowledge through scholarship." That somewhat flowery sentence was more Tilton than Agnese, but everyone who worked with Lou knew it represented what he thought.

The final point was the actual name itself: Why University of the Incarnate Word and not Incarnate Word University? Lou was determined on this one. Even today he still points to the wording as emphasizing the spiritual term "Incarnate Word." "If we were Incarnate Word University the emphasis would be on *university*. We wanted the emphasis to be on Christ, the Incarnate Word. Our university is His. Thus we are University of the Incarnate Word." Some may fail to see the difference and think of it as just a semantic issue. To most at Incarnate Word, it is fundamental.

The document ended with instructions that set up the agenda for the entire retreat: "Today I am asking our community to begin the process of examination of this *Millennium 2000: the Vision*, fleshing out the details and responsibilities with supportive action plans. The plan should be processed through the Councils and the College Planning Commission [the group aboard the plane] in a timely but deliberate manner. This will enable the Executive Council to present a finely honed proposal to our Board of Trustees at their March 1996 meeting. It is anticipated that the Board-approved recommendations will be publicly announced and formally initiated on the feast of the Incarnate Word, March 25, 1996. On that day, God willing and our community achieving consensus and cohesion in the process, Incarnate Word College will become University of the Incarnate Word."

The collective intake of breath as everyone finished reading the first document almost created a vacuum in the plane. It was a while before hands reached tentatively for the second document. Everyone knew Lou believed in the internationalization of the campus. His frequent trips to other countries and the agreements he brought back were exciting to most and mildly threatening to some. The second document's title, *Reaching for the Global Perspective*, made it clear there would be an increased emphasis on internationalization. But what would that mean?

For a long time Lou had urged that internationalization begin deep in the heart of education—with curriculum and faculty. He knew it was not enough to bring people here from other countries and show them off as "token foreigners." There had to be serious effort to understand other cultures and integrate them into the classroom experience. It required embracing and not just tolerating differences. One faculty member had pointed out that tolerance was a weak word. "One might tolerate the heat of summer, or tolerate poor service in a restaurant, but it is never appropriate to just tolerate cultural differences."

The big messages embedded in the second document included this paragraph: "The human infrastructure required for management and direction of a comprehensive program of international studies is extremely important for successful integration of the international programs with the everyday life of the community. In the 1996–97 budget, we will designate a top-level administrative position to take responsibility for direction of international programs."

Now there was a biggie. Speculation took off. Who would it be? What did he mean by "a top-level administrative position?" How high did that reach—dean, vice president? Some began to wish they had been more vocal in advocating the internationalization movement.

The document continued: "Today I am calling upon our community to give the support and commitment necessary to carry our efforts to fresh plateaus of achievement. In the next few days I will be asking for the formation of a task force and steering committee to develop the organizational plan for actualizing our international concepts. In the initial stages, I am asking Ed

Paderon, our vice president for academic affairs; David Jurenovich, our vice president for planning and marketing; Jim Tilton, vice president and assistant to the president, and Pat Watkins, dean of college preparatory programs, to act together as the core of leadership for this effort."

The document closed with a request that each member of the community give support and assistance to this endeavor.

Well, now there was nothing to do but land in Las Vegas and maybe find the bar! It was clear this was going to be more of a charge than a retreat.

Changing to a university and increasing internationalization were not the only topics that hit the table in Las Vegas. David Jurenovich and Brian Dalton, director of admissions, introduced the topic of football. They even had a regulation football which they tossed around to the group while presenting the idea. The outcry was immediate. Football was not a popular idea at that time in Incarnate Word's history. Finally one of the deans stated firmly: "If we are going to become a university, we have more serious things to think about than football." There was immediate agreement from the group. That was music to Lou's ears. Not that he was against football, but now the group was leading itself to a discussion of *how* the college would become a university, not *if* it would. Some still think the football presentation was a smoke screen to cause just the reaction it did.

But seriously, would Lou Agnese set up a smoke screen?

CHAPTER 15

JOHNNY'S BRIDGE

Kathleen Watson, board chair, and Sister Carol Ann Jokerst, who was completing her term as general superior, were part of the elaborate celebration planned for March 25—one of the last official duties for Sister Carol Ann.

This was a triple celebration—the Feast of the Incarnate Word, the celebration of the change to the University of the Incarnate Word, and Lou Agnese's tenth anniversary as president. Tom Plofchan chaired the steering committee for the event with help from Dick McCracken and Ed Paderon. There were more volunteers than could be counted. It seemed everyone wanted to make this a beautiful and meaningful occasion.

Delegates came from other universities, school districts, and organizations as they had for Lou's inauguration. This time his international influence was evident, as representatives arrived from sister schools in Mexico, the Dominican Republic, Taiwan, and Japan.

This was a ceremony with all the pomp and circumstance expected for the occasion. The academic procession into the fine arts auditorium was a spectacle of color. The San Antonio Pipes and Drums were followed closely by Dr. Kathi Light carrying the University of the Incarnate Word's mace. As the procession continued, Sister Maria Goretti Zehr's organ and Andrew Gignac's trumpet took over and set the tone and pace for the groups as they were announced:

"Representatives of Incarnate Word Student Societies and Organizations;"

"Delegates from Colleges, Universities, Learned Societies, and Educational Organizations;"

"Faculty and Administration of the University of the Incarnate Word, Incarnate Word High School, and St. Anthony Catholic High School;"

"The Board of Trustees."

The velvets and satins of academic regalia were spectacular under the auditorium lights.

Bill Gokelman led the Incarnate Word Chorale and soloist Deborah Bussineau-King in singing the national anthem. Sister Margaret Patrice Slattery gave the invocation, and Dr. Eduardo Paderon welcomed the assembly. Then many remember getting goose bumps as Board Chair Kathleen Watson read the Declaration of University Status.

What followed next took many by surprise. Since his inauguration, Lou had worn the red and gray academic robe, a gift from Dick McCracken presented to him on that occasion. The robe had been made by Esther Gabrysh, faculty member in Incarnate Word's fashion design program. That afternoon the president was presented with different academic regalia in a formal robing ceremony. The earlier robe was retired, a symbolic gesture of change. The new robe was black with velvet trim. The velvet chevrons of the sleeves were outlined with gold cord. The doctoral hood was a rich blend of blue velvet with purple and gold satin signifying his degree and alma mater.

This would be a long ceremony, one of the few long ones Lou has ever allowed. But it was too important to rush. It was a statement to the city and beyond. Introductions and greetings were given by representatives of the Congregation, faculty, and student government. The messages were followed by a musical interlude featuring the chorale.

Taking full advantage of the university status, Lou and others arranged for him to confer honorary degrees on three persons close to the hearts of the Incarnate Word and San Antonio communities. The first was to the Most Reverend Edmond Carmody, who was secretary to the Archdiocesan Tribunal for seventeen years while serving as chaplain of Incarnate Word High School. His Holiness Pope John Paul II had named him Prelate of Honor on April 24, 1979. He served as auxiliary bishop of San Antonio from 1988 to 1992, and on May 25 of that year he was installed as bishop of the Diocese of Tyler, Texas.

Sister Mary Boniface O'Neill was next. She had received her bachelor's degree in English and mathematics from Incarnate Word College and additional degrees from the University of Texas at Austin and Our Lady of the Lake University. In 1970 she became executive director of the Healy-Murphy Center when it opened as an alternative high school. Sister was referred to as "a beacon in the night, a lamp in the darkness and a salvation to thousands of high school drop-outs, pregnant teens, low achievers, young people in trouble with the law, youth involved in gang activities, and the homeless of San Antonio."

Sister Yolanda Tarango, who was serving as councilor on the general administration of the Sisters of Charity of the Incarnate Word, received the final honorary degree. She is the cofounder and was at that time director of Visitation House, a transitional residence for homeless women and children. The program listed one of her greatest contributions as the recognition and advancement of Hispanic women. She served as national coordinator of Las Hermanas and is coauthor of *Hispanic Women: Prophetic Voice in the Church.*

Lou then gave the president's address, and Sister Carol Ann Jokerst offered the Benediction. Sister Maria Goretti and Andrew Gignac once again added dignity to the recessional following the initial celebration of the San Antonio Pipes and Drums.

Sister Yolanda Tarango receives an honorary doctorate from Lou as Dick McCracken assists with the hooding.

At the reception the joy of the moment was evident in everyone, even those who might have had some reservations. This was Monday. There would be another celebration on Saturday night when university benefactors and many faculty and administrators gathered for the annual Associates Dinner.

For now everyone was tired— emotionally exhilarated but physically tired. Lou and the university had received hundreds of congratulatory messages. At home that evening, he read through the many warm wishes and shared them with his brother Mike who had flown in for the occasion. He was touched by the outpouring of good wishes and thanks from the various Sisters of Charity of the Incarnate Word who had taken time to write personal messages to him.

Lou places the final brick into the new corner wall on Hildebrand Avenue and Broadway in 1996, signifying the name change from Incarnate Word College to University of the Incarnate Word.

Sister Helena sent a card that read, "When it seems hard to keep on giving of your time, of yourself, remember—you're making a difference." She also included a personal message. Sisters Theophane and Alacoque Power wrote, "Congratulations on ten years of productive leadership. The Lord has been your teacher!" Another card asked, "How do you mail a standing ovation?!"

These were important messages to Lou. All of his energies for the past ten years had been directed toward continuing and enhancing the Sisters' work. The dozens of cards from them were more important than any he received. Sister Toni's card also included a personal message. Lou shared it recently.

March 28, 96

Dear Dr. Lou Agnese:

It seems like only yesterday that you arrived at I.W.C. with your two small children full of life and fun who brought sparkle to the campus. They even taught me some new games and watched me carefully in case I would cheat. Later your beautiful wife "Mickey" came to join the family.

God bless you Lou for the many accomplishments at I.W.C. during the last ten years. I'm happy that I saw the day "March 25, 96" when we became the University of the Incarnate Word. Thank you for carrying on the good work begun at the dawn of this century and extending it beyond the dream of the founders. Along with material growth you have preserved the spirit and charism of the Sisters of Charity of the Incarnate Word. Congratulations.

Love and prayers,
Sr. Antoninus Buckley.

Sister Toni sent Lou a note of congratulations on his tenth anniversary as president.

It was time to call it a night. Lou felt good about the day and about what was happening. He saw the University of the Incarnate Word starting to build its own safety nets for the future. He allowed himself a little satisfaction as he remembered Johnny saying, "You did something good here."

The next morning Mike Agnese and his friend left Lou and Mickey's home to drive to Horseshoe Bay where Lou had a small vacation house. It was a decent March day and it would be a nice getaway for a few days. Lou had other things to tend to. You can't celebrate forever—you have to get back to work.

Lou talks about what happened next. "Things were never smooth-going all the time. There were ups and downs, always something to steal the joy right at its peak." Lou took the phone call from his sister Susan. Johnny had been found dead in his New York home that morning by his son. His sudden and unexpected death had occurred on March 25, the Feast of the Incarnate Word.

Lou called Mike, and he came back from Horseshoe Bay. He and Lou made plans to leave for the funeral. But before Lou left he called in Steve Heying. "Steve," he said, "I told Johnny I had fixed that bridge, but I never have gotten to it. I don't know where he is right now, but he knows I lied to him. Fix that bridge while I'm gone, will you?"

By the time Lou returned on Friday, Steve and the carpenters and painters had finished the bridge. It looked new; all the boards had been replaced, and the whole thing was painted. At the next board meeting Lou's request to name the bridge for John Joseph Agnese was approved unanimously.

Lou and his brother Mike hold a drawing of a campus bridge named
in honor of their late older brother, Johnny, who passed away in 1996
(photo courtesy of Steve Holloway).

There was still the party on Saturday, the day after Lou returned from New
York. He explained recently, "There was never a thought to cancel that party. It
would have been the wrong thing to do. Everyone needed to celebrate the University, and I needed to be with friends who could help me start to heal."

Lionel Sosa had been back at the drawing board trying to come up with
something to match or even top "The College." He still had "Brainpower,"
but he needed another slogan. The first full-page ad about the University of
the Incarnate Word appeared on March 24, the day before the ceremony.
The new phrase filled one entire page. "The Universe Is Yours," it stated. The
facing page gave all the reasons why.

On May 24 the Agnese family had something to celebrate. Papa, Lou's
sister Susan and her husband, Stephen, joined the family and Sister Toni to
help celebrate Louis III's high school graduation. Toni was especially happy
that day because the doctor had just cleared her for travel following her back
surgery. Now she could make a long-awaited trip to Ireland.

The group ended up in Sister Toni's apartment in the independent living section of the Sisters' retirement center. The day before, on her eightieth birthday, Toni had received some new tapes of Irish music, and she was
teaching Papa how to dance a jig. A somewhat musically challenged Lou,
who can hum Jim Croce's "Time in a Bottle" and knows most of the words
to "Happy Birthday," just watched the fun.

Back home, the Agneses had a late dinner on their balcony. It was about
9:30 p.m. and Papa had just gone to bed when the phone rang. It was the
hospital notifying Lou that Sister Toni was in the emergency room, having

suffered a massive stroke in her apartment. Lou and Louis rushed to the hospital and were allowed to see her, but she was unresponsive. Sister Antoninus Buckley died moments later. Her death was hard on everyone. Even the priest had trouble completing the prayers at her service. But Sister Toni would have been unhappy if Lou had not continued with the plans and vision that had delighted her so much.

Football was one of the ideas that kept cropping up. In June 1996 *Express-News* staff writer Johnny Ludden wrote an article that could have been enhanced had he only been a fly on the wall during the Las Vegas retreat. "The University of the Incarnate Word is examining the long-range plan of its athletic department after a recent proposal to start a football program drew a mixed response from campus faculty and students," he wrote. "UIW president Lou Agnese temporarily shelved the football proposal in May and appointed a three-member committee to analyze the role of athletics at the university." The committee members were identified as Dr. Denise Doyle, dean of the School of Evening Studies; Dr. David Jurenovich, vice president for planning and marketing (who was out of town and unavailable for comment); and committee chair Dr. Reg Traylor, dean of the School of Graduate Studies.

"Both Traylor and Doyle said some faculty members, particularly the nuns, were concerned that the violent nature of football went against the mission of the university," Ludden reported. "Traylor said Agnese believed the football proposal was becoming 'too divisive' and was taking time and energy away from more significant issues facing the university." Traylor was quoted as saying, "It is now a philosophical issue, not a financial one. Some of the people against football see the abuses that go along with a Division I football program that don't necessarily apply to Division II. They see the violence aspect and the renegades that are not truly students."

Dr. Doyle summarized the situation this way: "I would say the campus is split (on football). The faculty in general seems to be against it, while I think the students, or some portion of the students, are supporting it." Football was an off-and-on debate for another twelve years until the community finally made the decision to add the sport to its athletic offerings in 2007.

In September 1996 *U.S. News and World Report* chose the University of the Incarnate Word as the Most Efficient institution among regional colleges and universities in the West. The institutions were judged on the relationship between cost of the institution and the quality of education they deliver.

Lou also received an award that fall. *Hispanic Magazine,* whose sixth Annual National Hispanic Achievement awards were sponsored by Anheuser-Busch, named Lou as Educator of the Year. The *Express-News* reported that he had been chosen "in recognition of the strides he has made to increase the number of Hispanic students at the San Antonio school in the past decade!" *Express-News* reporter Russell Gold wrote, "Ever the salesman for his students, Agnese said he was looking forward to attending the awards ceremony Tuesday, in part because it will give him the opportunity to rub shoulders with many corporate sponsors—like Ford, MCI, and Anheuser-Busch—and hopefully get some contributions for the school. 'I'll be able to pick some pockets while I'm there,' Agnese said."

At the dedication of the Grossman International Conference Center are, from left, Lou, Archbishop Patrick Flores and Miriam and Burton Grossman.

As the International Conference Center was being completed at the Hildebrand and Highway 281 corner that was blessedly not sold in 1986, Dr. Burton E. Grossman, widely respected as one of the kindest and most generous philanthropists of his generation, donated an undisclosed amount to the center. Lou responded to Dr. Grossman's generosity by naming the new complex the Dr. Burton E. Grossman International Conference Center. Later, on Grossman's eightieth birthday, Lou extended one more thank you. A full-page newspaper ad ran with a picture of the two men and wording that was pure Sosa. It read, "To congratulate you properly, we would need the entire newspaper . . . but they wouldn't sell it!"

The center's dedication, which took place on October 4, 1996, drew an international audience, as well as many Sisters who had lived in the building when it was a convalescent home. Sister Mary James, who watched the demonstrations of technology installed in her old community room, was quoted by the *Express-News* as saying, "Leave it to Dr. Agnese; he'll transform anything."

Jim Tilton, now vice president for international initiatives as well as Lou's communications assistant, was quick to give Dr. Cheryl Anderson credit for the state-of-the-art technology.

Anderson, then director of technology at Incarnate Word, explained the equipment built into the

Dr. Cheryl Anderson.

center would allow it to compete in the future when technology plays an important part in classes and conferences.

The dedication brought international visitors from Brazil, Taiwan, Mexico, and Spain. Several months later Mayor Yasuyuki Misumi of Kumamoto, Japan, specifically asked to tour the center when he was visiting in San Antonio. Lou had visited Kumamoto's International Conference Center and been impressed enough to decide Incarnate Word should also have one. Suzanne Hoholik of the *Express-News* stated Misumi was flattered the San Antonio center had been modeled after the one in his city. She quoted him as saying, "When I heard the building was inspired by the center we have, I was very impressed to know it was being built in the United States."

The International Conference Center was not the only thing that impressed Lou during his many visits to Kumamoto. He recognized the role Japan and other parts of Asia were to play in San Antonio and worldwide and encouraged his son to study at Kumamoto Gakuen University. Louis, who was eighteen, studied in Kumamoto for two years, becoming fluent in the Japanese language and learning the nuances of that culture. Later, Nancy continued the family's international focus and studied at Dante Alighieri School in Brazil.

There was only one more dedication in 1996. On November 23 the Buckley/Mitchell Graduate and Undergraduate Admissions Center was completed and dedicated to two women, one an Incarnate Word Sister and the other a Franciscan, who had been integral parts of the Agnese family. Sister Sally Mitchell had taken a three-year leave of absence to participate in pastoral work and was now back, serving as vice principal of Incarnate Word High School. And the spirit of Sister Antoninus Buckley—Sister Toni—would always be there.

CHAPTER 16

THE YEAR OF THE TIGER

Something big was now brewing or simmering, depending on who was reporting. Lou had given the nod to begin exploring a Ph.D. program, and like many difficult tasks in the past, this one was handed off to Reg Traylor. Reg had served as acting dean of nursing, mathematics, and science for only one year while Lou decided where he wanted to house those three disciplines. Denise Doyle observed, "Those three were like the Alsace Lorraine of the campus. They belonged first to one school or college, then to another, and back again." Regardless of their fate, 1996 saw Reg named dean of graduate studies. It wasn't long before the Ph.D. feelers were sent out.

Another task force was formed and the usual suspects were rounded up to serve on it. The members conducted open forums with interested faculty. As with any serious proposal, there were those in favor and those adamantly opposed. Input was sought from the business community and from successful Ph.D. programs around the state. Dr. Stan Carpenter of Texas A&M University and Howard Kimel, business owner and international entrepreneur, were among those who served as consultants.

By December 1996 a proposal was sent to the board with this preamble: "The University of the Incarnate Word proposes to offer a Doctor of Philosophy Degree in Education, effective January 1, 1998. The decision to offer such a degree is based on the heritage of the institution, the mission of the institution, and the assessed needs of the community served by the institution. It is expected that the degree will provide opportunity for four specialties [concentrations]." The four were listed as educational leadership, mathematics education, science education, and international education and entrepreneurship. Rather lengthy explanations gave the rationale for their selection.

The Ph.D. program did not start in January 1998. First the educational leadership concentration was changed to organizational leadership, and both mathematics education and international education and entrepreneurship continued developing. Dr. Tom Hudson, physics professor, took on the extensive revision of the proposed science education concentration.

However, when the time came to officially announce the Ph.D. program the next year, only organizational leadership and mathematics education were announced. There was a concern that the accreditation body would think the university had overextended itself with four concentrations. This was a bit awkward since three concentrations had been announced internally, and there were applicants in the pipeline for all three. The issue was resolved to everyone's professional security, if not satisfaction, by the fact that all doctoral students took the same courses in the early stages of the degree, regardless of their concentration.

Sister Dorothy Ettling was hired on August 18, 1999, as an associate professor to take charge of the organizational leadership concentration. Dr. Richard Henderson joined her later, and they shared coordinator duties for the next ten years.

The international education and entrepreneurship concentration was officially announced the next year. The extra planning, though unexpected, allowed time for a team from the U.S. Department of Commerce to serve as valuable consultants. Science education was never completed because Dr. Hudson became ill. His illness progressed, and the concentration never found another champion after Tom's death.

The 1997–98 academic year saw more than the resolution of the Ph.D. degree. Another program was blossoming. Before Dr. Annemarie Walsh arrived, Incarnate Word's fashion program was about to close. Annemarie poured so much energy into it as director that it became one of the university's most popular majors. Its annual fashion show, the Cutting Edge, is a favorite event during San Antonio's Fiesta.

In 1997 Lou and Annemarie's energies converged to give fashion design and fashion management students the experience of a lifetime. Lou had become a frequent visitor in Taiwan and a frequent host when Taiwanese civic and educational leaders came to San Antonio. Fu Jen Catholic University and Tainan Woman's College of Arts and Technology were two of Incarnate Word's sister schools and would be part of Tainan, Taiwan's 1997 International Costume Carnival. The two sister schools saw to it that Incarnate Word's fashion programs were invited to participate as well.

The costume carnival would include fashion shows from New Zealand, Korea, Brazil, Japan, and Taiwan, in addition to the United States, which would be represented by UIW and the company, Naturally Texas, described by the *Express-News* as a group of designers, manufacturers, and fiber producers. It wouldn't require much work on the part of Annemarie and her students—just design 104 fashions ranging from traditional Western wear to elegant ball gowns, produce the clothing, find someone to produce the show, hire models, and take the whole setup to Taiwan. "Why not?" said Annemarie.

Incarnate Word graduate Robert Mitchell produced the show, and several graduates already in the fashion industry participated. Forty-one persons, including professors, students, the professional models who had been hired, and Lou Agnese, flew to Taiwan for the production. The Incarnate Word show was praised in the Taiwanese newspapers and enthusiastically received by an audience of several thousand. Annemarie and the students stayed for nine days, participating in the carnival and enjoying sightseeing and Taiwanese food as students from Tainan College hosted them. Annemarie retired in 2008, but she left a legacy that her fellow faculty are happy to continue.

Lou, who squeezes every possible value out of any trip he takes, used the Taiwan carnival as an opportunity to visit Korea, Thailand, Japan, and the People's Republic of China. Lou had several good friends in China, the best being Harley Seyedin, a naturalized American citizen from Iran. Harley had been an exchange student in the United States under the former Shah's extensive study abroad program. He was a businessman, entrepreneur, informal politician, and longtime friend. He and Lou met in 1985 through mutual friend Jose E. Martinez, who years later became the first president of the Free Trade Alliance and a special assistant to President George H. W. Bush. It was discussions with Harley that led to what happened in early 1998, the Chinese zodiac's Year of the Tiger.

Lou asked Pat Watkins, now dean of University Collaborative Programs, to come to his office. He casually started the conversation with "How would you like to go to China and open a school for us?" Lou didn't realize it at the time, but he had just offered that to a lifelong China-phile. As a four-year-old, Pat had believed the stories about digging a hole deep enough to reach China and had nearly destroyed the family garden trying. Here was a chance to go with a lot less digging.

Higher education had only begun to flourish again in Chi-

UIW fashion department students on a parade float in Taiwan during the 1997 International Costume Carnival.

na, having been almost destroyed during their Cultural Revolution. It sought the support and innovation of an American presence. Being that presence in China would be a public relations coup for UIW, but at a more serious level, it would address many aspects of the university's Mission.

Opening a school in China could also be a promising venture for the investors who backed it. And investors would have to be a major part of anything UIW decided to do in China; Lou would not use UIW money as startup funding for the venture. "We had the knowledge and experience of higher education," he explained recently. "That would be our contribution; that and administrative personnel. Money had to come from the Chinese partner." Beyond the obvious, Lou had another reason for not funding the operation. "In joint ventures, we need to be invited; the partner has to want the program as much as we do, and that's demonstrated by matching our efforts and expertise with their money."

Even with Chinese educators seriously seeking an American partner, Lou could not just walk in and volunteer. Trust is slow to build in a country that traces its first dynasty to 2200 B.C. and has seen repeated famine, revolution, and political domination. The term guanxi, loosely defined by the Chinese as "connections," is an important part of their culture. That would be Harley's biggest contribution. He had been living in and investing in China for twenty years and lived at the time in Guangzhou, where he was president of its American Chamber of Commerce. But even Harley needed a little guanxi boost from time to time. His wife, Sun Hui, epitomized the concept. In China the family name is always stated first. Lou Agnese would be Agnese Lou in that culture. So Sun Hui is known to close friends as Hui, her given name. Hui was educated in both China and the U.S. with a law degree from China and additional law certificates from Georgetown University in Washington, D.C. She is the senior partner with the Shanghai Universal Law Firm.

Careful probes had already gone out. There was clear interest on both sides. The goal was to establish a joint venture with South China Normal University, one of the top schools in the country, ranked 45 out of 1,100. It was located in Guangzhou, a sprawling, bustling city in Guangdong province, once known as Canton. The area is in the heart of the Pearl River delta. The joint venture would develop an American university on shared campus space with a branch of South China Normal University.

That branch was still in its talking stage and would be located in a rural setting about forty-five minutes from the city. The grounds were spacious, with acres of rural land and grazing water buffalo. The owner-investor had already established large preschool, elementary school, and high school facilities on the grounds where all students, including the three-year-olds, boarded. Now he would begin construction of the university buildings. One of the Americans who later taught there dubbed the complex "a Chinese Brainpower Connection on steroids."

Pat arrived on June 6, 1998, intending to begin university planning with a timeline of at least a year to eighteen months. But the Chinese partners had added another component. They wanted to start with a group of UIW–selected teachers to offer English in the pre-K, elementary, and high schools. They currently had teachers from Canada, but the partners wanted to change from the British English being used to American English. They wanted all their foreign eggs in the same basket. And they wanted the basket of teachers delivered by the fall semester—less than three months away. Lou and Harley agreed that the addition was a necessary and positive one, but the date was negotiated to fall 1999, allowing time to select and train the teachers.

Now there were two projects—the first involved developing a new ESL curriculum and hiring and training teachers for the K-12 program. The second and original project was to bring the University of the Incarnate Word to China. The two projects had considerable overlap, and the fact that Lou had agreed to the K-12 plan added trust to the partnership. It made the planning process for the university project a little easier. "People always think the religious nature of our university must have been the hardest problem to solve, but that was never the case," Lou explained in a recent discussion. "We made it clear we were there for educational purposes. We showed how we would teach world religions as a history course, not as a religion course, and we stated up front that we would be teaching U.S. history and U.S. government. Curriculum was just never a problem."

Pat recalled the issues that caused the most upset and led to endless meetings were the little ones like wanting to serve readily available McDonald's hamburgers for lunch on a special occasion or forgetting to put the ping pong balls back in the right case. The only serious conflicts dealt with length of classes and the number of teachers needed. Lou held tightly to the teacher-student ratio UIW recommended. Its accreditation was also protected by hiring faculty with the proper credentials. It puzzled the Chinese partner, especially the party secretary, that one teacher couldn't just teach history and English, and psychology, too, if he had the book. The party secretary had one other small problem when the initial agreements were being worded. He could not quite bring himself to agree to the word "profit" in the financial section. After much thought, he substituted the word "benefit."

The nine teachers for the K-12 project became the core of everything that happened in China. They arrived in August 1999, with then doctoral student Norman St. Clair as lead teacher. "You don't have room to include a

Dr. Norman St. Clair in China.

fraction of what we learned," Norm said. "It was the most profound experience of my life—and I met my wife there." Bobbie Holmes was one of the nine teachers that year. Norm and Bobbie married in 2000 when they briefly returned from China. Norm is now Dr. Norman St. Clair, assistant professor in the Dreeben School of Education, but he was to play a large role in the China story before settling in to that position.

In the midst of increasing international activity, the university lost its vice president for international initiatives and Lou lost a valuable friend and assistant. Jim Tilton died on July 6, 1998, after fighting cancer for several years. Visitation was held in Our Lady's Chapel at the university. Marge Draeger and Lou stood at Jim's casket trying to say good-bye. "He needs a pen to click," Lou said. He reached in his coat pocket, took out his pen, and discreetly placed it in Jim's casket.

At the retreat that summer—again in Puerto Vallarta—a new administrative structure was presented. The position of provost was established and Lou appointed Ed Paderon as the university's first provost. The academic vice president position, however, was not being abandoned; the university would have both. At that point no one knew—though many guessed—who that vice president would be. The new structure also called for a vice president for administration, filled early on by Dr. David Jurenovich. David would continue his other vice presidential duties, but his title changed. In the absence of the president, who was traveling internationally a great deal by then, Ed would be in charge of academic issues and David would handle decisions related to the administration of the university. Robert Barnett was hired as dean of international initiatives to pick up the work Jim Tilton had started. This new dean position was the one Lou had alluded to during the Las Vegas retreat and had been intended to give Tilton more time to focus on presidential communications.

The groupings in the academic divisions also changed. They had been tweaked slightly since Lou's earlier plan. Professional Studies was now divided into three schools. This was the moment of birth for the School of Business, School of Education, and School of Nursing. It was also the birth of the School of Science, Mathematics, and Engineering—though engineering was still in the hoped-for stage.

There was spirited debate about whether the School of Graduate Studies, which had been a separate school since 1996, would be subsumed into the other schools and colleges. The question had serious ramifications, as the reporting structure of the new Ph.D. would be affected. The debate continued well after the retreat.

Details regarding restructuring and staffing continued to be resolved. Many new administrators were selected, some by searches and some by direct appointment of the president. Those "direct appointments" eventually became more dry kindling for a fire. Here was the turnover anticipated earlier. When the dust settled, a new lineup was in place for the fall 1999 semester.

Dr. Denise Doyle, in a surprise to very few, was named academic vice president. The surprise, however, was that the position was now vice president for academic and student affairs. Frank Ayala, who had been vice president for student affairs, moved to a new position as dean of academic progress. Frank later accepted a position at Occidental College in Los Angeles. Denise's new title revived and paraphrased one of academe's old jokes: "Denise is vice president for faculty and student affairs, of which we pray there are none!" Dr. Reg Traylor was named vice president for extended academic programs, another new position. The Brainpower Connection, now under Sister Sally Mitchell, and the ADCaP program would report to him. Lou also had Reg exploring the potential for an online, or virtual, university; if it materialized it would also report to him. Both Reg and Denise would report to the provost.

There were a host of new or rearranged dean positions. The decision had finally been made to keep the dean of graduate studies, and Lou appointed Dr. Gil Hinojosa to replace Traylor. Dr. Donna Aronson was named acting dean of the School of Humanities, Arts, and Social Sciences, replacing Gil. Lou appointed

Theresa Altomare briefs Sister Sally Mitchell as Sally takes over the Brainpower Connection.

Dr. Pat LeMay Burr the first dean of the School of Business and Applied Arts and Sciences; Pat had previously been the director of the academic program in international business. Dr. Kathi Light was named the first

Sister Mary Elizabeth Joyce cuts the ribbon at the renovated Joyce Building, named in her honor. Looking on are Lou and John Lodek, chair of the Interior Design Department.

dean of the School of Nursing and Health Professions. Drs. Lois Soefje, Jim Sorensen and Jane Cardea had served as director or dean during the years when nursing was combined with other disciplines. Dr. Pat Watkins, still back and forth in China, was named acting dean of the School of Education. Dr. Paul Nowak, an outside hire, was the first dean of the School of Science, Mathematics, and Engineering.

As folks were grabbing a seat in this round of musical chairs, a tall, stately tower was being constructed near the newly renovated Joyce Building.

The building was named for Sister Mary Elizabeth Joyce, founder of the fashion design program, and now enhanced by a gift from Alumna Marjorie Ann Jordan. Jordan, a graduate of the class of 1967, donated the grand clock tower with its majestic carillon. It was an addition to the campus that brought with it the traditional sounds of a university. The chimes and tolls of the music and bells were immedi-

ately embraced by faculty and students. The tower was dedicated on November 22, 1998, Marjorie Jordan's birthday. She donated it "for the future enjoyment of the Incarnate Word community and in memory of the members of the Jordan family."

Dick McCracken took on the responsibility for hymns and other music that would emanate from the tower. At first it seemed like just one more task assigned to Dick, but the truth was the carillon became McCracken's newest and probably favorite toy.

Lou stands in front of the Jordan Carillon, a gift of alumna Marjorie Ann Jordan.

CHAPTER 17

BLIND OR BLINDSIDED?

I t was bound to happen. Process was not Lou's strong suit. He knew opportunity rarely kept knocking if no one answered the first time. And his natural impatience made him bypass anything or anyone who could conceivably slow him down. On the other hand, those opportunities were knocking at the door of an institution of higher learning, and in that environment process was revered. The only surprise was that it had taken this long for the spark to ignite. But when the fourteen-year-long fuse finally touched off the fire, it was more than a marshmallow roast.

The college was now a university; it had tripled in size; it and Lou Agnese managed a large portion of San Antonio's Catholic high school education; there was an evening studies program that might or might not be following all the faculty handbook rules; there was a Ph.D. program; and now the university was about to open in mainland China where only God knew what would be happening. Equally alarming, there would probably soon be a virtual university with "our curriculum just floating around somewhere in cyberspace." The fast-moving Agnese train had left some at the station, but more important, many of those who made it aboard had no idea where that train was heading. They didn't really care right then that the endowment fund was five times greater than it had been in 1986.

The irony is that by 1999 Lou was what Denise Doyle describes as a "recovering micromanager." Lou had always seen the big picture, but he had also been in the trenches worrying about every detail. By now he had a cadre of administrators and faculty he felt could handle the details. He saw his role as continuing to break new ground for the university, envisioning the future, and clearing obstacles to get there. He was a builder, not a maintainer. When he created the provost and academic vice president roles, he told Denise: "Take care of details. Stay on the campus when I am gone. The provost can travel, but you stay here." He knew Denise understood the faculty, and he was comfortable with her role.

No one will ever know for sure, but it appears likely that the fire would not have blazed were it not for one thing. The faculty held passionately that the Faculty Senate was their official decision-making body. Now under the new structure outlined at the Puerto Vallarta retreat, there was growing concern about the faculty role in governance. In November 1998 the administration disseminated a chart showing the senate reporting only to the vice president for academic and student affairs. Even though that would be someone as trusted as Denise, this appeared to sideline the senate, now that the university had a provost at the top of the academic administration.

Dr. Ed Paderon, right, with Father Richard Hall, left, and Lou.

The December senate meeting produced a recommendation stipulating that the senate coordinate directly with the provost when the new structure was implemented in August. By the January 1999 meeting, there was a little more to the issue. The senate strongly and unanimously stated that their line of communication must be either with the provost (Ed Paderon) or with both academic vice presidents (Denise and Reg). Part of the concern was that Reg Traylor was known to be as fast-moving an entrepreneur as Lou, and there was some underlying feeling that the extended education parts of the organization he oversaw might not always be communicated with the faculty. That concern heightened as the virtual university concept grew.

As senate president in those years, Dr. Bob Connelly must have thought he was living out the old Chinese curse, "May you live in interesting times." In August 1999 Bob met with Ed, Denise, and Reg, and the group developed the "triangle model" in an attempt to clarify the faculty role in governance. That model showed the senate at the base of a triangle recommending and communicating in different directions depending on the issues at hand (to the provost at top of triangle, or to the vice president for academic and student affairs or the vice president for extended academic programs to either side).

There is a clue embedded in this unfolding chronology that gives insight into the clash of cultures between Lou and the senate. It has nothing to do with who is important and who isn't. But it is interesting to see that in January 1999 the senate wanted the communication lines changed, but the meeting with Paderon, Doyle, and Traylor took place seven months later. Seven months of Lou's time would have been enough to develop ADCaP, build a dorm, or raise several more million dollars. It wasn't who would win the race but rather how it was run that sometimes caused the conflict.

The leadership retreat in 1999 took place in October instead of the usual August. This was the first retreat with the new administration and new structure in place. But in a startling move no one saw coming, Ed Paderon laid a plan on the table. Ed presented a model that eliminated the university-wide Faculty Senate altogether! In this model it was replaced with a provost's council that would be advisory to the provost. He also called for individual faculty senates and committees in each college or school.

Dr. Bob Connelly was president of the Faculty Association and later of the Faculty Senate.

Most administrators still think the concept of a provost's council blindsided Lou. It certainly stunned the retreat participants. Denise Doyle recently shared her opinion that Ed and the faculty never completely connected, adding that perhaps he had a different concept of how to share governance with faculty. On a personal level, Ed was considered one of the university's most respectful and kindhearted administrators. With Ed's obvious loyalty to Lou and to the university, it is doubtful he would have presented that model had he anticipated the faculty reaction.

The Faculty Senate was quick to react. At their October meeting, they endorsed their triangle model but expressed no desire to rework the senate concept into smaller units within the five colleges/schools. The senate also committed to developing policies and procedures that would facilitate decision-making in the new structure. That latter statement suggests the faculty were aware that lengthy processes could risk opportunities the university might have and they wanted to take that possible administrative argument off the table.

On November 9 Lou presented his own model. Although it appeared to be an attempt to save face for all, many felt that it proved he was not really listening. Compromises are difficult to achieve once the lines have been tightly drawn. Lou's model showed three reporting lines: the full Faculty Senate would report only to Denise; a yet to be formed advisory group would report to Reg; and some type of provost council would be created.

It would be an understatement to say all hell broke loose. Lou then called for a Summit on Decision Making, to take place on January 11, 2000. The senate called its own meeting to prepare for the summit, and some expressed far-reaching concerns about what they saw as "the growing fragmentation of faculty voice in governance." There were references to the marginalization of the senate, a decreasing sense of ability to exercise oversight of curriculum and faculty affairs, and a growing tension between faculty and administration.

The senate invited all tenured full-time faculty to a discussion on Monday, December 13. The minutes of that meeting show an escalation from the issue of which governance model to implement to a much greater concern. The quality of the president's leadership and leadership style became the focus of discussion. The tone and a bit of internal dissonance within faculty are seen in quotes from the meeting:

"I'm not comfortable when a president of a university refers to himself as a CEO."

"We have to consider our alternatives: We could form a teacher's union, or maybe a teamsters' union; we could develop a statement of censure or maybe a vote of no confidence."

"A vote of no confidence is a serious step. I've seen an institution torn apart by such action. A whole system brought down."

One speaker cited a long list of concerns, including "appointment of certain academic administrators without conducting formal searches" and disagreement with the eight-week format of ADCaP.

The assembled faculty agreed that in order to be effective partners in shared governance, the senate must be recognized as the sole official voice expressing the faculty position on all curriculum, faculty affairs, and rank and tenure issues at the university. But it also planned another meeting for after Christmas to address concerns about the president's leadership.

The record shows that Bob Connelly received a letter from a faculty member on December 22 stating, "I would like to express a concern that I have about any potential action that may be contemplated by the Faculty Senate as a result of our meeting on December 13. I believe that first of all there must be an understanding of the difference between an action of Censure versus an action of No Confidence." The letter went on to explain the differences, ending with the suggestion that No Confidence was the safer way to go. That the letter was sent at all indicates the suggestions in the meeting were being taken seriously. The war had begun.

CHAPTER 18

THE OTHER SHOE

The summit met on January 11—but without Lou. On January 9 Lou was notified that his mother, Nancy Garguilo Agnese, had died. Sister Helena accompanied him to the funeral in New York. Anger can sometimes steal perspective, and despite the circumstance, a few faculty expressed annoyance that Lou had opted to miss such an important meeting with them. In his absence, Ed Paderon conducted the meeting. It ended uncomfortably, with the decision to reconvene when the president returned.

Sister Dorothy Ettling and Dr. David Jurenovich facilitated the reconvened summit on January 13 with twenty-six faculty and academic administrators, including Lou. A positive-sounding memorandum was released, stating there was agreement that the Faculty Senate was the faculty's decision-making body and would report to both vice presidents as it had requested. It also stated the senate would assure its membership was appropriate for the new structure and could provide timely response to new academic issues and programs. It ended with the reassuring words: "The Faculty Senate and the Administration will respect these agreements and the processes that will be developed as these agreements require, and commit to resolve differences in a spirit of collaboration." It sounded like time to exhale.

Denise explained recently that Lou was truly engaged with the group at this meeting. "He heard them," she said, "and that seemed to be a turning point." However the summit did not lead to lasting peace. On January 24 the faculty met and decided the agreement was not enough. Thirty-eight of the sixty-two tenured full-time teaching faculty participated. Bob Connelly reported the faculty felt the agreements were a positive first step but other concerns still needed to be addressed and "the conversation should continue."

The rest of his memo gave insight into how that conversation would likely continue. It stated that the faculty would consider requesting a meeting with the board or board representatives in order to share concerns. Those included institutional support for academic quality and collaboration in developing a constitution for the university. But the final portion of the memo was the most critical. It stated that the senate would "explore the ramifications of a faculty vote of no confidence in the leadership of the president and determine the procedure for taking such action."

Later it was decided that a meeting with the president should take place before approaching the board. Bob Connelly wrote to Lou and requested a February 7 meeting. He included points compiled by a faculty member:

"It is disruptive to have the structure constantly changed."

"It is demoralizing to have Deans and Vice Presidents appointed without a search committee with significant faculty representation and without term limits."

"It is insulting to have a Provost appointed solely for the academic area, implying that faculty are less responsible than other employees under other Vice Presidents."

Some have tried to explain what was happening. Clearly, the faculty had some justifiable concerns, but they were becoming mixed with an anger and resentment that was feeding on itself. As one supporter at the time put it, "Lou Agnese saved this place, and they're never going to forgive him for it."

A written account of the February 7 meeting does not seem to exist. One can only imagine it did not go well since the next document, dated February 10, states simply, "Faculty Senate met with President . . . Faculty Senate charges Executive Committee to develop action plan . . ." Part 2 of the action plan was to form a committee to explore ramifications of a vote of no confidence in the president, and part 3 was to develop a fifteen-question survey to confirm faculty concerns. Reading the questions eleven years later they seem to have been constructed in a rather negative voice. But it is important to remember there was substantial anger in some quarters at that time.

Most responses, as expected, showed considerable faculty unrest, though some took issue with the survey itself. "The questions do not describe my attitude. I believe that I am not nearly as frustrated as the authors of the questions." One respondent who clearly did want action taken against the president still commented on the questionnaire, "It's what we call a 'loaded survey' in market research. The questions are stacked—poorly designed."

But it was Sister Margaret Patrice who tried to restore reason. As academic dean in 1969, she had first introduced a plan for faculty participation in governance. It was based on a 1962 American Association of University Professors document. She addressed each question and summarized her comments in a final paragraph: "My general response to your survey is that it is lacking in objectivity. If so, then the results will not be reliable. As educators who pride ourselves on being involved in research, we should be able to offer a questionnaire that is open-minded and leading to valid opinions. I do not think you have offered us that opportunity."

By early March the issue was far from settled. The senate planned to study responses and prioritize problems to be discussed with the president. Both pro and con voices were still being heard when the other shoe fell.

It may never be clear how or by whose authority, but, in the midst of dissension and tension, another dean was hired without a search. This time it was Dr. Cyndi Porter, as dean of the virtual university. According to correspondence between Ed Paderon and Reg Traylor, she joined a large group of administrators similarly hired. Reg made a noble effort to point out all those appointments. He acknowledged his own positions had been appointed without searches and reminded the reader that it is a presidential prerogative to appoint interim and acting administrators. Unfortunately, this was neither.

On March 10, 2000, Bob Connelly wrote to Lou, "At our Senate meeting yesterday I reported on what I knew about the recent appointment of a dean of the virtual university. After some heated discussion Senate approved action to request a meeting with you to discuss faculty concern with the way this hire and those last year were done." He added, "Senate suggests that the whole Senate be present, whomever you choose from administration, the Academic Subcommittee of the Board, and a facilitator."

Lou, no doubt wishing his own administrators would stop "helping" him so much, responded at once. Bob sent another memo to the senate the same day: "I met with Lou at 1:30 today after the Board meeting . . . His initial reaction to the concern about the Dean of Virtual U. was to acknowledge a problem with the search process . . . He was more than willing to meet about the topic of academic administrator appointments or whatever can move us to a better place. But, he suggested a two-stage process and I agreed."

The two-stage process involved a March 23 meeting of the senate, Lou, Ed Paderon, Denise Doyle, Reg Traylor, and a facilitator if necessary. Pending the outcome, a second could be set up on March 30 with representatives from the senate and the board's Academic subcommittee.

The first meeting required no facilitator and produced open discussion of concerns. The group agreed to set up a task force to develop guidelines for academic administrator searches. Lou announced a creative solution to the unsearched-for dean: Dr. Porter would be an assistant vice president instead of a dean, therefore not as directly involved with faculty as a dean. Lou assured the senate that no deans would report to the assistant vice president.

The second meeting was with the same group. That no board representation was required suggests trust was starting to rebuild. Lou planned to tap Reg once more for an assignment. The dean's position in the School of Mathematics, Science, and Engineering was again open, and the engineering program was dear to Lou's heart. This time he announced directly to the senate he was going to appoint Reg interim dean of that school until a new dean could be found. That left Cyndi Porter as assistant vice president in a program with no vice president. Lou solved that one by announcing that Ed Paderon would take over duties in that area for the next year until a new vice president was selected.

On April 27, 2000, the final memo about the president's leadership was sent to the entire faculty as follow-up to their participation in the meetings and questionnaire. Bob Connelly wrote, "As you recall, we had planned to prioritize problem areas to be discussed in meetings with the President. Information received about the pending appointment of a dean of the Virtual U. pushed the topic of searches for academic administrative positions to the top of the list. Senate requested a meeting with the President." He explained what had happened in those meetings.

Later in the memo, under Presidential Leadership, Bob wrote that the "Senate called a special meeting on April 10th to discuss the report from the committee set up to explore the ramifications of a vote of no confidence in the President . . . After hearing perspectives from Senate members who were on the committee and discussion, the Senate decided that it was not ready at this time to take action on this matter." He added the senate would determine its five most important concerns to discuss with the president.

Several collaborative innovations resulted from efforts on both sides. The Faculty Senate president now sits on the Executive Council and attends meetings the vice president for academic and student affairs has with the deans. Longtime board member Alan Dreeben hosts an annual reception for faculty and administrators at the San Antonio Country Club, the campus has an annual Faculty Appreciation Luncheon where awards and recognition are given, and the Presidential Teaching Award was established.

But perhaps the most valuable change was the reconfiguration of the University Planning Commission. That group now includes fifteen faculty chosen by peers. Having representative faculty and administrators together in planning sessions and retreats allows immediate dissemination of all planning discussions. Even during the awkward and disagreeable months of dissension, Bob Connelly, as chair of the Faculty Senate, was a Board of Trustees member and attended its meetings, still a responsibility and privilege of that office.

Bob Connelly and Lou recently talked about the 1999 and early 2000 difficulties. "People thought Bob and I were at odds with each other. We rarely had differences about the final product; we just had differences in how to get there. Bob is good at process, and I'm getting better at it," Lou said. Bob, now an academic dean himself, reflected on his role at that time. "Sometimes I think my role was to just keep people talking so that real communication could take place."

Lou appreciated the support he had from the Congregation, the board and Sister Margaret Patrice throughout the process. "Dr. Dennis Juren was on the board and also teaching as an adjunct in the School of Business," Lou said. "He and Sister Teresa Stanley, superior of the Congregation at that time, gave me good advice." Sister Stanley had been on the nursing faculty earlier and could share perspectives from both positions.

Lou and Dr. Denise Doyle present Dr. Roger Barnes with the first Presidential Teaching Award.

While acknowledging right on both sides, Lou took a lot of the blame on his shoulders. "I realized I had not communicated enough with the faculty in those years. I was so intent on getting the college/university to a safe place that I didn't even notice I had lost the rest of the parade somewhere." He added, "I'm still impatient and I still want things done yesterday, but I know how to control that better now—a little better," he laughed.

"It's all about growth—in all of us," he said. "The faculty was being asked to handle one change after another. I still think those changes were necessary, but today I would probably approach them a little differently."

Lou became very serious, very intent. "The important thing to remember is that all that bad stuff had to happen. It had to happen to help us finally get in place the structure we have today—and to develop it together. The institution was changing from a college to a university, with all the demands that kind of change brings. What happened could have caused me to leave. It could have caused the university to go backwards. But it didn't. The struggle continued and it got us where we are now. You can't be afraid of dissension or struggle. It makes you better. That whole situation improved me personally, and it improved the university."

As John Updike once wrote, "A leader is one who, out of madness or goodness, volunteers to take upon himself the woe of the people. . ." In this case it was the woe of an institution.

· III ·

RAISING ALL SHIPS

A Mature Campus; A Mature President

CHAPTER 19
A MOUSE IN THE HOUSE

L ife at the university did not stop during the months of open dis-
cord. People came, left, and made major contributions. Some valued
friends died.

Bill Crain, whose Budweiser puppy logo had infuriated Amy Freeman
Lee, died on July 29, 1999. He had been a member of the Board of Trustees
for the previous ten years. Lou felt Bill's death personally and wrote a post-
humous letter to him that appeared on a full page of the *Express-News*. He
spoke of Bill's public and private sides and how he always kept his help to
people a private matter. Speaking for all who loved Bill, the letter ended, "We
hope to live our own lives well enough to see you again."

Burton Grossman was eighty-one when he died on November 12. Lou
told the *Express-News* that Grossman was a wonderful benefactor and a good
friend. "He supported not only the university but just about every kind of
project in this community for years." As if in testimony of that, Jeannie Frie-
den, executive vice president of the Cancer Therapy and Research Center,
told the *Express-News* that Grossman "never wanted
people to know what he gave . . . one time he saw a
need and said, 'Well, the tooth fairy is going to have
to do something about it.' He was just a very special,
special man."

Sister Helena Monahan had been doing double
duty ever since the death of another special man, Jim
Tilton. She was serving as legal counsel and as Lou's
assistant for communications. Lou knew he had to
find an assistant to replace Tilton, and since Sister
Helena was leaving in 2000 for an elected position in
congregational leadership, he also needed a new legal
counsel. It meant searching again for persons whose
work styles would be compatible with the president's.

Bill Crain, a member
of the Board of
Trustees, passed
away in July 1999.

Just communicating with Lou can be an adventure at times, and on a daily basis is not for the fainthearted. Lou tried to hold back any profanity when he was with the Sisters, but it didn't always work. One day, in a particularly frustrated moment, he barked some instructions and then told Sister Helena he didn't "want that sonofabitch involved." Without missing a beat, Sister Helena nodded and said, "Got it! But which sonofabitch are we talking about?" Lou needed to find another assistant with that composure.

Vincent Rodriguez applied for the advertised communications position. A veteran journalist at several large news organizations and then a Graduate Fellow at the University of Iowa, Vince knew about Lou and had even been on the campus for an event once—though he left because he couldn't find a parking place. Vince describes his interview with Lou in 1999:

"It was a Saturday afternoon and Lou had just completed the December commencement ceremony. It wasn't dark enough for the Christmas lights to be on, but they would be soon. It was the end of what must have been a tiring day. I didn't know anything about the turmoil going on, nor did I know Lou's mother was seriously ill. But you could tell it had been a long day." Vince continued, "I went into his office, and he was impeccably dressed. He greeted me cordially but informally. As he indicated a chair for me I noticed this professional man I had been both briefed and warned about was talking to me without his shoes on. He was clearly beat. Then I saw the tiny hole in his otherwise perfect socks and one very tired toe trying to peek out. Hey, this is someone I can work for, I thought, and fortunately he thought so, too.

"My learning curve was steep," he added. "I had to learn to think like Lou, and I had to learn the UIW culture." Lou's fast pace allowed only a small window of opportunity in which to accomplish both. "I found myself frequently drawing on my experience at the United Press International wire service. Whenever we were assigned a story at UPI, we'd always ask our editor the deadline. The answer was almost always the same. 'Five minutes ago!' That frequently was the case with Lou."

Over the years Vince was to find UPI deadlines generous compared with some of Lou's. Often operating behind the scenes, Vince has been a valuable asset, directing presidential communications, creating presentations, serving as liaison to the public relations office, and advising Lou and other senior administrators on critical media issues.

The day before he left for his mother's funeral in January, Lou participated in yet another dedication. Even with the property surrounding the International Conference Center, the university needed to expand beyond the physical borders of Broadway and Hildebrand. The university was able to purchase the building on Broadway directly across from the Motherhouse Chapel with its famous steeple. Andrea Cyterski-Acosta, UIW's dean of enrollment, and her staff moved their highly successful recruitment and enrollment functions across the street to what was dedicated that day as the Kathleen Watson Enrollment Center. Kathleen and her husband, Mark Watson, were generous longtime supporters of the university.

Kathleen was still chair of the Board of Trustees, but she was now quite ill. A gracious and always stunning Kathleen participated in the dedication ceremony. She died later that year, and Lou once again chose a full-page dedication in the *Express-News* as tribute to her. It included her picture and the painful words, "You Left Us All Too Soon."

Ruth Eileen Sullivan was an emeritus member of the board, but Lou recommended that she fill the remainder of Kathleen's term as chair. Ruth Eileen's late husband, Dan Sullivan, had been devoted to the university's baseball program, but her favorite had become the fashion design program that Dr. Anne Marie Walsh had revived. The program, which received major support from both Ruth Eileen and Dennis and Ruth Juren, was named the Juren-Sullivan Center for Fashion Design in 2003.

There was one farewell and one welcome still to come. On March 31, 2000, Marge Draeger retired, leaving a huge void in the office. Marge had supported two presidents in the years she was there. That she would be missed went without saying, but she retired in good health and good spirits. Marge and her husband, Ralph, still participate in many UIW events. With her old sense of humor, Marge says, "They're a lot easier to enjoy now."

The search for Marge's replacement brought Damita Fedor to the university in April of that year. Damita arrived with a contagious laugh and a Mississippi accent that transforms "yes" into a three-syllable word. She and

Dick McCracken, second from left, retired in 2005 as Dean of Alumni, one of several administrative positions he held during his 41-year career at Incarnate Word. Marge Draeger, at his left, retired in 2000 after 15 years as Lou's executive assistant. At far left is Dr. David Jurenovich, at far right is Sister Ann Finn.

Dr. Dennis Juren, emeritus member of the board of trustees.

Vince are still there after eleven years, contrary to Lou's long-ago warning that he is hard to work for. It took a little longer for Lou to fill the legal counsel position permanently. Bob Kunczt served in that capacity for several years until becoming director of human resources. Others who were hired after that eventually accepted positions outside the UIW community. Cynthia Sanchez Escamilla, about as tiny as Sister Helena and with an unflappable personality, is now general counsel for the university.

By now Cyndi Porter had hit the ground running. The Virtual University (VU) was launched as soon as she arrived, bringing new changes. Unaware of the excitement her appointment had generated, Cyndi went about those changes with gusto. The first term started with only twenty-two students, but she was undaunted. It was probably good the first term was small because Cyndi, like Denise before her, was running a one-person operation. She did have a secretary, but her expected assistant, Norman St. Clair, was still in China.

Cyndi soon received a call from Fort Sam Houston. The Army had decided to be a major player in online education. Cyndi was invited to a summit in Washington, D.C., to hear the vision of the Secretary of the Army. This was the start of "eArmyU," a distance education program that would grow worldwide and put UIW's virtual university on the map. The Army called for proposals to choose a company to manage the entire program. Interested universities would be their subcontractors. Cyndi had an immediate decision to make. With which of the competing companies would she align Incarnate Word? She opted for PricewaterhouseCoopers. It was an agonizing decision, but she didn't have time to agonize. She chose it because it had a minority focus and was reaching out to Hispanic Serving Institutions, Historically Black Colleges and Universities, and Tribal Colleges and Universities. Fortunately, PricewaterhouseCoopers was awarded the contract, and UIW's virtual university became a founding member of the eArmyU consortium.

This was a success—and a whole new challenge. Cyndi recently explained just how big the challenge was. "The big stumbling block for colleges and universities at the beginning was the Army's insistence on a common college application. There was resistance from other campuses that couldn't or wouldn't change their application forms for the program." Cyndi hadn't known Lou long, but she had gathered quickly that when he said, "Make this happen," she needed to do just that.

She agreed immediately to the common application. The Army was delighted; UIW's registrar was not. Bobbye Fry, who had added the sentimental bridge meeting with faculty at graduation, had adjusted to ADCaP and was bracing for China. At least she knew those players. They had been there a long time and they understood the problems those programs created for her office. But now this new person was walking in and stating with great authority, "We aren't going to be using UIW's application, and oh, by the way, you probably won't see any high school transcripts either. But don't worry about it; the Army guarantees the transcripts and vouches for their existence."

San Antonio Spurs Hall of Famer David Robinson towers over Lou's office staff in the new millennium, from left, Cindy Sanchez Escamilla, General Counsel; Vince Rodriguez, Assistant for Communications; and Damita Fedor, Executive Assistant.

Both laugh about it now, but it was a hurdle to jump. Bobbye's common sense and Lou's persuasive reasoning helped them over it. Cyndi explained that with thirty-one schools in the consortium, a soldier had to be able to pull up a single common form in order to apply. The soldier-students would indicate to which schools they wanted their applications forwarded, and it would be done. The Army also maintained course comparison charts to ensure that various courses matched for transfer purposes.

The common application had been difficult, but the billing issue proved more so. The consortium held it to be a contract violation for a soldier to receive a bill. All bills went to the Army and the Army paid them. That was hard to tell a computer—especially one whose program is expressly designed to bill all students taking UIW courses. No one doubted the soldiers would get those bills after all, and they were right. After the first glitch Cyndi solved the problem by registering each soldier with the street address of the University of the Incarnate Word. The computer happily sent all the bills to its own house, and Cyndi forwarded them to the Army.

As a result of eArmyU's success, the Army deployed the concept across all Army education, forming GoArmyEd.com. Cyndi and UIW continue to be on the ground floor of everything involved with the military's distance education, although the armed forces are not the only source of VU's students. Many creative print and television ads were designed for the virtual university. One was carried on the side of buses belonging to VIA, San Antonio's transit company. "Is there a mouse in your house?" it asked. A large computer mouse and its tail-like cord spread across the bus. Today, the virtual university has over 1,000 students and is still growing.

While Cyndi, Bobbye and the computer were resolving their issues, there was another technology innovation taking place. Faculty members at UIW were beginning to use more computer-assisted instruction in their classes. In addition it was clear the age of computers would leave students and faculty behind if something were not done to provide technology across the board for all. UIW decided to become a laptop university. It would start by issuing laptops and color printers to all full-time sophomores and juniors.

Technology was part of David Jurenovich's wide expanse of responsibility. He explained some of the creative measures taken to help both students and the university fund what could have been a prohibitively expensive project. ThinkPads and printers would cost students $550 a semester for six semesters, but the university would absorb $300 of that expense each time. The remaining $250 per semester would be rolled into the students' financial aid package. At the end of six semesters, having paid a total of $1,500, the students would own the laptops and printers.

This was a generous way to help students enjoy current technology. Many already owned computers, but then many others did not. The playing field needed to be level. Students paid the extra money and were eagerly looking forward to receiving their computers as soon as classes began in August.

"Never let inanimate objects know you're in a hurry" has been well-used, if anonymous advice. It certainly applied here. The laptops did not arrive as planned. Bridget Gutierrez of the *Express-News* interviewed Lon Levitan, an IBM spokesman, to find out why. It seemed the delay was caused

by a "shortage of plastic pieces used in the production of cell phones and computers, combined with a high demand for a new IBM product." The computers were delayed about a month, but IBM sweetened the delay by providing wireless upgrades so students "would not need modems."

Today the idea of needing a modem is hard for students to imagine. The entire campus, like most homes and businesses, is wireless and students use an array of computers, phones, e-readers and other devices. Marc Prensky, author of *Don't*

With Harley Seyedin at right looking on, Lou signs the guest book at the opening of China Incarnate Word in October 2000.

Bother Me Mom—I'm Learning, calls students who were born into the age of technology "digital natives," while the faculty teaching them are "digital immigrants"—just one more gap for the generations to bridge.

Meanwhile the university was building even longer bridges. The formal opening of the China Incarnate Word Education Center was celebrated on October 12, 2000, amid a sea of red—balloons, lanterns, flowers, silk sashes, and dresses. The miles of empty countryside had been transformed into the beginnings of a small city. Roads and dormitories had been constructed almost overnight, and even the usually muddy water buffalo appeared to have been scrubbed for the occasion.

The center's main building was 60,000 square feet and included classrooms, lecture halls, and multiuse areas. Guests arrived at the center in a steady parade of taxis and expensive Mercedes, a surprise to many Westerners who were experiencing China for the first time. Anyone who watched the opening ceremony of the 2008 Summer Olympics remembers that China knows how to throw a party. Students from South China Normal University and from Kangda elementary through high school danced, sang, and charmed the growing crowd. Speeches were long, and everyone made one—in the soft flow of Mandarin, the harsher emphasis of Cantonese with its long drawn-out "ahh" sounds, or in English that few understood. Translations made long speeches longer, but no one seemed to mind. It was a celebration. And everyone had a camera, a cell phone, and a cigarette—all in use at once.

Incarnate Word sister schools from many countries sent representatives. Good friends Erol and Emel Altaca arrived from Istanbul. Ali Sahin, affectionately known to UIW as "Ali of the Black Sea" arrived without his lost luggage. He never got it. Sister Luz Romay, who represented Incarnate Word's Board of Trustees, and Lou, Pat, Harley, and Sun Hui were seated on a huge stage with South China Normal's president, the party secretary, and at least thirty other Chinese educators, administrators, and business partners.

Norm and Bobbie St. Clair were there in new roles. Norm had been named on-site director of China Incarnate Word and

UIW was the first American university to open an undergraduate degree-granting program in China. Lou speaks at the opening of China Incarnate Word before a crowd that included dignitaries from many countries.

Answering questions at a student recruitment fair in China are Dr. Pat Watkins, second from right, and her Chinese assistant, Wang Ping, right.

was charged with implementing the academic decisions made at UIW. Bobbie was now a faculty member teaching college-level ESL. Pat would continue frequent travel back and forth in order to support Norm and provide overall supervision. There were fifteen other Americans, teaching all the courses for associate degrees in international business and in accounting and finance, plus the complete ESL program. Bachelor degrees were added later.

The American teachers watched from their seats, keenly aware of the historical significance of the day and their role in it. This was the moment when a Catholic university in San Antonio, Texas, became the first American university to open an undergraduate degree-granting program in the People's Republic of China. Lou was one happy president!

CHAPTER 20
WHERE WERE YOU WHEN . . .?

Ed Paderon and his wife decided to move back to the New York area they missed. Ed said good-bye on July 24, 2001, and became vice president and later provost at Georgian Court University in Lakewood, New Jersey. Lou knew Dr. Terry Dicianna, president of Del Mar Community College in Corpus Christi, because ADCaP had a branch there. Terry was considering retiring and coming back to San Antonio, where he had been founding president of Palo Alto Community College. Lou made sure Terry knew about the provost search.

Meanwhile Lou faced another decision. Rob Barnett had left UIW and Lou now made an internal appointment. He selected Dr. Pat LeMay Burr as dean of international programs at the International Conference Center. Dr. Bob Ryan was named acting dean of the School of Business and Applied Arts to replace Pat. Bob, who was as good in his field as brother Nolan Ryan was at pitching, became one of the best friends China Incarnate Word had. His flexibility helped establish meaningful bachelor's degrees there and later in Mexico.

When the provost search ended, Terry Dicianna emerged as the successful candidate. He arrived on August 1, planning to "just help out for a year or two and then really retire." Terry found himself aboard the Agnese train for the next eight years. That August the enrollment was over 4,000 and the endowment was seven times what it had been in 1986. Pat Burr was inheriting an international student population figure of 9 percent. Everyone was ready for a good year.

On September 10 Lou was in Taiwan having dinner with the head of Taiwan's aviation security. Ironically, their conversation included the differences between airport security in Taiwan and the United States. Pat Watkins and Norm St. Clair were in China working late into the night on the semester's schedule due the next day. It was about 11 p.m. in that part of the world when it happened. Probably everyone remembers where they were when they learned of the attacks of 9-11. Norm's wife heard the news and called the office where he and Pat were working. In less than fifteen minutes all of the American teachers had gathered. Accustomed to the frequent blank screen when certain stories were blacked out by Chinese authorities, the group was relieved to find Dan Rather on TV. They followed the story through the night—daytime in the United States.

The next day they had to go into Guangzhou on university business. Chinese pedestrians approached the Americans sympathetically. If they spoke any English they shared their grief verbally. Most reached for newspapers with pictures of the burning towers and holding them up, put their hands over their eyes or heart in a non-verbal communication that was more eloquent than words.

Lou wrote in the *Express-News* about the outpouring of sympathy received across borders during that time. "Millions of people from across the world joined in our sorrow and supported us with heartfelt expressions of sympathy. For a moment that, in retrospect was all too brief, people transcended national, ethnic and religious boundaries in their grieving."

Within forty-eight hours of the attack, Lou was with the Americans at China Incarnate Word, deliberately arriving early for the quarterly board meeting. The meeting was scheduled for September 15 and as usual the table was set with small Chinese and American flags. As the participants gathered around the table Lou adjusted the tiny American flag to a half-staff position. The party secretary took the cue and called for a moment of silence—not prayer, but at least silence.

Lou has been quick to model support for the troops and the country. He has also held strongly to the continued internationalization of UIW. Shortly after the attack he discussed the university's international efforts. "They bring together young people who can develop positive dialogue while bridging the cultural gaps that might otherwise separate them," he said. Pat Burr was taking on the international dean position at an important time.

Lou and Mickey Agnese with five-time Olympic swimming champion Josh Davis at the dedication of the Ann Barshop Natatorium.

The university was wishing for something positive by then, and it came in the form of the Ann Barshop Natatorium. The natatorium, a $5 million state-of-the-art swimming facility, was dedicated on October

11, a month after the terror attacks. Sam Barshop, a member of the board of trustees, donated a large portion of the money that built the structure, and he and Lou chose to name it for Sam's wife. Lou was asked about naming a building on a Catholic campus for someone of the Jewish faith. "This is very fitting, given current world events," he said in the *Express-News*. "It illustrates our desire for tolerance and understanding at a time when there has been an unfortunate increase in religious and cultural bigotry, both at home and abroad."

Josh Davis, five-time Olympic medalist, was one of the speakers that day. As a child Josh had learned to swim at Incarnate Word College when his father, Mike Davis, was an administrator in Sister Margaret Patrice's administration. The natatorium allowed the university to add varsity swimming, diving, and synchronized swimming to its sports offerings, and the teams today regularly compete against top programs in the country. The synchronized swim team began competing with Stanford University that first year, and the tradition has continued. They also compete with Ohio State, University of Florida, and University of Michigan. Synchronized swim coach Kimberly LoPorto says, "It's great to compete against Stanford as they are (always) either number one or number two. We've won against them in overall points during dual or tri meets but then lost to them or to Ohio State at national competitions." UIW's synchronized swim team is currently ranked third in the nation.

Less than ninety days after Lou lowered the American flag on a conference table in China, he was ordering the flag on the university's Mission Plaza also lowered. Tom Plofchan lost his battle with cancer on December 7—another significant date in American history. As with Jim Tilton, Lou arranged for Tom's visitation to be in Our Lady's Chapel at the university. Tom had been one of the rocks Lou could lean on regardless of circumstances, and it was a heavy blow.

Tom was much loved by his staff, and they felt the loss as deeply as Lou. Robert Sosa, Lionel's brother, worked closely with Tom as one of the directors in the Office of Institutional

Since debuting in the 2001–02 season, the synchronized swimming team has consistently been among the best in the nation. In 2011 the team took third place at the Collegiate Championships, behind Ohio State University and Stanford University.

Advancement. It was Robert who developed the grants program, which has brought millions of dollars to the campus over the years. After nearly twenty years, he is still director of foundation, government, and corporate relations at UIW. Robert recalls his feelings about Tom, then and now. "Losing Tom was difficult. Even though we all knew he'd been in poor health, his death was a shock. Not only did I lose a boss—I also lost a friend." Robert went on to describe the Tom he knew and still misses. "He was an exceptional human being, a good husband, father, and grandfather. He was gentle, never talked down to anyone, never raised his voice, never criticized or gave orders."

Those last comments could just as easily be attributed to Robert; it's no wonder he and Tom were close. He added one last thought: "All these years after his death, I still think about him. He still creeps into my thoughts from time to time. So in that sense I haven't really lost him after all."

Tom Plofchan, a member of Lou's executive team for 15 years, lost his battle with cancer in 2001.

Lou chose not to initiate a search for Tom's position right away. He appointed Laura Shaw, one of Tom's directors, to fill in on an interim basis. About a year later he selected Sister Kathleen Coughlin, former CEO of Spohn Health Care in Corpus Christi and president of the Catholic Health Association of Texas in Austin, as vice president.

The December commencement that year saw the first graduates of the Ph.D. program. Dr. Bill Schurter and Dr. Mickey Tehan had risked entering the program while it was in its infancy and not yet accredited. They knew the courses would count as postgraduate work if the unthinkable happened, but fortunately for all the approvals came as expected. Bill's concentration was mathematics education while Mickey's was organizational leadership.

The mathematics education concentration never drew as large a number of students as had been expected. Whether this was due to the death of several dynamic mathematics professors or just indicative of the times is uncertain. Dr. Judith Beauford, current director of the Ph.D. program, worked to save the concentration, but eventually the decision was made to phase it out. A higher education administration concentration was later added. Adult education had been an increasingly popular graduate degree under the energetic direction of master teacher Dr. Jessica Kimmel, so it was no surprise when it became a specialty in the higher education administration concentration.

News that year alternated between good and bad. *U.S. News and World Report* recognized UIW's online graduate business program as one of the country's best, and the U.S. Department of Education ranked the teacher preparation program second in Texas. That well-ranked School of Education was about to start on its own adventure as its building, one of the oldest on the campus, was scheduled for complete renovation.

Mike McChesney again used innovative design to provide space where it seemed there was none. His wraparound renovation of the original building would result in additional offices, classrooms, and conference rooms. But while McChesney worked, the education faculty needed offices. They sought whatever space could be found. Some moved to temporary offices in the Gorman-Mitchell room—the glassed-in room overlooking the basketball court where the Spurs had practiced. Others were given the far end of a girls' dormitory, where male students had to be announced before entering and the dean's secretary stored supplies in a spare bathtub. They would soon be rewarded with more than

UIW's first doctoral degrees were awarded in December 2001, when Dr. William Schurter earned a Ph.D. in Education with a concentration in Mathematics Education and Dr. Mickey Tehan earned a Ph.D. in Education with a concentration in Organizational Leadership.

a new building; the School of Education was about to become the first named school in the university's 121-year history, in honor of Barbara and Alan Dreeben.

"Alan has made a lifelong commitment to education," Lou said of the man he's known for years. "I met Alan when Louis was at Alamo Heights High School and Alan was president of the school board. He has also served on the Texas Board of Regents." Alan is a fervent believer in the value of education, but he is even more fervent about faith-based education. "As a member of the Jewish faith, Alan understands what we mean when we say Incarnate Word is a Catholic university that is a welcoming campus for students from all faiths," Lou explained. "There were many ways we could have honored Alan and Barbara, but naming the School of Education for them was the most fitting one I could think of."

The School of Education was named in honor of Alan and Barbara Dreeben. It became the first named school at Incarnate Word.

That summer the university announced plans for another international campus. Buoyed by the successful beginnings of China Incarnate Word, the decision was made to open a campus in Mexico City. It was a natural considering the years of congregational commitment in that country. Plus, a university had long been the dream of the Sisters in Mexico. Board member David Cibrian told the *Express-News*, "If we could do that in China, which is halfway around the world, it really didn't make sense for us not to do something on a similar magnitude in Mexico." Lou explained that a Mexican corporation would be formed, and officials would apply for the necessary licenses to operate a university. The campus, whose target opening was August 2003, would be patterned after the one in China and would offer degrees in four majors.

Sister Luz Romay, who had attended the China Incarnate Word opening, would establish the Mexico campus, with support and oversight by Dr. Pat Burr. Sister Luz began with the building vacated by one of the Sisters' K-12 schools, Instituto Miguel Angel Valle. It required massive renovation to minimize its K-12 look in preparation for university students. She was also confronted with the many bureaucratic steps involved in opening an educational facility in Mexico. She was walking the same fine lines the China campus had walked earlier—making sure UIW's accreditation body would be satisfied with the final product. There were no party secretaries this time, but Mexico's secretary of public education was even more demanding.

San Antonio attorney David Cibrian is a member of the UIW board in San Antonio and the CIW-Mexico board in Mexico City.

As September 11, 2002, approached, Provost Terry Dicianna was trying to decide if he really wanted to board an airplane on the one-year anniversary of the 9-11 attacks. Terry's main academic role was the development of new programs. Lou had been invited to a meeting with the American Association of Colleges of Pharmacy to discuss the need for more pharmacy schools in the country. He and Terry had talked earlier about how health care programs were the key to the future. Lou handed Terry the invitation and said, "Go to this if you think it has merit." Terry thought about the science facilities then available at UIW and thought again about having to fly on a day people had speculated might see more terror attacks. He pretty much decided against going. But the potential kept nagging at him, and he decided to make the trip after all. He claims he didn't take a Valium at the airport, but no one really believes him.

Terry arrived safely in Washington, D.C., and heard dynamic presentations by Dr. Kenneth Roberts, dean of the University of Kentucky pharmacy school, and Dr. Art Nelson, dean of Texas Tech's pharmacy school. He was amazed that few of the other participants seemed interested. "I realized I might be one of the few people there who was serious about this thing," he said. He was impressed with the quality of the speakers and their willingness to share information. Texas Tech's dean was openly hopeful for another pharmacy school in the state. But Terry also heard about the "twelve-year plan." According to that plan any university starting a school of pharmacy should expect to lose money the first four years, break even the second four, bring in enough money the third four to make up the loss, and somewhere around year twelve or thirteen begin to earn more than they were spending. Terry recently laughed as he asked, "Would you want to present that scenario to Lou Agnese?" He thought he might use the term "OPM." Other People's Money was always a good way to approach Lou.

CHAPTER 21
THE RIGHT PRESCRIPTION

Construction was everywhere in 2002. Lou was determined to grow the western side of the campus, where there was only the International Conference Center (ICC) and a lot of empty space. The university needed more dormitories, and there was never enough parking. He also wanted to place strategic services on that side to force awareness and use of the entire area. In October the university's largest building was completed adjacent to the ICC. The building, later named the McCombs Center in honor of Charline and Red McCombs, combined a parking garage, dormitory space for ninety students, and an approximately 6,000 square-foot space where Lou would move the university bookstore—a popular and strategic service.

But the crowning touch was the top floor, with a 12,000 square-foot, glassed-in banquet hall offering a stunning view of downtown San Antonio on one side and the campus on another. The banquet hall accommodated 800 and had sliding walls that divided the space into as many as four venues. It was appropriately christened the Sky Room and later named for Sandra and Stanley Rosenberg. The Sky Room became one of San Antonio's favorite venues for meetings, galas, luncheons, and just about any celebration. This was only the first of the Rosenbergs' generous gifts. A later one would set a record in special donations and allow the university to expand academically and geographically.

Meanwhile the Dreeben School of Education took its supplies out of the bathtub and moved into the Gorman Business and Education Center, the building it would share with the School of Business. Jim and Tena Gorman, long-time Incarnate Word supporters, had approached Sister Margaret Patrice in the early 1980s asking "How can we help?" That

The McCombs Center was named in honor of Red McCombs and his wife, Charline.

was the beginning of one of the most valued relationships with which Incarnate Word has been blessed.

Tena and Jim are also active in the local community, serving on several boards and having received numerous civic awards. A former Air Force officer, Jim continues to maintain close ties with the armed services. Those ties were evident on October 11 when two assistant secretaries and two deputy assistant secretaries of the Air Force participated in the ceremony naming the building for Jim and Tena.

(L-R): Alan Dreeben, Sister Helena Monahan, Jim Gorman, Tena Gorman and Lou. The Gormans were awarded honorary doctorates in 2006 for their advocacy of higher education.

Terry had now broken the news about what financial expectations Lou should have if UIW started a school of pharmacy. "We can do this academically, but not financially," he told Lou. "We need a dedicated building, for one thing." Terry remembers his own surprise. "Lou didn't think about it for even thirty seconds. 'Hell,' he said, 'if it's only money we need, start the project. I'll take care of the money.'"

That confident response stood in clear contrast to the anxiety of a younger Lou Agnese, who had once drawn inspiration from a story about bartering chickens. Lou had become a CEO. He was now connected with the San Antonio community. He understood it, and it understood him. Board Chair Charlie Amato alluded to that corporate maturity in a tribute to Lou several

years later, saying that under Lou's leadership Incarnate Word had "forever transformed the educational landscape in South Texas" and had increased its own endowment from $3 million to over $80 million.

It wasn't that money was in abundance or that Lou had grown blasé about it. But he now understood how people chose to donate and what they believed was important enough to warrant their donations. He knew a school of pharmacy for San Antonio would draw support.

Charlie Amato, 2011 Chair of the UIW Board of Trustees.

With the division of labor clear, Terry began the academic process while Lou handled funding. "I had to work backwards," Terry explained. "I had no idea what the accreditation of a school of pharmacy involved, so I started conversations with the Southern Association of Colleges and Schools (SACS) and the Accreditation Council for Pharmacy Education." Each had a long list of requirements, including wanting to see a curriculum and a budget.

Lou's vision of the school included a pre-pharmacy program. Whereas only the school required board approval, all majors and curriculum issues require faculty approval. Denise Doyle explains, "When you seek faculty approval you are always speaking the language of scarcity—'If your program gets the money it means mine won't.'" That was one of several problems Terry would face. Everyone knew a pharmacy program would be expensive, especially with its own dedicated building.

But Terry still had his OPM concept. He and Lou agreed that no money from the university's general fund would go toward the program. That was one of the best-selling points, along with the fact that the pre-pharmacy program would also necessitate a new science building. Lou knew the science and mathematics faculty had made do with seriously outdated facilities and equipment for years. Tom Plofchan's last capital campaign had been to raise money for a new, or at least renovated, building. Adding a pre-pharmacy program could draw more donations and make the building a reality. The improvements would also enhance the engineering management major opening in August 2003.

Cyndi Porter not only knows how to run a virtual university, she also has a doctoral degree in chemistry. Terry asked her to look into the curriculum. In two days Cyndi had surveyed all eighty-eight schools of pharmacy in the country and put together a sample curriculum consisting of what 80 percent of the schools had in common. That was a starting place for the faculty to begin their own study.

Terry then had the good fortune to find a man clearly destined to become a dean—Dr. Joe Dean, then dean of Samford University's pharmacy school in Birmingham, Alabama. After several conversations, Terry discovered that Joe also did consulting work. He agreed to help Terry find a dean and develop a budget. They started with the budget because the accreditation agencies wanted to see that before discussing even preliminary approval. Doug Endsley, vice president for business and finance, worked with Joe while Terry began the yearlong process of presenting the programs and gaining faculty approval.

Faculty was asked to "conceptually" approve the pharmacy curriculum until a dean could be hired. It would be that dean's responsibility to make final curricular adjustments. Conceptual approval, which included giving final revision to an unknown and un-hired dean, was not an easy sell, but it was finally granted. The curriculum was designed to provide the only pharmacy program in the country with an optional English-Spanish track. Bilingual pharmacists are scarce and valuable to the people of South Texas and other areas where Spanish is as common as English.

That spring it was time to renovate the science facilities. The logistics of teaching science courses with equipment-intensive labs would be a challenge. Lou knew he could not move science laboratory classes to rooms equipped only for lecture and discussion. This presented a different challenge from that faced earlier by the Dreeben School of Education. The originally planned renovation was put on hold, allowing teaching to continue, and ground was broken for a new building. The situation was inconvenient, but there was no interruption of classes. When completed, the new building would provide space for everyone while the original building was renovated.

Lou's luck was still holding. Before the pharmacy school was even a consideration, Brian Wallace of UIW's institutional advancement office told him about someone who would likely be a good board member. John and Rita Feik's son and daughter were Incarnate Word graduates, and Brian thought John might be inclined to accept a seat on the board if invited. Feik was owner and founding president of DPT, a locally based pharmaceutical development and manufacturing company with branches in several other countries.

John accepted the invitation and was already a board member when the science building and renovation were about to start. With his expertise and intense focus on quality control and safety, John donated his time to consult on planning and to suggest changes. He and his staff examined the drawings of the science building, checked for appropriate drainage systems, and urged more gas and water lines. John also pointed out that the facilities for chemistry and biology would be seriously under-built unless another floor were added to the building, allowing two dedicated floors for each discipline. Under his guidance the science building grew into a larger state-of-the-art facility.

The two-stage operation would not be completed until 2006, and there was a lot to do in the meantime. Terry was still mentally building the pharmacy school. He was confident about board approval, but he needed a dean and a location for the school once it was approved. Mike McChesney was good at making things fit, but this might be asking too much.

Meanwhile, with the expanded ICC, dozens of sister school agreements, and a Mexico campus about to open, Lou elevated Dr. Pat Burr's dean of international programs position to a vice presidency in January 2003. "Oversight of the many international activities is a growing responsibility," he explained. Pat responded to the new title: "I am honored to be a part of the in-

ternationalization of the UIW campus and programs .
. . the international mission that we all believe in is becoming a greater reality across our campus with each
new international program we develop." The opening
of the Mexico campus was only a few months away.

But first a local issue was raising eyebrows and
tempers. The university announced that St. Anthony
Catholic High School would become a coed institution. The move was intended to boost enrollment,
which had only increased from 144 students to 244
since the university took over its management. Incarnate Word had already invested $1 million in renova-
tions at the school, and the debt was substantial.

The announcement was not positively received
by the Oblates of Mary Immaculate, who wanted the
school to remain all male. In fact, they felt strongly
enough to file a lawsuit against UIW. A great deal of
negotiation eventually led to the university buying the school outright and
continuing with the coeducational plan. Forty-three young women enrolled
during St. Anthony's first year of coeducation. Today the school is a thriving
part of Catholic education in San Antonio and has an enrollment of 450.

May 2003 saw the 1,000th ADCaP graduate, the first associate degree
graduation at the China campus, and the naming of the H-E-B School of Business and Administration. James "Fully" Clingman Jr., retiring COO and president of H-E-B, was commencement speaker for the school's May graduates. In
2004 Clingman would become chair of the UIW Board
of Trustees, the first man to hold that position.

In June Mickey Agnese received the Insigne Verbum award for her years of service as the university's
First Lady. That seemed appropriate for her work at the
university, but as Mrs. Lou Agnese most thought canonization would have been more fitting. Being the wife
of a university president can be challenging, as there
is always public time and seldom private time. Mickey recalls the moments that have helped her through
the crazy parts. "I remember the evening Lou became
president of the North San Antonio Chamber of Commerce. The children were all dressed up, and Nancy
had fallen asleep before Lou spoke. When he was called

Dr. Pat LeMay Burr,
former Vice President
for International
Programs, became
the Distinguished
Chair in International
Business.

Dan Ochoa served
as Principal of St.
Anthony Catholic
High School from
2001 to 2004.

Lou was as surprised as Mickey when she was awarded the Insigne Verbum award for her years of service as UIW's First Lady. Standing with them is former Board Chair Fully Clingman.

to the stage and took the microphone, he looked out at us and said, 'I can't thank my wife enough for my children.'" In the busy life of a president and his family, private thoughts can sometimes only be embedded in public moments. But they still mean as much.

In August, while the new science building was being built and Terry was still searching for a pharmacy dean, another school was created. The School of Interactive Media and Design became the university's sixth school. Dr. Cheryl Anderson, who had supervised the technology for the Burton Grossman International Conference Center, was named its first dean.

August was also time to celebrate the grand opening of Centro Internacional Universitario Miguel-Angel-Incarnate Word, the Mexico campus. The seven-word name suggested challenges, but the crowd of 200 at the inaugural ceremony did not seem to mind. Matt Flores of the *Express-News* covered the event. Blake Hastings, then executive director of the Free Trade Alliance of San Antonio, and Antonio Flores, president and CEO of the Hispanic Association of Colleges and Universities (HACU), attended. Lou was a founding member of HACU and has remained a strong supporter. Antonio Flores told the *Express-News* that Incarnate Word's move to establish a campus in Mexico was strategic. "The world is becoming a global society, and higher education is a part of that village," he said.

In contrast to the financial arrangement with the Chinese partners, Incarnate Word and the Congregation invested over $1.5 million in the Mexico project. Both are partners in this internal joint venture and are committed to making it a reality.

Lou discussed the Mexico campus's potential with the *Express-News*, explaining that classes would begin with 25 students, but as many as 300 should be registered for the next year. Mexico's accreditation body cleared the new university to offer four-year degrees in international business, international finance, and computer information systems, with other majors expected in the near future. Classes would start on August 18, 2003.

Through all this activity Terry tried to stay focused on a dean for the proposed school of pharmacy. A national search and Joe Dean's contacts had produced quite a few applicants. Interviews began even though no one would be hired until the December board meeting, at which program approval was expected.

Lou and Mickey at a North San Antonio Chamber of Commerce event.

Lou's part of the interview process was generally a twenty-minute conversation with each applicant.

Dr. Arcelia Johnson-Fannin arrived for her twenty minutes. An hour and a half later she was still there—and she was doing the interviewing. It had not taken long for Lou and Terry to realize she was their top candidate. But Arcelia, the founding dean of Hampton University's School of Pharmacy, was not so sure. She had seen situations where the dean was expected to be the fundraiser and only a figurehead academically.

Arcelia ran a tight ship. Hampton, which had been started in 1868 for children of former slaves, was a Historically Black College, and many students had the expected challenges of first-generation college students everywhere. Despite the difficulties encountered in developing a pharmacy program at Hampton, the academic freedom granted to the dean and her faculty allowed the graduates to be extremely successful on the pharmacy licensing examination.

Looking back at her interview Arcelia says, "I told Dr. Agnese that if he wanted excellent results, whoever became the dean would

Dr. Arcelia Johnson-Fannin, Founding Dean of the Feik School of Pharmacy.

need, among other things, academic freedom, appropriate financial support, state-of-the-art physical facilities, and no interference with the admissions process."

Arcelia remembers Lou said he was afraid she couldn't get the faculty. "Let me worry about that," she said, adding, "I'm afraid you won't get the facility." Lou tossed her earlier words back to her: "Let me worry about that!" The two appeared well matched.

In December 2003 the board approved the pharmacy school, which would grant doctoral-level degrees. A few months later Dr. Arcelia Johnson-Fannin became its founding dean.

CHAPTER 22
BUILD IT AND THEY WILL COME

O r maybe they won't. When doors opened for the 2003 classes in Mexico, only four of the expected students showed up. By midterm three had dropped out and the fourth transferred to UIW in San Antonio. This was a crushing blow to those who had worked so hard for the success of a Mexico campus. Lou reminded everyone that he and Lionel had a similar experience when they first started their ad campaign and were turned down flat.

Sister Luz Romay knew the potential was there. Approvals from Mexico's secretary of public education had perhaps come too late for the necessary publicity and recruiting. But Sister Romay was rotating back to the San Antonio campus and the recruiting would have to fall to someone else. In the meantime Dr. Pat LeMay Burr, whose heart had always been in teaching, accepted the newly created faculty position of Distinguished Chair in International Business at what is today the H-E-B School of Business and Management. Both Dr. Burr and Sister Romay would be changing positions in summer 2004.

Lou announced a search for Dr. Burr's vacated position. Dr. Pat Watkins was named vice president for international affairs effective July 1, 2004. Dr. Denise Staudt, then assistant dean of the Dreeben School of Education, was named the school's acting dean, replacing Pat. Denise later became dean and still serves in that capacity.

Confronted with a school but no students, Pat enlisted the consulting help of longtime personal friend Oscar Rodriguez. Oscar was director general of the successful Universidad de Londres (University of London), owned by Dr. Gabriela De La Vega, another close family friend. Both Oscar and Gabriela were also friends and supporters

Dr. Denise Staudt, Dean of the Dreeben School of Education.

Oscar Rodriguez, Director General of the University of London, served as a consultant for CIW-Mexico.

of UIW, and had been present at the celebration when the college became a university in 1996.

Meanwhile Lou decided to ask Marcos Fragoso, a Mexican national, to take the job of director and continue developing the Mexico campus. Marcos, a UIW graduate who helped Dick McCracken manage Brackenridge Villa during his student years, had just been hired to work with Watkins at the ICC.

Marcos was working in higher education in Mexico City at that time and still remembers the day he joined Pat and Oscar for what should have been an uneventful lunch. Pat planned to break the news as gently as possible. "I had no idea where the conversation was headed as Pat started talking," Marcos recalls. "I had visited the campus and knew the situation, but I also knew I was about to leave Mexico for a new job at UIW. I just listened and felt kind of sorry for Pat because she had a big job. All of a sudden she got to the real point of the lunch. I was completely surprised, but it sounded like a challenge I could enjoy. Besides, Lou had done a lot for me, and I was willing to help him and Pat in any way I could."

Marcos jumped right in. He began extensive publicity and added new majors. Oscar was a generous consultant and shared the University of London's entire law curriculum. Law, an undergraduate degree in Mexico, was the first new major Marcos introduced. It proved to be one of the most popular. Marcos also had substantial damage control to address because the initial failure of the campus hung like a cloud over recruitment efforts. In August, a month after Marcos took over, the campus reopened with twenty-five students. Today enrollment is over 400, with a projected enrollment of 600 for 2011. Marcos and Pat became close friends and a good team, and when Pat retired in May 2010 he succeeded her as vice president for international affairs. But a lot was to happen in the six years following their initial meeting.

In another part of UIW's world, China Incarnate Word had just celebrated one more milestone, the first graduation of students earning bachelor's degrees. Norman St. Clair's six-month internship as a doctoral student had stretched into a five-year stay at the China campus. The university was now relocating to Zhencheng, a small town about forty-five minutes from the original site. Still good friends with the administrators and party secretary at South China Normal University, China Incarnate Word was moving to allow other use for the space at the Kangda campus. It also was embracing another partner, Hua Li University, affiliated with Guangdong University of Technology, whose philosophy continued the original mission and provided even more growth opportunity. This was a good time for Norm and Bobbie to come home. Norm had finished his coursework and needed to complete his dissertation. Besides, he would now be director of international initiatives at the ICC, continuing his years of international work.

Two other International Education and Entrepreneurship (IE&E) doctoral students took over at the new site. Harry Littlewood, a young British citizen with an uncanny ability to speak Cantonese with no trace of an accent, and retired military officer Ernest Amende became director and assistant director respectively for several semesters.

Norm and Bobbie's marriage is not the only one credited to China Incarnate Word. UIW graduate Ann Marie Cowan, one of the original nine teachers who went to China, and Osman Ozturgut, a UIW friend from Turkey who joined the CIW faculty soon after, married in 2002. The China experience apparently influenced Ann's future study, as she later pursued a master's degree in East Asian studies and became proficient in both written and spoken Mandarin. Ann and Osman returned to China in 2005 where Ann served as on-site director of the China campus for three years and Osman directed the ESL program. When Ann and Osman returned to the U.S., Ernie Amende was named lead teacher and served as the on-site administrator for two years. Another IE&E student, Mohsen Omar, currently holds that position.

The interface of doctoral students with UIW's international campuses has been a natural symbiosis, benefiting the university's international initiatives and its traditional academic programs. The international campuses receive dedicated staff with an array of experience, and the doctoral students have international internship opportunities. Dr. Murat Tas, a graduate of the program, was UIW's major recruiter for international students. Through him, Lou was able to establish valuable linkages with universities in Ankara and Istanbul.

Many graduates in organizational leadership and in mathematics education have strengthened UIWs ties with

The library at China Incarnate Word.

Dr. Murat Tas, second from right, during a recruiting trip in Turkey, where UIW has several sister schools. Turkish students comprise one of the largest contingents of international students at Incarnate Word.

sister schools as they have moved into faculty and administrative positions in their home countries. Dr. Shu-Yuan Chang is now assistant professor and vice-director of the nursing department at Fooyin University in Taiwan, and Dr. Meng Hsun Wu teaches statistics and management at Cheng-Kuo University.

In addition, full-time UIW faculty have chosen to spend anywhere from six weeks to a year teaching at the China and Mexico campuses. Sister Germaine Corbin temporarily dropped her "Sister" title and was known simply as Miriam Corbin, the official name on her passport, while she taught speech and drama at the China campus for an entire semester.

Interaction with students from other countries and cultures increased faculty and student sensitivity to the extent they made a decision of conscience that year. Incarnate Word sports teams had been the Crusaders since 1980. Now with the growing number of Middle Eastern students, many felt that the mascot was neither welcoming nor inclusive. Sister Martha Ann Kirk, a professor of religious studies, told the *Express-News*, "We need a mascot more in line with the mission of the university . . . Crusaders presents an image of domination and destruction." Most agreed it was a good idea to change, but some felt the change was an attack on school spirit.

Dr. Michael Risku, then associate professor in the Dreeben School of Education, chaired a task force to find another mascot. Risku echoed Sister Martha Ann when he told the *Express-News*, "We need a mascot that is more culturally sensitive if we are going to continue to have international students and international programs."

Sister Martha Ann Kirk, Professor of Religious Studies.

The task force gathered close to fifty possible options for a community vote. Suggestions included everything from weather-related names such as Tornadoes, Cyclones, Wave, and Red Storm to the religious suggestions of Angels, Archangels, and Saints. Spotted creatures made the list with Dalmatians and Ocelots, and there were crawling Scorpions, Crickets, and Fire Ants. It was probably wise the voters did not choose option

11, Concolours. Explaining "Incarnate Word" often took a little time. It might have taken even longer to devise a good cheer for the "Incarnate Word Concolours." In the end, the community chose Cardinals—the birds, not the clergymen. The name and a red fuzzy mascot suit were ready for fall 2004.

In the meantime Marcos was presenting a more simplified name for the Mexico campus. It became Centro Universitario Incarnate Word and was abbreviated by students as CIW. Like the

Lou and the Cardinal mascot pose for the camera. The Cardinals replaced the Crusaders as UIW's mascot in 2004.

Chinese students, those in Mexico are proud to be part of Incarnate Word. Both campuses reflect UIW with pictures, symbols, banners, and flags. But the real reflection is in their commitment to Incarnate Word's mission, evidenced by the matching curriculum as well as school newspapers, clubs, organizations, and student government, all designed to mirror the San Antonio campus and goals while celebrating the rich overlay of their own cultures.

The abbreviation CIW was no accident; it was the closest Marcos and the Mexico students could come to UIW. Since Chinese students had already staked out CIW for their simplified name, China Incarnate Word, the two campuses became known informally as CIW-China and CIW-Mexico.

Several years after CIW-Mexico was stabilized and CIW-China had settled into its new and larger home, students from all three Incarnate Word campuses celebrated together. Dr. Lydia Andrade, chair of UIW's political science department, gathered students from her classes, and Marcos gathered a group from CIW-Mexico. Drafting a very willing Pat as another chaperone, the two groups flew to Beijing, where they were guided by Juan (Misty) Chen, an IE&E student and director of the Institute of World Cultures at the ICC. Misty would eventually take over UIW's coordination of the China campus and all Chinese initiatives when Pat retired in 2010. They toured together and were joined by CIW-China students, who flew to Shanghai to guide the group to their home campus in Zhencheng. The students spent several days together, attending classes and exchanging stories of their campuses. There are many examples of the success of Lou Agnese's original plan to internationalize the campus, but none makes so touching a statement as that visit.

UIW faculty have been increasingly active in urging students to study abroad, but one of their greatest services has been actually taking them there. Dr. Andrade, whose passport must need extra pages by now, is not the only one designing travel opportunities for students. Drs. Lopita Nath, Pat Burr, Scott Ditloff, Sara Jackson, and Irene Gilliland are among the many who have taken students to Russia, Korea, Germany, Mexico, The Hague, and many other destinations.

The UIW Jazz Ensemble's performance at the Montreux Jazz Festival in Switzerland in 2009 included a mean sax blown by its director, Jim Waller.

But while people were flying around the world, Terry Dicianna was staying put. He and Lou had a pharmacy school to complete. John Feik had done much more than examine building plans and give advice. In December 2004 Lou announced a major gift from the Feik family. Although the amount was not revealed, Lou confirmed to the *Express-News* that it was in the seven-figure range, adding that the school would be known as the John and Rita Feik School of Pharmacy. Sister Kathleen Coughlin would launch a capital campaign in 2005 to raise the additional funds needed for the estimated $9 million total.

Lou recently shared the story of a 2004 dinner with John and Rita. "We were just having a friendly dinner, and the conversation moved to the number of buildings that had been built in the past few years. I was mentioning them by name, like 'the Gorman building' and the 'Barshop natatorium.' Rita, who is full of life and quick to joke, said, 'John, don't you get it? The Gorman building, the Barshop building—he's trying to get you to make it the Feik building.' And I was, and he did." Lou added, "John and Rita really made it possible for us to build the school and open it on time."

Even though the school now had a name, it still didn't have a home. The pre-pharmacy program it spawned had a home—or at least one was being built, but the Feik School of Pharmacy was homeless. In the beginning, the preferred site for the school was the corner of Hildebrand and Highway 281, the corner almost sold years before. There were mixed feelings about using that site. Some felt the building would be so large as to overshadow the rest of the campus. They feared UIW would eventually be seen as simply a "school of pharmacy." That was better than "the school across from Earl Abel's," but it wasn't satisfactory to the majority involved in the discussions.

Lou and Terry examined buildings at Brooks City Base, but they would require major renovation and still would not be right. They looked at land in that area where they could build to suit their plan, but that didn't feel right either. Then Lou returned to his old bartering days. The university owned the rights to the historic Miraflores Park across Hildebrand from where the science building was being constructed. It had been a gift from AT&T, but as a historic site, it could not be altered with the addition of a building. What UIW did not own was the land at Hildebrand Avenue and Devine Road, the perfect site for the school of pharmacy. The City of San Antonio owned that.

Lou and Doug Endsley began negotiations. The rest is history. When the time came to break ground for the Feik School of Pharmacy on May 2, 2006, the ground they broke was at the corner of Hildebrand and Devine.

At the groundbreaking for the Feik School of Pharmacy were, from left, State Senator Leticia Van de Putte, Sister Helena Monahan, Winell Herron, Dr. Arcelia Johnson-Fannin, Lou, John Feik and John Montford.

CHAPTER 23
BAD YEAR AT GOODYEAR

L ou glanced at Terry and said, "Which one should we look at next?" The question, coming at that time, was classic Lou Agnese. It was just a quick conversation between the two of them, but Lou was dead serious. In his mind the Feik School of Pharmacy was wrapped up. The science buildings were still under construction, and there would soon be that groundbreaking on Devine Road. But Lou didn't construct the buildings. He would enjoy watching, but essentially his work was done. Even though he and Sister Kathleen would continue raising the rest of the pharmacy money, Lou was already moving to the next project. A veterinary school? A dental school?

Whatever they investigated, it had to continue expanding UIW's venture into health-related programs. Lou was unwavering in his conviction that those were critical if UIW were to thrive in the twenty-first century. With 4,800 students, the University of the Incarnate Word was now the largest Catholic university in Texas. In just a few months there would be over 5,200 students, and the university would become the state's fourth-largest private school. Only Baylor, SMU, and TCU had larger enrollments at that time.

Terry began researching the programs Lou had on the list. A school of veterinary medicine would be quite an undertaking, and in all honesty could not match Texas A&M's. "We would have always been known as 'the other veterinary school,'" Terry explained. "It would be too expensive and would require both large animal and small animal hospitals, which we did not have room to build." He added, "We looked at alternative models in California where students used the hospital facilities of the zoo and racetracks in lieu of building their own, but we opted not to pursue that either."

Andrea Cyterski-Acosta, Dean of Enrollment.

Lou and Terry revisited veterinary medicine several months later when San Antonio began competing for the National Bio and Agro-Defense Facility. That facility would be relocated from Plum Island, New York, with at least $500 million in lab relocation funds from Congress. It would require extensive veterinary service for humane research involving animals. Lou committed to the city that UIW would build a school of veterinary medicine if the city won the contract, and that pledge was written into San Antonio's official bid. As part of so large an operation, the danger of being a second place program would not be a concern and space could be found within or near the new facility. These things don't move quickly. In 2007 San Antonio made the final list of five, and things looked good for what would be named the Texas Biological and Agro-Defense Consortium. In 2008, to the city's bitter disappointment, the bid went to Manhattan, Kansas and UIW made no further plans for veterinary medicine.

Terry had continued down the list in the meantime. He looked at chiropractic care but anticipated too much controversy. Podiatry and dentistry were also stricken from the list. Both Lou and Terry liked the idea of physical therapy, but insurance companies were not favoring claims in that area—a serious drawback to starting a program. In addition, physical therapy was in the process of elevating its terminal degree from a master's to a Ph.D. The accreditation body would not allow a new program to start until that was resolved.

Terry was now at optometry, and he and Lou thought that might be it. But if there was anticipated controversy with a chiropractic program, Lou and Terry found a Pandora's Box of it as they began delving into optometry. Surprisingly, many local optometrists were opposed to the idea of an optometry school in San Antonio. The biggest fear cited was that Incarnate Word would flood the market with optometrists who would be hired by the "big box stores," and small existing clinics would suffer. Lou decided to push through the controversy. He was correct.

Research showed that Texas had a great need for more optometrists. Figures from the Texas Department of State Health Services in 2006 showed 30,000 practicing optometrists in the country, only 2,690 of whom served Texas's 23 million-plus residents. In addition, 109 Texas counties, including 23 of the 43 border counties, did not have a single optometrist. Local need was also great due to the prevalence of diabetic eye disease in San Antonio.

Terry would soon begin a process similar to the one he had followed for pharmacy. But first there was celebration in the School of Science, Mathematics, and Engineering. After living with the old science facility, built in 1950, the faculty and its new dean, Dr. Glenn James, now had their promised complex. Both science buildings were formally dedicated on January 27, 2006. The new building had five stories to accommodate the two dedicated floors for chemistry and two for biology urged by John Feik. The other floor fulfilled the dream of a research center primarily dedicated to water quality studies. With the San Antonio River's headwaters on campus, the initiative was close to many faculty and student hearts. The new building was named the AT&T Science Center. The renovated science hall, which bore little resemblance to the original, complemented the AT&T facility and was renamed the Henry Bonilla Science Hall in honor of the former congressman.

Four days after the science complex was dedicated, Sister Margaret Patrice Slattery, who had served as chancellor through all of Lou's years at Incarnate Word, retired. There would be no chancellor for the next two years until Lou further restructured the administration to address the university's growing needs. Sister Audrey O'Mahony took over Mission Effectiveness, one of Sister Margaret Patrice's previous responsibilities. Lou offered to elevate the position to a vice presidency, but Sister Audrey preferred a lower profile and Lou allowed her to structure her own comfort zone.

Two years later, when Sister Audrey retired, the position was expanded to include supervision of all campus ministry activities. Sister Walter Maher accepted the position, and this time Lou insisted on the vice president title.

Two other initiatives were conceived that year. In partnership with the University of Monterrey and at the request of CHRISTUS Muguerza Hospital in Monterrey, UIW's School of Nursing and Health Professions agreed to offer a Bachelor of Science in Nursing to select hospital employees who were already registered nurses. As meetings and discussions progressed, the hospital realized the most useful process would be to first offer the master's degree to bachelor-degreed nurses. Those nurses could then be the "seed corn" of a more extensive program, serving as UIW adjunct professors. With their help more students could be reached for the bachelor's program than UIW could reach with just a small number of visiting faculty. This type of program was only possible with a dean like Kathi Light, whose response is usually yes, even before the question is asked.

Lou considered the program a model of the Mission and agreed to offer it, including transportation

Sister Audrey O'Mahony retired as Assistant to the President for Mission Effectiveness in 2009 after a 34-year career at Incarnate Word in various administrative positions.

Dr. Jim Sorensen taught the first classes to CHRISTUS nurses in Monterrey, Mexico.

of UIW faculty to Monterrey, for only what it would actually cost. No profit was built into the program. In response, CHRISTUS Muguerza Hospital agreed to underwrite the cost of the program, waiving all tuition for the nurses. In the end the hospital would profit from having U.S.-trained nurses with master's degrees and could look forward to more bachelor-degreed nurses once the process was fully operational. It would take almost two years for the program to be launched once the change was made to the master's program. The hospital had to select nurses, and arrangements had to be made for a year of English study prior to starting the master's program. The first nursing course wasn't taught until January 2008, when Dr. James Sorensen began the long commute between San Antonio and Monterrey.

The other 2006 initiative was also at a remote site. Under the direction of Dr. Cyndi Porter, Incarnate Word agreed to study the feasibility of a campus in Goodyear, Arizona. The city was courting a university, and all indications were that Incarnate Word would have a long and successful relationship there. Cyndi and Vince Porter spent a considerable amount of time in Goodyear and actually had a small program up and running for a while. The future looked promising enough for Lou to hold the 2008 leadership retreat in Goodyear.

(L-R) Steve Swatzell, Director of the EAP Call Center; Dr. Cyndi Porter, Vice President of Extended Academic Programs, and Vince Porter, Dean of ADCaP.

But a Goodyear campus was not to be. The national economic downturn hit Arizona especially hard, making it impossible to pursue a new university at that time. Lou responded philosophically to the situation. "It wasn't the first idea that didn't work, and it won't be the last," he said. One of the best parts of working for and with Lou Agnese is that if an idea doesn't work, it isn't considered a failure. To Lou, failure is when you refuse to try something reasonable because you're afraid it won't work or it just seems too hard. He values innovation and people who take on entrepreneurial efforts like ADCaP and the programs in Goodyear, China, and Mexico.

Lou lost a longtime friend in 2006, someone who was never afraid of hard work. Sister Ann Finn died suddenly on Valentine's Day. Lou had earlier honored Sister Ann by naming the new coffee shop in the Mabee Library "Finnegans." Professor John Lodek, who had helped decorate Lou and Mickey's first San Antonio home on Canterbury Hill, assigned his interior design students the task of designing the coffee shop. Having food and drink inside a library building might seem counterintuitive, but library dean Mendell Morgan could not have been happier. He had lobbied for a library snack bar for years. It was part of the new approach to making libraries more user-friendly, and Mendell knew it would bring in more people.

Sister Ann Finn had always played a large part in decorating for Light the Way. Her major responsibility was the large crèche in front of the administration building. Unfortunately, the life-sized statue of the infant Jesus was a frequent object of theft. Following the 2005 Christmas season, Sister Ann decided to hide the statue immediately after the crèche was dismantled in January. Sister knew every nook and cranny of the campus and did a great job of hiding it. No one could find it when the 2006 celebration began. Dick McCracken swears the search took on the tone of a tent revival, with people constantly asking, "Have you found Jesus?" Sister Ann would have loved her inadvertent joke.

In 2006 Dr. Kevin Vichcales arrived from Kalamazoo, Michigan, to become dean of the School of Graduate Studies and Research. Dr. Gil Hinojosa

Lou with Sister Ann Finn at the opening of Finnegans, the coffee shop in the Mabee Library named in her honor. Beside them are, from left, David Allwein, Assistant Director of Health Services, and Sister Helena Monahan.

had returned to teaching history, and Dr. Michael Mulnix, who served as the school's third dean for two years, had moved away. Kevin arrived at an important time. With the doctorate in pharmacy already approved and one in optometry likely, a strong graduate culture was developing. Kevin stressed the research aspect of graduate work, establishing an annual research symposium. He also developed and edits "Illuminatus," a newsletter devoted to research excellence and opportunity. Kevin's additional responsibilities included establishing and shepherding an honors program for undergraduates.

By fall 2006 Dr. Arcelia Johnson-Fannin had her first class of seventy-nine pharmacy students. On September 15 the impressive White Coat Ceremony was conducted in the Sky Room. Arcelia describes receiving the white coat, a symbol of medical professionals, as the students' public declaration of their intent to work toward becoming pharmacists and the oath "as their pledge to work toward the relief of human suffering." The pharmacy building would not be completed until 2007, so first-year classes were held at the Datapoint Drive property owned by Stanley Rosenberg and primarily occupied by Rackspace. ADCaP was already using part of the space as an additional site.

The five-story building that houses the John and Rita Feik School of Pharmacy was officially opened on October 17, 2007. It received a double blessing by then Archbishop José Gomez and Sister Audrey O'Mahony. A crowd of nearly 500 enjoyed tours and a champagne toast appropriate for a structure that sits as majestically as this one does on the sloping corner of Hildebrand and Devine.

At dedication ceremonies for the Feik School of Pharmacy are, from left, Sister Teresa Stanley, Dr. Arcelia Johnson-Fannin, Rita Feik, Lou, Emily Thuss, John Feik and Dr. Terry Dicianna.

Having found the rough spots in the road during his work with the pharmacy program, Terry was better able to steer around the many obstacles he encountered in developing a school of optometry. He spent the better part of 2007 on the program, and the faculty and board approved it that year. Now the search for a dean would intensify.

CHAPTER 24
STILL UNDEFEATED

In 2007 the university made the decision to add football to its sports offerings. As early as 2005 Athletic Director Mark Papich had developed
a feasibility study at Lou's request, determining what it would take to
make football a reality. When first conceived, a UIW football team would
have to play off site at either St. Anthony Catholic High School or Alamo
Stadium. Both options had drawbacks and both required some degree of
construction. The high school facility would need substantial improvement,
and even if the team played at Alamo Stadium it would need a locker room
and an exercise facility at Incarnate Word. The location was still undecided
when the board approved adding the sport in April 2007. As with the optometry school, board approval meant the search could move forward—this
time for a head coach.

Knowing it would be much better if a team played on its own turf, Lou
had Mike McChesney develop plans for a field house and playing field with
stadium seating on one side. Lou was also having quiet conversations with
Tom Benson, owner of the New Orleans Saints and a UIW benefactor.

Mike Santiago had just left Utah State when personal friend and former
UIW basketball coach Danny Casper called him.
Danny had heard about the addition of football at
UIW and thought Mike might be just the person to
launch the program. Mike was one of those interviewed during the search process, and he was hired
as head coach on June 18, becoming the nation's
only Hispanic Division II head football coach.

Mike shared the story of his interview and how
for a while it looked like his wife, Dr. Rochelle Caroon-Santiago, was the one they were hiring. "Rochelle and I were in Dr. Agnese's office for my interview when he found out Rochelle had a Ph.D. in

Head Football Coach
Mike Santiago.

psychology. He made a quick phone call, and all of a sudden a lady named Cyndi Porter walks in and takes Rochelle with her. At that time I didn't know Dr. Porter, and I had no idea what was going on." Mike continued with the interview all morning, still without his wife. "The next time I saw Rochelle was during lunch at Tomatillo's. She arrived, and as she slid in next to me she whispered, 'They just offered me a job.' 'Great,' I said, 'they haven't offered me one.'"

Of course the offer was soon made to Mike, and later at Lou's home they laughed about it. "I told Dr. Agnese about our whispered lunch conversation and how I thought for a while they were hiring only one Santiago. Dr. Agnese responded, 'Well, I thought you could have figured out you were being hired.'"

While the search was in progress, Tom and Gayle Benson decided to give football a first-class home at UIW. Tom Benson shared his thoughts about the decision later. "When Lou talked to me about football at Incarnate Word, I thought it would be another great thing for the university." Benson knew some people still might be thinking Incarnate Word was a girl's school or a nursing school. With the addition of football the university could say, "Hey, we've got a full school here." He added, "That stadium and the football program have helped establish more things than ever . . . I didn't think it was going to be this great, but I thought it would be a great thing for the university."

Dr. Beth Senne-Duff, UIW Professor of Nutrition, helped develop the nutrition curriculum at CIW-Mexico to mirror the one at UIW. At the podium is Marcos Fragoso.

Excitement built as the stadium was being constructed. Cardinal T-shirts appeared with the words "Still Undefeated." It would be almost two years until the first game was played, but football had arrived. Players would be selected the next year, but all would be redshirted the first year.

That 2007–08 academic year saw an increase in international activity, including expansion of the Mexico campus. Nutrition had been announced as one of the new majors, and UIW faculty member Dr. Beth Senne-Duff helped develop the curriculum for CIW-Mexico so that it mirrored UIW's while satisfying Mexico's secretary of public education. Beth also helped set forth the specifications for new labs to be built in Mexico and even helped Marcos select pots, pans, and other cooking equipment required for accreditation standards. Cooperation and commitment like that is one answer to the frequent queries about how UIW is able to establish and maintain campuses at international sites.

The labs would be housed in the old convent building that holds many memories for the Mexican Sisters who each lived there at some point. The building required extensive renovation, especially in order to preserve much of its historic architecture. It was dedicated in December 2007 and houses laboratories, dormitory space, and offices.

Incarnate Word's international programs require detailed attention in the planning phases because their implementation occurs so far from home. In addition to deans, faculty, and the international affairs staff, the support of the registrar and comptroller are essential. Lou is fortunate to have Bobbye Fry seeing to it that grades given in China show up on transcripts in San Antonio, and that the names of international students are spelled correctly on the diplomas that will hang proudly on walls around the world.

With good humor and patience, Comptroller Edie Cogdell maintains the financial records of the UIW campuses in San Antonio, Mexico and China.

Diplomas and transcripts show; it is not hard to recognize the work that goes into them. It might be a little harder to know the role of Edie Cogdell, comptroller since 1999. Edie maintains financial records in three countries, understands the intricacies of budgets as those countries expect to see them, and knows to the penny how much was spent. And she does it all with good humor. Marcos remembers, "One of the first things Pat told me when I started was 'Make friends with Bobbye and Edie. You can't do this without them.'"

CIW-Mexico held its first graduation on June 11, 2008. Effort went into making the ceremony as close to those in San Antonio as possible.

Celebrating the first graduation at the Mexico campus are, standing from left, Lou, Alejandra Espinosa Lopez, Oscar Rodriguez, Dr. Pat Watkins and Marcos Fragoso. Seated is Dr. Gabriella De La Vega.

Mariachis alternated with bagpipes at the reception following commencement at the Mexico City campus.

Marcos arranged for faculty to line a walkway, simulating the bridge-crossing at UIW graduations. Faculty cheered and applauded the nine graduates as they passed in their UIW academic regalia. (Seventeen law students would graduate that December.) Richard Rose's bagpipes were a greater challenge. Marcos now knows the location of every bagpipe musician in Mexico—and there aren't many. Somehow, to Lou's surprise, the wail of bagpipes announced the approach of the academic procession he would join as they passed through their moment of applause. With a healthy mix of cultures, the bagpipers alternated with mariachis in the celebration following graduation.

Back in San Antonio, Lou knew it was time to restructure administrative lines for the approaching academic year. The university's growth was now so rapid that areas of responsibility were becoming unbalanced. In June 2008 Terry Dicianna was named chancellor. He was still wistfully eyeing retirement, and warned Lou this could only be for a short time.

Denise Doyle moved from vice president for academic and student affairs to provost. As provost Denise would concentrate entirely on academic issues. David Jurenovich's title changed to vice president for enrollment management and student services, picking up an area that had been with Denise. Terry continued his concentration on new programs, a responsibility that would fall to the new chancellor if Terry ever managed to retire.

Cyndi Porter was named vice president for extended academic programs. Rita Russ replaced Cyndi as dean of the virtual university, and Vince Porter became dean of ADCaP. The search for a dean of the optometry school was completed; Dr. Hani Ghazi-Birry had arrived just a few months earlier. Sister Sally Mitchell had turned the reins of the Brainpower Connection over to Dan Ochoa a few years before. Dan, previously the principal at St. Anthony Catholic High School during the teapot tempest of coeducation, was still serving as dean of university preparatory programs.

Mendell Morgan, dean of library science, made the decision to fully retire that year. His wife of forty-five years, Jean Marie Winn Morgan, was quite ill, and Mendell wanted to spend his time caring for her. Jean died that October, just a few days after celebrating her sixty-fifth birthday. Cheryl Anderson, dean of the School of Interactive Media and Design (SIMD), temporarily took on the library deanship as well. Later Dr. Sharon Welkey replaced Cheryl as dean of SIMD, and Cheryl was able to devote her full attention to the Mabee Library.

Doug Endsley's title changed to vice president for finance and technology, and he, Pat Watkins, and Sister Kathleen Coughlin remained in their vice president positions. Lou Fox, former city manager of San Antonio, joined the Executive Council as assistant to the president. Fox later took over police, safety, and logistics issues for the university. Cindy Escamilla, the university's general counsel, added Human Resources to her areas of responsibility.

Now that Dr. Hani Ghazi-Birry was aboard, work toward preliminary accreditation of optometry began. Files prepared for that and the later accreditation state "UIW's School of Optometry will be only the second college-based optometry school in Texas." The program mirrors pharmacy in one important aspect: "It will be the only optometry school in the nation to offer a Spanish-language certification. Based on the demographics of South Texas and consultations with professional optometrists, there is a great need for optometrists who speak Spanish, both here and in other regions in the U.S." The optometry school would be one of only twenty in the United States mainland and the only one at a faith-based university.

The UIW Executive Council in 2009, from left, standing, Dr. David Jurenovich, Doug Endsley, Vince Rodriguez, Sister Walter Maher, Lou, Dr. Annette Craven and Lou Fox; seated, Cindy Escamilla, Dr. Cyndi Porter, Dr. Pat Watkins, Dr. Denise Doyle, Sister Kathleen Coughlin and Sister Helena Monahan.

After trying to retire for nearly a decade, Dr. Terry Dicianna was finally able to do so in 2008.

Terry finally escaped to retirement in August 2008, and Sister Helena Monahan was named chancellor, officially beginning that work in January 2009.

On February 13, 2009, the Accreditation Council on Optometric Education granted the school the pre-accreditation classification of "preliminary approval," the only classification available to a new optometric degree program. That allowed student recruitment and admission to begin and courses to be offered.

During that 2008–09 school year of changes, retirements, hires and approvals, the Gayle and Tom Benson Stadium was completed. Watching it grow had been a thrill for everyone who argued in favor of football over the years. The first game would be played in August 2009. Lou thought it would be a good idea if the match had an international flavor. Incarnate Word has its own university in Mexico City, the nursing program was still in place in Monterrey, and there were many sister schools in Mexico. Why not invite one of them to play the first game?

It sounded like a great idea. Mark Papich and Mike Santiago looked over the schools that had football teams. Soccer was big in Mexico, but they were looking for a nice game of American football for their opener. UIW had many contacts with Monterrey Tech, an outstanding academic university often referred to as the M.I.T. of Mexico. Raul Rodriguez, former president of

Tom Benson, owner of the New Orleans Saints, whose gift allowed UIW to start a football program in 2007, stands with Lou and UIW Athletic Director Mark Papich.

the North American Development Bank and now the Benson Chair of Banking in the H-E-B School of Business and Administration, had even taught there. What a nice arrangement!

Phone calls were placed, dates were cleared, and the deal was made. Shortly after everything had been finalized it came to light that Monterrey Tech's team was on a twenty-six-game winning streak that dated back to 2006. Those "Still Undefeated" T-shirts could soon be obsolete.

The August 29 game began after hours of celebration. Fans arrived early for their first-ever UIW tailgate parties. Tom and Gayle Benson helped open the festivities and received everyone's thanks. Sadly, Reg Traylor had not lived to see the football program for which he had worked so vigorously. But Lou and David Jurenovich saw to it this first game was dedicated to his memory.

The Monterrey Borregos Salvajes (Wild Rams) ran the kickoff back 62 yards for what looked like a sure six points. The day seemed doomed. But, somehow, UIW's Cardinals held them to a field goal. No one expected the high-scoring game they saw that day. It ended with UIW winning 42–39. The Wild Rams' winning streak was over, and the Cardinals were "still undefeated." There were many interviews, quotes, and sound bites following the game, but none so perfect as Coach Santiago's statement to the *Express-News*: "I wanted this so much for Dr. Agnese. That man waited twenty-three years to see his first (UIW) football game. And what a hell of a first football game to see."

Before a standing-room only crowd of more than 6,000,
the UIW Cardinals won their inaugural football game by
ending Monterrey Tech's 26-game winning streak.

CHAPTER 25
To Be Continued

Sister Helena's contract as chancellor shows a starting date of January 1, 2009. Knowing Lou, one can only hope she really did not spend New Year's Day at work. Sister Helena sorted through Lou's growing list of ideas, one of which was to revisit a physical therapy program. The degree had now officially been declared Ph.D. level, and insurance companies had also made changes in their regulations. Both new decisions made physical therapy a viable option.

As early as March 2009, five months before the Cardinals ruined the Wild Ram's winning streak, Helena had brought together the Allied Health Advisory Group. In addition to UIW administrators Denise Doyle, Kathi Light and Kevin Vichcales, Helena had included Jim Van Straten, Incarnate Word's dean of professional studies in the late 1980s and later dean of allied health at the University of Texas Health Science Center. Representatives from St. Philip's College, the UT Health Science Center, and the military completed the group.

Sister Helena explained that their meeting focused on physical therapy but also explored other emerging allied health care needs. She added that the UT Health Science Center "reported hundreds of applicants for the forty openings a year, making it clear that Central and South Texas are strong markets for physical therapists." Space for clinical labs was identified as a potential problem, but Sister Helena noted, "We have an advantage because of our affiliation with CHRISTUS Health."

Sister Helena Monahan plans to end her 40-year UIW career with retirement in 2012.

As a result of the meeting, UIW administrators recommended a feasibility study that led to the decision to proceed with the Doctor of Physical Therapy (DPT). That program and the search for its dean would occupy much of Sister Helena's time in 2009–10. She had the optometry ball in one hand

and the physical therapy ball in the other when SACS tossed in a third. They were looking closely at the Mexico campus.

SACS had never decided exactly how to handle UIW's latest international site, and now they began asking big questions. Since CIW-Mexico had already graduated classes in June and December 2008, this was a little unnerving. Helena revisited the many reports Terry had sent to SACS earlier and added the new responses now being sought. Good records had been maintained regarding Mexico, and the UIW faculty and administration's involvement was clear to SACS. The process was long and complicated, and it almost caused a run on antacids, but on September 27, 2010, SACS sent approval of the joint-venture campus. Mexican bagpipes would soon play again.

Sister Helena had become a juggler. She was keeping the optometry and Mexico balls in the air while making sure the physical therapy one didn't bounce. She really wanted a dean, someone with expertise in physical therapy. The search would not be simple, and Helena, Denise, and Kathi would be the physical therapy think-tank for a while longer. The DPT degree would be taught 100 percent online, not by the virtual university but by UIW professors using Blackboard, a university delivery system.

Dr. Hani Ghazi-Birry had completed selection of the sixty-two students in the first optometry class for fall 2009. And they had a home. Stanley Rosenberg made substantial adjustments to the Datapoint space vacated by the Feik School of Pharmacy, and the optometry program was able to move in its equipment.

The leadership retreat was held in August at the Purple Sage Ranch near Bandera, Texas. Lou and Kathi—and just about everyone else who ever saw it—knew the nursing building and its equipment were seriously out of date. Lou talked to Kathi while they were in Bandera and told her to start in-depth discussion with her faculty about where nursing should be housed in the future. Should the nursing building be renovated, or should the program move off campus, maybe to the Medical Center?

The nursing faculty began the process of deciding "renovate or move." They had established criteria for making the decision and were several weeks into the process when Lou called Kathi. "You're staying," he said. "Start planning what you want in your new building." Kathi had been at Incarnate Word when Lou arrived. She had received many "Lou calls" over the years, so not much surprised her. The committee simply shifted the focus of their weekly meetings to the design of their dream building. They met frequently with the architect and braced happily for the hectic move they would soon have.

The School of Nursing faced another significant decision that year. The American Association of Colleges of Nursing had issued a ruling that required any nursing program offering master's degrees in nurse practitioner, clinical nurse specialist, nurse anesthetist, or nurse midwife to convert those master's level programs to a Doctor of Nursing Practice degree by 2015. UIW offers a master's degree in clinical nurse specialist in adult health. Kathi was about to join Helena's juggling act in what would become UIW's delightful circus before things settled.

The mandate to convert the master's program to the doctoral level was neither as extreme nor unwarranted as a casual observer might think. The programs had grown to contain over seventy credit hours while master's degrees in most other fields averaged thirty to thirty-six hours. Graduates of these specialized programs are already a big step ahead of others in the profession. They still take the National Certification Examination like other nurses. But once they pass the exam they can apply to the Board of Nursing for recognition as a clinical nurse specialist with limited prescriptive authority. In spite of the program's intensity and the authority to write certain prescriptions, the master's degree still does not position graduates competitively with those holding a doctoral degree. Universities were given the option to elevate the programs in those specialized fields or end them.

UIW's School of Nursing discussed the option for several years. They asked themselves if they had the resources to make the change. They determined they had the appropriate faculty for the doctorate which is a practitioner's degree, not a research doctorate (Ph.D.). Kathi explained the practitioner's doctorate is the type of degree granted in other specialized disciplines, including education's Ed. D., medicine's M.D. and pharmacy's Pharm. D. The nursing faculty decided to elevate the degree in order to provide greater opportunities for their graduates.

Dr. Mary Elaine Jones, UIW nursing faculty, took responsibility for chairing a committee that would spend months gaining approval from all internal UIW groups—the full nursing faculty, the university Graduate Council, the Faculty Senate, and the Board of Trustees. Sister Helena took charge of the substantive change request that would seek approval from SACS.

As the busy year progressed, the nursing faculty prepared to leave their building as soon as the academic semester ended. Steve Heying and Kathi Light designed an exit strategy worthy of a military operation. Starting at the east end of the building and moving relentlessly westward, faculty moved out as they finished their final exams, administered a week early by special arrangement. As each exam ended, the faculty member was escorted out and the asbestos abatement team moved in.

By May 1 the building was empty. Nursing faculty in full academic regalia participated in the graduation ceremony, homeless but happy. Some would work from home for a semester, some would move in with the optometry program at the Datapoint site, and some would use the Gorman-Mitchell room once utilized by the Dreeben School of Education when their building was renovated. Kathi says proudly, "Steve Heying says it was the most orderly, well-planned move-out in the history of all buildings at UIW."

On June 18, 2010, the Mexico campus celebrated the appointment of its new rector, Matthew Whitehouse, and said good-bye to its previous and much loved rector, Marcos Fragoso.

Marcos and his family moved to San Antonio where he became vice president for international affairs at UIW as Pat Watkins retired after twenty-two years. The family became an immediate part of the Brainpower Connection as Marcos's daughter, Ana Julia, entered St. Peter Prince of Apostles School, and his wife, Adriana, began teaching Spanish as a volunteer. The littlest Fragoso, daughter Ivana, also became a Brainpower Connector by spending a few days a week in daycare at St. Peter's.

In June SACS affirmed the two programs that had consumed most of Terry's time in the past few years. Its brief but welcome message read, "The Commission on Colleges continued accreditation following review of the

Ivana Fragoso, front left, stands beside her sister Ana Julia Fragoso, both students at St. Peter Prince of the Apostles School. Behind them are from left, Catheryn Orihuela, a teacher; Adriana Fragoso, their mother; Amy Migura, a teacher; and Marcos Fragoso, their father.

Doctor of Optometry and Doctor of Pharmacy degrees."

Summer also saw the expansion of the Gayle and Tom Benson Stadium. Seeing the overflow crowd supporting the Cardinals, Benson readily agreed to fund the expansion Lou proposed. If there is any truth to the idea that problem solving can help create more neural connections, Mike McChesney is about to max out the IQ scale. Mike needed to find

The generosity of Tom and Gayle Benson allowed UIW to double the seating capacity of Benson Stadium in 2010.

a way to have stadium seating on both sides of the field without closing vehicular access between the two sides of the campus.

The ICC side had exploded in growth. Two new dormitories, including the one named for Gary Joeris, and the Alonzo Ancira Tower, an 800-capacity parking garage, had been added near the ICC and the McCombs Center. A new entrance to the campus had been constructed allowing cars to enter directly from the Highway 281 access road. All the traffic generated by that growth had to move freely between the two sides of campus. Mike solved the problem by building the stadium seating so cars could pass through a covered tunnel created by the sloping side of the new stand.

It was now August 2010. Lou began his twenty-fifth year at Incarnate Word like he had all the other years. There was an opening Mass on August 5, but this time the chaplain, Father Thomas Dymowski, had prepared a special moment for Lou and his family. As the assembled Congregation, faculty, students, and friends watched, Lou and Mickey walked to the altar and received the "Blessing of the Family." The blessing, which Father Tom logically found in the *Book of Blessings*, seemed written for this moment. It began, "We bless your name, O Lord, for sending your own incarnate Son to become part of a family, so that, as He lived His life, He would experience its worries and its joys." Everyone, whether thinking of the Incarnate Word family or their own personal family, felt the moment of inclusion.

Father Tom extended his hands over Lou, Mickey, and their family and said: "We ask you, Lord, to protect and watch over this family, so that in the strength of your grace its members may enjoy prosperity, possess the priceless gift of your peace, and, as the Church alive in the home, bear witness in this world to your glory." Father Tom concluded with the usual closing of prayers at Incarnate Word, saying, "We ask this through Christ your Son, the Incarnate Word." Everyone added "Amen."

At UIW no one leaves after "Amen." They know that's Lou's time. Claiming he always wants the last word, Lou saves his comments for the end. This day was no different. Lou took the microphone to thank the assembled crowd and accept their congratulations. "As I stood there looking at the audience," he recalls, "my eyes went to my son, Louis. It suddenly struck me at that moment that my son was only one year younger than I had been when I became president of Incarnate Word College. It was a sobering moment."

A reception followed on the lawn of Brackenridge Villa. The bottomless platters of Bill Miller tacos supplied by board member John Miller were the crowd's favorite. Those tacos became a standard at board meetings once John was a trustee. After the reception, it was work as usual. This was the beginning of the 2010–11 academic year, as full of action and decisions as the past twenty-four had been. Lou walked from the villa to his office to start the workday. He was grateful for the gift of another year, and for the gift of family and friends, but other than that there was nothing unusual about the day.

In October Sister Helena had her wish. The announced search for a dean of the physical therapy program brought Dr. Caroline Goulet, director of the physical therapy program at Creighton University, a Jesuit campus in Omaha, Nebraska. Caroline would have almost two years to establish the program and recruit the first class, which begins in 2012.

The Spurs Coyote tries to upstage Lou at Light the Way.

Light the Way moved to a new venue in November of 2010. The event, still sponsored by H-E-B, drew over 5,500 guests in 2009, creating a standing-room-only crowd that overflowed the convocation center.

This year it moved to the Gayle and Tom Benson Stadium. Although Patsy Torres, a UIW graduate, headlined the entertainment, the stadium venue also gave UIW an opportunity to show off its new marching band, a natural outgrowth of its football program.

Light the Way may have marked the start of the holiday season, but it was Stanley Rosenberg and his wife, Sandra, who gave the gift. At $11.5 million, it was the largest single gift in the university's history. Lou explained that it was also one of the largest in recent national history from a Jewish family to a Catholic institution. He announced the gift to the *Express-News* the day after Hanukkah, stating that it was a most appropriate day for the announcement.

Incarnate Word has always felt the support of the non-Catholic community, especially those of the Jewish faith. The Rosenbergs made an earlier gift to the university in 2006 when they donated funds toward the Rosenberg Sky Room. This new gift allowed the university to purchase the large Datapoint building it had used for several years.

In 2010, Stanley and Sandra Rosenberg made an $11.5 million gift to UIW, largest in school history and one of the largest nationally by Jewish donors to a Catholic university in recent years.

The *Express-News* reported "though the gift is for the university in general, UIW has named its new optometry school in honor of the benefactors." It quoted Lou as saying the Sandra and Stanley Rosenberg School of Optometry is the only named optometry school in the nation. "It is a real honor when you have a school named for you as a legacy. Every diploma granted will be from the Rosenberg School of Optometry . . . and every graduate will have that on their wall," he said. On January 19, 2011, the Sandra and Stanley Rosenberg School of Optometry opened its Eye and Vision Care Center to the general public at the Datapoint location.

January also saw the completion of the new nursing building. The Ila Faye Miller School of Nursing was dedicated on January 17. John Miller and his wife, Vladimira, an alumna, contributed a major gift in memory of John's mother, Ila Faye Miller. John told the assembled crowd of over 300 how his mother, a nurse herself, had taught him and that he was proud to contribute to the education of other nurses in her name.

Lou with, from left, Dr. Kathi Light and Vladimira and John Miller. In 2011, the School of Nursing was named the Ila Faye Miller School of Nursing in honor of John's mother, a nurse.

On March 2, 2011, the Ila Faye Miller School of Nursing received an answer from SACS about its application for approval of a Doctor of Nursing Practice. The letter read as follows: "We approve the Doctor of Nursing Practice degree program, shall include it within the scope of accreditation previously granted, and wish you and your colleagues much success with it. The institution is also approved to deliver 50 percent or more of the program's credits electronically. By means of this letter and the approval of the fourth doctoral program, I also authorize the advancement of the University of the Incarnate Word from Level V to Level VI." Sister Helena explained, "Level VI is the highest level recognized by SACS. Being there is a tribute to the work of all of you and of the entire UIW community."

March 25 had almost arrived. Lou Agnese was only days away from the twenty-fifth anniversary of his inauguration as president of then Incarnate Word College. There had been a little tension as Lou began that twenty-fifth year in August, and it was still in the air. This time the tension was in the whispered concerns, "What if he leaves?" Lou heard the concerns but could not or would not allay them right away. It was one thing for individuals to express hope that he would stay. He wanted to stay, too. But twenty-five years is a long time.

Whoever first said "The older we get, the more like ourselves we become" must have known Lou Agnese. He may be more certain of his ability, more confident that the university is secure and maybe even more reconciled to aches, pains, and hair that is no longer "prematurely" gray, but inside he hasn't changed. Back in 1986 Lou delayed his inauguration in order to be sure the board knew what they were getting. He developed his five-year plan and set it out for examination. He wanted to be president, but only if he had the support to move forward with what he knew should be done.

Now Lou did the same thing. He was ready to give more of his life to Incarnate Word, but it wasn't entirely up to him. He wanted to put forward plans for the next five years and see what support those plans had. He knows Incarnate Word will become the state's largest private university in a few more years. He knows the virtual university, graduate and international programs, and health professions will all be key. The university launched its Nursing Practice Doctorate in August 2011. The physical therapy program begins in August 2012, and the first optometry class graduates in 2013. An increasingly internationalized campus resulted in a new Asian studies program, launched February 1, 2011, and China and Mexico may soon be joined by another international site.

The balloons went up, and no one shot them down. Lou recently felt it was fair to say, "God willing, I will stay with you as long as I am useful." The whispered word is "another ten years."

If anyone expected Lou to slow down in this next phase, they now know they were wrong. And if they happen to be around during one of Papa Agnese's visits, they will understand why the campus is talking about Lou's next ten years of service. Papa is still a frequent visitor to the campus, and at ninety-six can out-walk most of the students. With genes like those, maybe folks should be thinking about Lou's next twenty years, not just ten.

Lou with Papa Agnese.

EPILOGUE

aving turned sixty, Lou is no longer referred to as one of the country's youngest presidents but rather as one of the longest-serving presidents. The last figures released by the American Council on Education show that the average length of presidential service is 8.6 years. Only 3 percent of college presidents have served twenty-five years. Even more amazing is the fact that the average age of first-time presidents is fifty-nine, a year younger than Lou is now.

Lou and Mickey are now grandparents. Louis III and his wife, Melissa, both attorneys in Austin, are the parents of Jack Louis, born June 17, 2010. Nancy, a practicing veterinarian, and her electrical engineer husband, Bryan Vrla, presented Lou and Mickey their first granddaughter, Brooklyn Michaeline, on July 11, 2011. Brooklyn had Lou wrapped around her little finger the next day after taking quick lessons from the big boss, cousin Jack.

Lou is surrounded by the accomplishments of twenty-five years, but he is the first to point out he didn't do it alone. One of his gifts has always been finding the right people for the jobs. Another gift has been the ability to

Louis III, his wife Melissa and their son Jack Louis.

Nancy with husband Bryan and their daughter Brooklyn Michaeline.

(L-R) Dr. Kathi Light, Lou and Dr. Denise Doyle.

engender loyalty. If Lou isn't the most exhausting person to work for, he surely is second. In spite of that, or maybe because of the excitement he generates, he has always been surrounded by people who choose to stay with him, some for life and many until retirement.

Sister Helena Monahan will retire as chancellor in 2012, and Dr. Denise Doyle will fill that position during her own three-year phased retirement. Dr. Kathi Light will take over as provost and Dr. Glenn James will become associate provost. Until then, Sister Helena and Denise will continue to be part of Lou's current Executive Council, along with Vice Presidents Dr. David Jurenovich, Doug Endsley, Dr. Cyndi Porter, Sister Kathleen Coughlin, Marcos Fragoso, and Sister Walter Maher. Vincent Rodriguez, Cindy Escamilla, Lou Fox, and the Faculty Senate President, Dr. Annette Craven, complete the council.

Dick McCracken is semiretired but assists with alumni affairs and entertains with stories of the past—some of which, he will admit with a wink, might just border on the apocryphal. Lisa Schultz, who followed Dick, is now director of alumni, adding her own touch to the strong program he developed.

Dr. Gil Hinojosa is semiretired and teaches some history courses. Sister Sally Mitchell restricts her activity to teaching for the virtual university. Besides his vice presidential duties, David Jurenovich's life centers around his sons Christian, age nine, and Matthew, age eight.

Misty Chen continues her work with the China campus. She and Mohsen Omar presided over the May graduation with a UIW alumnus as

Dr. David Jurenovich with sons Christian, left, and Matthew.

special guest speaker. Mohsen's brother, Dr. Husam Omar, an IE&E graduate now teaching at Dubai Women's College in the United Arab Emirates, sounded a bit like a young Lou Agnese when he told the graduates not to be afraid of the decisions they will face in the future. "We don't have to be right all the time. We just have to do what we do with devotion and commitment . . . . Mistakes can serve a purpose in life."

Sister Dorothy Ettling still teaches in the organizational leadership concentration

Villagers in Bukoba, Tanzania, with, top row, Velica Calvert, left;
Sister Dorothy Ettling, sixth from left; Dr. Richard Henderson,
front, second from left; and Dr. Carolin Sinkfield, far right.

of the Ph.D. program and has founded the organization Women's Global Connections. She frequently takes students and faculty with her to work in Africa, especially in Zambia and Tanzania.

Dr. Rick Henderson died of cancer on March 19, 2011, the morning of his sixty-seventh birthday. Dr. Absael Antello and Dr. Noah Kasraie complete the full-time faculty in the organizational leadership concentration. Dr. Osman Ozturgut, Ann Cowan's husband, who handled all ELS at the China campus, received his Ph.D. from University of Missouri and has joined Dr. Norman St. Clair as faculty in the international education and entrepreneurship Ph.D. concentration.

Dr. Terry Dicianna and Dr. Pat Watkins are retired, but both teach a few courses—Terry for AD-CaP and Pat in the international education and entrepreneurship program. Sister Audrey O'Mahony is retired and stays active with various ministries of the Congregation.

Dr. Bob Ryan retired, and Dr. Shawn Daly followed him as dean of the H-E-B School of Business and Administration. A new position, dean of student success, was created and is currently filled by Sandy McMakin. Dr. Bob Connelly, who had been eyeing retirement, decided to leave his position as dean of humanities, arts, and social sciences and will assist Dr. Glenn James in his new role.

Dr. Glenn James is to become Associate Provost in 2012.

Other deans include Drs. Denise Staudt, Cheryl Anderson, Kevin Vichcales, Sharon Welkey, Arcelia Johnson-Fannin, and Renee Moore, as well as Dan Ochoa, Andrea Cyterski-Acosta, Rita Russ, and soon-to-be-doctor Vince Porter.

The Center for Medical Tourism and Research is flourishing under the direction of Dr. David Vequist, with assistance from Dr. Michael Guiry, and oversight support from Dean Shawn Daly. The center has been working closely with its counterparts in Korea.

Dr. Caroline Goulet is working to open the School of Physical Therapy on time. It now has a home in the Debbie and Naty Saidoff Center located at the newly acquired Tezel Road site in northwest San Antonio.

Dr. Andrew Buzzelli, acting dean of the Rosenberg School of Optometry, will help establish the UIW Eastside Center for Visual Science and Health Care. The Center will have three floors, one for ADCaP and the other two for the eye clinic. The clinic will be unique in that it will not only address the pathology of vision but also be the first institution to look at the functionality of vision.

All these changes mean searches will soon begin for Kathi Light, Glenn James, and Bob Connelly's current dean positions.

The Cutting Edge Fashion Show production was on April 11, 2011, and Tainan, Taiwan, was once again part of it. This time Dr. Welkey and her fashion design students hosted the Taiwanese sister school students and their fashion creations in San Antonio.

The master's degree in nursing continues being taught for the Monterrey nurses in the CHRISTUS system, although violence in Monterrey has made online instruction a necessity for the time being. Language remains a challenge, but Kathi Light and her Monterrey counterpart are determined to see the program to successful completion. Visits by student nurses to the UIW campus motivated both sides. The new School of Nursing and Health Professions has also given increased energy to all the players.

Dr. Bobbye Fry and Edie Cogdell are still registrar and comptroller, respectively. Steve Heying continues to direct physical plant affairs and Roger Labat, who joined Steve after completing his term as Incarnate Word principal, has retired.

The Sky Room is the magnet it was intended to be and is often booked two years in advance. The Alonzo Ancira (parking) Tower made the Sky Room an even better choice for large events. The university's special events staff is kept busy and continues under the direction of José Herrera. Light the Way has become so popular it needed a larger home and moved to the Benson Stadium last year.

The campus is benefiting from the 160 new trees planted in 1987 and the 63 elms transplanted on the west side of the San Antonio River that same year. Lou is particularly proud of the other sustainability measures architect Mike McChesney has incorporated into buildings and sites. They include gray water for landscaping, sunscreens and double-glazed low E windows to reduce heat, as well as air conditioning boxes that sense body heat. If no one is inside, the air volume is reduced and electrical power is saved.

The Grounds Department, under the direction of Bill Mulcahy, continues with tree planting and landscaping that make the campus beautiful year round. The university now owns the beautiful old Den-

The Korean Pavilion, a $1.5 million gift from the city of Gwangju, South Korea, is near San Antonio's South Texas Medical Center on the former Denman Estate, being renamed Cardinal Park.

man estate in the Medical Center area. The estate, which will soon be renamed Cardinal Park, recently became home to an extravagant $1.5 million Korean Pavilion donated to San Antonio by its Korean sister city, Gwangju.

Sister Margaret Patrice Slattery, honored with the title president emerita, is fully retired but occasionally graces university activities with her presence and wit.

Only a few Sisters are left in teaching or administration besides Sister Dorothy, Sister Helena, Sister Kathleen, and Sister Walter. Sister Eilish Ryan and Sister Martha Ann Kirk still teach in religious studies, and Sister Germaine Corbin, semiretired, teaches some courses in theatre arts. Music professor Sister Maria Goretti, who appropriately christened herself the Pun Nun, died of a massive heart attack on the second day of classes in 2001. At the age of seventy, she was preparing for what she loved best—teaching.

B. J. Nelsen is the current principal at Incarnate Word High School, and Rene Escobedo is principal at St. Anthony Catholic High School. The Keaveney sisters, Sister Agnes and Sister Ailbe, retired from the high school several years ago but can frequently be seen enjoying activities on both campuses. Sister Clarita Burke, the Testing Center general, died in 2005 at the age of ninety-one.

SR. MARGARET PATRICE SLATTERY
LEADERSHIP CENTER
OFFICE OF THE PROVOST

President Emerita Sister Margaret Patrice Slattery in front of the Leadership Center named in her honor.

Ann Lauder is principal of St. Peter Prince of the Apostles Elementary School and Patricia Ramirez has just been named interim principal at St. Anthony's Elementary School.

Martin Klingbacher helped increase the student numbers at St. Anthony Catholic High School as director of enrollment for five years and then became director of International Student and Scholar Services at the ICC. After 11 years he has turned the job over to his assistant Jose Martinez and settled into the associate director position, but everyone knows he is eyeing retirement almost as eagerly as Terry Dicianna once did.

Under the guidance of Dr. Javier Lozano and Alana Taylor, sister school activity is flourishing and the study abroad program continues to open vistas for UIW students. Opportunities have increased in Taiwan, with the help of San Antonio businessman Jimmy Hu, and in Korea, through the efforts of another San Antonio businessman, Daniel Han. Dr. Lydia Andrade and Ambassador Jim Creagan are planning a faculty-led trip to Cuba in the spring for their students.

Earl Abel's, which eventually became known as "the restaurant across from Incarnate Word," has moved to another location. At the university it's business as usual. Sister Kathleen has already raised $85 million in a capital campaign that had an original goal of $75 million, and she doesn't plan to stop. Ernest Bromley, in partnership with Lionel Sosa prior to Lionel's retirement, heads Bromley Communications, Incarnate Word's primary advertising agency. Lionel's retirement didn't diminish his presence on the campus. He even found time to teach the first course of the Lionel Sosa Visiting Professorship founded in his name in the H-E-B School of Business and Administration.

Among the new leaders at the University of the Incarnate Word are, from left, Dr. Sharon Welkley, Dr. Shawn Daly, Rita Russ and Dr. Caroline Goulet.

As UIW and Lou move forward together, the results of their first twenty-five years are impressive. In 1985 the enrollment was 1,298 students, of whom only 780 were full-time. In fall 2011, the freshman class alone surpassed 1,000 full-time students. The total enrollment is nearly 8,500, a figure that has more than doubled in just the last decade. Amy Carcanagues, director of financial assistance, continues to work her magic in stretching the financial aid dollars to as many students as possible.

Today's student body is nearly sixty percent Hispanic and African American, keeping pace with the changing racial/ethnic demographics of Texas. UIW is ranked number one nationally among faith-based universities in awarding of bachelor's degrees to Hispanics and ranked number two among all private universities. Only the University of Miami, whose total enrollment is twice that of Incarnate Word, awarded more in 2010.

In 1985 the college had few international students. Today nearly fourteen percent of UIW's student body is international, representing sixty-seven countries. A new international campus will soon open in Heidelberg, Germany. The physical growth has kept pace with student and programmatic growth. In 1985 the college had 410,000 square feet of space. By 2001 that had increased to slightly over one million square feet. Today University of the Incarnate Word occupies more than two and a half million square feet of space, in addition to campuses in China, Mexico, Corpus Christi and various satellite locations in San Antonio.

Most folks at Incarnate Word agree that there is an odd sense of comfort in the hectic but familiar pace of Lou Agnese. There are projects developing everywhere on the main campus and elsewhere, but no one is surprised when Lou asks "What's next?" and expects an answer.

Lou, 60, the longest serving president of a comprehensive
public or private university in Texas, as he began
his twenty-sixth year at Incarnate Word.

Academic Council, 116
Academy of the Incarnate Word, xi
Administrative Council, 116
Adult Degree Completion Program/
 ADCaP, 99–104, 108, 135, 169, 185,
 186
Agnese, Jack Louis, 205
Agnese, John, 106, 124
Agnese, Louis J. Sr., 15, 38, 40, 42, 53,
 125, 203
Agnese, Louis J. III, 4, 8, 9, 10, 11,
 23–24, 35, 38, 69, 82, 86, 105, 125,
 128, 200, 205
Agnese, Melissa, 205
Agnese, Michaeline, 3–4, 8, 17, 21, 23, 35,
 42, 60, 85, 86, 105, 158, 169–71, 199
Agnese, Mike, 38, 106, 123, 124, 125
Agnese, Nancy (Mrs. Louis J. Sr.), 38,
 42, 53, 141
Agnese, Susan, 38, 106, 125
Agnese-Sosa Living Center, 105
Alamo Heights High School, 82
Albrecht, Juanita, 39
Allied Health Advisory Group, 195
Allwein, David, 185
Altaca, Emel, 155
Altaca, Erol, 155
Altomare, Theresa, 135
Amato, Charlie, 166
Amende, Ernest, 175
Ancira Tower, Alonzo, 199, 208
Andrade, Lydia, 177, 178, 210
Anderson, Cheryl, 127–28, 170, 191, 207
Antello, Absael, 207
Armer, Joseph Marie, 54–55
Arnell, Melvin, 218
Aronson, Donna, 135
Ashe, Ken, 25–26
Athletic program, 46–47, 50, 84–85, 90,
 98, 120, 126, 159, 176–77, 187–88,
 192–93
AT&T Science Center, 183
Avoca, 54
Ayala, Frank, 67, 92, 135

Barnes, Roger, 145
Barnett, Robert, 134, 157
Barshop, Ann, 113
Barshop, Sam, 113, 159
Barshop Natatorium, Ann, 158–59

Beauford, Judith, 160
Beeman, Mary, 81
Bell, Phil, 51
Bensman, Charles, 38, 39, 41, 108–09
Benson, Gayle, 188, 193, 199
Benson, Tom, 56, 90, 91, 187, 188, 192,
 193, 199
Benson Chair in Banking and Finance,
 90–91
Benson Stadium, Gayle and Tom, 188,
 192–93, 199, 200, 208
Bonilla, Henry, 183
Bowie, Mike, 25–26
Brackenridge, George, xi, 7
Brackenridge Villa, 7, 10, 40, 41, 49, 200
Bradley–McChesney, 45
Brainpower Connection/Senior
 Connection, 78–79, 81–82, 107–08,
 135, 190, 198
Briar Cliff College, 6, 23, 24, 34, 38, 39,
 46, 51, 68
Bromley, Ernest, 210
Bromley Communications, 210
Buckley, Antoninus, 9–11, 18–19, 21, 38,
 123–26, 128
Buckley Alumni Courtyard, Sister
 Antoninus, 85
Buckley/Mitchell Admissions Center, 128
Burke, Clarita, 77, 209–10
Burke, Sean, 26
Burr, Pat LeMay, 67–68, 81, 135, 157,
 158, 162, 168–69, 173, 178
Bush, George H. W., 69, 131
Bussineau-King, Deborah, 121
Bustamante, Albert, 66
Buzze;, Andrew, 208

Calgaard, Ron, 14–15, 38
Calvert, Velica, 207
Canterbury Hill House, 17–18, 105, 185
Carcanagues, Amy, 210
Cardea, Jane, 135–36
Cardinal Park, 209
Carlton, Bill, 98
Carmody, Edmond, 67, 122
Caroon-Santiago, Rochelle, 187–88
Carpenter, Stan, 129
Casanova, Itza, 95, 218
Casey, Rick, 52, 53
Casper, Danny, 187

CCVI Spirit Award, 98
Center for Fashion Design, Juren-Sullivan, 130–31, 151, 208
Center for Medical Tourism and Research, 208
Centro Universitario Incarnate Word, 168, 168–71, 173–74, 177, 188–89, 196, 198
Cervera Wellness Center, Richard and Janet, 86
Chang, Shu-Youan, 176
Cheever, Charles, 74
Chen, Juan (Misty), 177, 206
China Incarnate Word Education Center, 131–34, 154, 155–56, 157–58, 169, 174–75, 177
CHRISTUS Health Care, xi, 195
CHRISTUS Muguerza Hospital, 183–84, 208
Cibrian, David, 162
Cisneros, Henry, 38, 50, 51, 53, 61, 66–67, 79, 81, 95
Cisneros, Mercedes, 95
Clayton Fund, 65
Clingman, James Jr., 169, 170
Cockrell, Lila, 111
Cogdell, Edie, 189, 208
Colbert, Columkille, 7, 9, 37, 113
Commission on College/University Planning, 23, 30, 41, 109, 115, 144–45
Condos, Barbara, 38
Connelly, Bob, 85, 98, 110, 138, 139, 140–42, 144, 145, 207, 208
Corbin, Germaine 176, 209
Corpus Christi, TX, 211
Coughlin, Kathleen 160, 178, 181, 191, 206, 209, 210
Cowan, Ann Marie, 175, 207
Crain, Bill, 60, 61, 75, 84, 149
Craven, Annette, 191, 206
Creagan, James, 87, 210
Crosby, Kate, 102
Cyterski-Acosta, Andrea, 151, 181, 207

Dalton, Brian, 120
Daly, Shawn, 207, 208, 210
Daniel, Mary, 14
Davis, Josh, 158, 159
Davis, Mike, 159
De La Vega, Gabriela, 173, 189
Dean, Joe, 167, 171
Denman Estate, 209
Dicianna, Terry, 157, 162–63, 166–67,
168, 170, 171, 178, 181–82, 186, 190, 192, 196, 198, 207, 210
Ditloff, Scott, 178
Del Toro, Debra, 218
Dossmann, Ann, 14, 21, 23
Doyle, Denise, 67–68, 98, 99–104, 115, 126, 129, 135, 137, 138, 139, 141, 143, 145, 167, 190, 195, 196, 206
Draeger, Marge, 8–9, 11, 116, 134, 151
Draeger, Ralph, 151
Dreeben, Alan, 144, 161, 162, 166
Dreeben, Barbara, 161, 162
Drury, Thomas J., 53–54
Dunlap, Lillian, 38, 73, 85
Dymowski, Thomas, 199

Earl Abel's Restaurant, 25, 43, 60–61, 210
eArmyU, 152–53
Eccell, Raphael, 19–20, 109
Ehrenberg, Oscar, 111
Ellwanger, Jim, 46
Endsley, Doug, 98, 167, 179, 191, 206
Escamilla, Cindy Sanchez, 153, 191, 206
Escobedo, Rene, 209
Escobedo, Ruben, 4
Ettling, Dorothy, 39, 84, 130, 141, 206–07, 209
Ewers, Lorraine, 98, 218
Fanning, Buckner, 112
Fanning, Lisa, 112
Fedor, Damita, 151, 153
Feik, John, 168, 178, 179, 183, 186
Feik, Rita, 168, 178, 186
Feik School of Pharmacy, John and Rita, 162–63, 166–68, 178–79, 181, 186
Finn, Ann, 9, 11, 151, 185
Flores, Antonio, 170
Flores, Patrick, 39, 51, 56, 60, 105, 128
Football program, 120, 126, 187–88, 192–93
Fox, Lou, 87, 191, 206
Fragoso, Adriana, 198
Fragoso, Ana Julia, 198
Fragoso, Ivana, 198
Fragoso, Marcos, 174, 188–89, 190, 198, 206
Frank, Charles Marie, 86
Frank Nursing Building, Sister Charles Marie, 85–86
French, Thomas A., 54–55
Fry, Bobbye, 91, 153, 189, 208
Fu Jen Catholic University, 130

Gabrysh, Esther, 122
Gannon University, 45, 51, 59, 68
Garcia, Margaret, 218
Garriga, Mariano Simon, 7
Ghazi-Birry, Hani, 190, 191, 196
Gignac, Andrew, 121, 123
Gilliland, Irene, 178
Gokelmanm Bill, 121
Gomez, José, 186
Goodyear, AZ, 184
Goretti, Maria, 123, 209
Gorman, Jim, 165–66
Gorman, Tena, 165–66
Gorman Business and Education
    Center, 165
Gorman-Mitchell Room, 161
Gott, Adela, 218
Goulet, Caroline, 200, 208, 210
Gower, W. N., 73
Greenburg, S. Thomas, 7
Grossman, Burton E., 127–28, 149
Grossman, Miriam, 128
Grossman International Conference
    Center, Burton E., 111, 127–28, 170
Guiry, Michael, 208
Gwangju, South Korea, 209

H-E-B, 61, 200
Hall, Richard, 138
Halligan, Maureen, 54
Han, Daniel, 210
Hastings, Blake, 170
Hayes, Patricia, 18, 38, 45
Heidelberg, Germany, 210–11
Heidt, Herb, 45
Henderson, Richard, 130, 207
Henry Bonilla Science Hall, 183
Herrera, José, 208
Herron, Winell, 179
Hesburgh, Theodore M., 7
Heying, Steve, 46, 49, 56, 59–60, 101,
    124, 197, 198, 208
Higher Education Council of San
    Antonio, 14–15
Hillestad, Ann, 58
Hinojosa, Gilberto, 98, 118, 135, 185–
    86, 206
Hispanic Association of Colleges and
    Universities, 170
Hood, Mike, 218
Hu, Jimmy, 210
Hua Li University, 175
Hudson, Tom, 129, 130

Hyland, Rosita, 110

Incarnate Word College, see University
    of the Incarnate Word
Incarnate Word Day, 37
Incarnate Word Health Care System, 65
Incarnate Word High School, xii, 74–78,
    81–82, 92, 94–95, 101, 106, 108, 128, 209
Incarnate Word House, 14
Insigne Verbum award, 55, 169
Institute of World Cultures, 177
International Association of Business
    Communicators, 59
International Costume Carnival,
    130–31

Jackson, Sara, 178
James, Glenn, 182, 206, 207, 208
James, Mary, 127
Johnny's Bridge, 106, 124–25
Johnson-Fannin, Arcelia, 171–72, 179,
    186, 207
Jokerst, Carol Ann, 84, 121, 123
Joeris, Gary, 199
Jones, Earl, 7
Jones, Mary Elaine, 197
Jordan Carillon, 136
Jordan, Marjorie Ann, 136
Joyce, Mary Elizabeth, 136
Joyce Building, 136
Junior Chamber of Commerce, 68–69
Juren, Dennis, 145, 151, 152
Juren, Ruth, 151
Jurenovich, Christian, 206
Jurenovich, David, 67, 68, 92, 115,
    120, 126, 134, 141, 151, 154, 190,
    191, 193, 206
Jurenovich, Matthew, 206

Kasraie, Noah, 207
Katherine Ryan Development Center,
    49, 78, 83–84, 106
Kathleen Watson Enrollment Center, 151
KCOR, 29, 31
Keaveney, Agnes, 77, 209
Keaveney, Ailbe, 77, 209
Kenedy Foundation, 55
KENS-TV, 31–32
Kilpatrick, Charles O., 29–30, 32, 56, 74
Kimel, Howard, 129
Kimmel, Jessica, 160
King, Pam, 110
Kirk, Martha Ann, 176, 209

Klingbacher, Martin, 104, 210
KLRN-TV, 33
Korean Pavilion, 209
KTSA–KTFM, 60
Kumamoto, Japan, 61–62, 81, 128
Kumamoto Gakuen University, 62, 127–29
KWEX-TV, 27, 29, 31, 33

La Quinta Reservation Center, 92, 103
Labat, Roger, 77, 101, 107, 108, 208
Lauder, Ann, 210
Lee, Amy Freeman, 4, 7, 17, 38, 39, 64,
    84, 108, 149
Leopold, Mary Ann, 108
Lesuik, Teresa, 110
Light, Kathi, 98, 121, 135, 183, 195, 196,
    197, 198, 201, 206, 208
Light the Way, 21, 50–51, 59–61, 102,
    185, 200, 208
Littlewood, Harry, 175
Lodek, John, 17–18, 136, 185
Lomas, Yolanda, 95
Lonchar, Pat, 22, 81
Lopez, Alejandra Espinosa, 189
LoPorto, Kimberley, 159
Lozano, Javier, 210

M-Bank, 45
Mabee Charitable Foundation, 98
Mabee Library, J. E. and L. E., 98, 109,
    185, 191
Mabry Tennis Center, Clarence, 110
Maher, Walter, 90, 183, 191, 206, 209
Maloney, Pat, 58
Martinez, José, 210
Martinez, José E., 131
Martinez, Marisol R., 218
Mary Grove College, 48
Maverick, Maury Jr., 57–58, 64
Mayol, Anne Therese, 94, 95
McCabe, Hugh, 18, 22, 30
McCarthy, Jerry, 59, 83
McChesney–Bianco, 45
McChesney, Mike, 45, 57, 105, 161, 168,
    187, 199, 209
McCombs, Charline, 165
McCombs, Red, 15–16, 60, 165
McCombs Center, 165, 199
McCracken, Richard J., 4, 6, 11, 13, 24,
    54, 57–58, 60, 75, 89, 95, 105, 121, 122
    123, 136, 174, 185, 206; Assistant to
    the President, 33, 42–43, 50, 51; Dean
    of Alumni, 59, 151

McDermott, Alice, 67
McDermott, Robert, 67, 74
McDermott Convocation Center, 66–67
McLain, Donald, 39
McMakin, Sandy, 207
Mead, George, 4, 39
Mengden, Carol, 82, 108
Mexico City campus, see Centro
    Universitario Incarnate Word
Migura, Amy, 198
Millennium Vision 2000, 116–19
Miller, Ila Faye, 201
Miller, John, 200, 201. 218
Miller, Vladimira, 201
Miraflores Park, 179
Mitchell, Dolores, 67, 84, 86
Mitchell, Robert, 131
Mitchell, Sally, 23–24, 128, 190, 206
Moll, Marilyn, 32
Moll, William G., 31–33, 43, 56
Monahan, Helena, 50, 58, 67, 85, 89, 95,
    96, 97, 98–99, 116, 121, 149–50, 152,
    166, 179, 185, 191, 192, 195, 196, 197,
    200, 202, 206, 209
Montalvo, Roberto, 218
Montford, John, 179
Moore, Renee, 102, 107, 207
Morgan, Jean Marie, 191
Morgan, Mendell, 98, 185, 191
Mueller, Mary Lou, 47
Mulcahy, Bill, 209
Mulnix, Michael, 186
Nath, Lopita, 178
Nelsen, B. J., 209
Nelson, Art, 163
Newman, John, 110
Nicholas, Richard, 23, 24
Nicolas, Emilio, 56
North San Antonio Chamber of
    Commerce, 169–70, 171
Nowak, Paul, 136

O'Connor, Bernadette, 98
O'Connor, Peter, 22–23, 30, 47
O'Mahoney, Audrey, 47, 183, 186, 207
O'Malley, Dennis, 61
O'Neill, Mary Boniface, 122
Oblates of Mary Immaculate, 107, 169
Ochoa, Dan, 169, 190–91, 207
Office of Institutional Advancement,
    159–60
Omar, Husam, 206
Omar, Mohsen, 175, 206

...ula, Catheryn, 198
Ottiz, Jeanne, 101
Our Lady of the Lake University, 26
Ozturgut, Osman, 175, 207

Paderon, Eduardo, 109, 115, 118–20, 122, 134, 138–39, 141, 143, 144, 157
Palo Alto College, 65, 157
Papich, Mike, 187, 192
Paul Daher Computing Center, 86
Pawel, Nancy, 56
Ping, Wang, 156
Platzer, Bill, 85, 118
Plofchan, Paula, 48, 82
Plofchan, Tom, 48–49, 55, 82, 89, 98, 104, 121, 159–60, 167
Pontililo, Peter, 107
Porter, Cyndi, 143, 144, 152–53, 167, 184, 188, 190, 206
Porter, Vince, 184, 190, 207
Power, Alacoque, 7, 74, 195
Power, Theophane, 54–55
President's Advisory Council, 82–83, 116
President's Scholarship Find, 37
President's Spaghetti Dinner, 51, 52, 59

Ramirez, Patricia, 210
Rangel, Jesus, 87
Ray, John, 13–14, 16, 24, 30, 45, 47, 98
Reaching for the Global Perspective, 116, 119–20
Richards, Ann, 95–96
Risku, Michael, 176
Roberts, Kenneth, 163
Robinson, David, 153
Rocheleau, Jim, 99–100, 103
Rodriguez, Oscar, 173–74, 189
Rodriguez, Raul, 87, 192
Rodriguez, Vincent, 33, 150, 153, 191, 206
Rogers Cable, 60
Romay, Luz, 155, 162, 173
Rose, Richard, 91, 190
Rosenberg, Sandra, 165, 200–01
Rosenberg, Stanley, 165, 186, 196, 200–01
Rosenberg Sky Room, 165, 201, 208
Run for Brainpower, 84–85
Russ, Rita, 190, 207, 210
Ryan, Bob, 157, 207
Ryan, Eilish, 39, 209
Ryan, Nolan, 157

St. Anthony Catholic High School, 106–08, 169, 190–91, 209, 210

St. Anthony's Elementary School, 76, 83–84, 108, 210
St. Clair, Bobbie, 134, 155–56, 175
St. Clair, Norman, 134, 152, 155–56, 157–58, 174, 175, 207
St. Joseph's Convent, 110–11
St. Mary's of the Plains College, 38, 59
St. Mary's University, 26, 43, 47
St. Peter–St. Joseph's Children's Home, xi, 75
St. Peter Prince of the Apostles School, 11, 78, 108, 198, 210
St. Philip's College, 65, 195
Saegert, Merry, 63
Sahin, Ali, 155
Saidoff Center, Debbie and Naty, 208
San Antonio College, 64
San Antonio Express-News, 29–30
San Antonio Jaycees, 53
San Antonio Light, 29
San Antonio River headwaters, 51, 56–58, 183
San Antonio Spurs, 67, 161
Santa Rosa Hospital, 65, 75
Santiago, Mike, 187–88, 192, 193
School of Business and Administration, H-E-B, 134, 169, 173, 192, 207, 210
School of Education, Dreeben, 134, 135, 161, 168, 173
School of Graduate Studies and Research, 135, 185
School of Humanities, Arts and Social Sciences, 98
School of Interactive Media and Design, 170, 191
School of Nursing and Health Professions, Ila Faye Miller, xii, 64–66, 73–74, 85–86, 98, 109, 132, 134, 183–84, 196–98, 201–02, 208
School of Optometry, Sandra and Stanley Rosenberg, 182–83, 191–92, 195, 201
School of Physical Therapy, 208
School of Science, Mathematics and Engineering, 135, 182–83
School of the Americas, 82
Schultz, Lisa, 206
Schurter, William, 160, 161
Segovia, Gino, 218
Semmes Art Gallery, Douglas and Donna, 98
Senne-Duff, Beth, 188–89
Seyedin, Harley, 131, 154, 155

Shaw, Laura, 160
Short, Gary, 107, 108
Sinkfield, Carolin, 207
Sisters of Charity of the Incarnate Word, 3, 5, 16, 35, 37, 42
Slattery, Margaret Patrice, 14, 37, 40, 49, 67, 91 113, 121, 142–43, 145, 159, 209; president, 3, 7–8, 90–91; chancellor, 39, 54–55, 183
Slattery Leadership Center, Sister Margaret Patrice, 209
Smiley, Mona, 68
Soefje, Lois, 135–36
Sorenson, Jim, 135, 136, 184
Sosa, Lionel, 17, 24–27, 84, 90, 99, 125, 173, 210; advertising barter campaign, 24–36; The College campaign, 31, 42–43, 47, 49, 51, 52, 56, 60, 63, 79, 93, 117
Sosa, Robert, 159–60
South China Normal University, 132, 155, 174
Southwestern Bell, 60
Sports complex, 50
Stanley, Teresa, 145, 186
Staubach, Jennifer, 50
Staubach, Roger, 50, 56
Staudt, Denise, 173, 207
Sullivan, Daniel, 84–85, 90
Sullivan, Ruth Eileen, 84–85, 151
Sullivan Field, 84, 90
Summit on Decision Making, 139–40
Sun Hui, 132, 155
Swatzell, Steve, 184
Swofford, Mary Beth, 58

Tainan Woman's College, 130
Tarango, Yolanda, 122–23
Target 90, 24, 30
Tas, Murat, 175, 176
Taylor, Alana, 210
Tehan, Mickey 160, 161
Thompson, Annette, 218
Thompson, Paul, 63
Thuss, Emily, 186
Tilton, Jim, 81, 116, 127, 134, 149, 159
Torres, Patsy, 200
Traylor, D. Reginald, 97–99, 109, 118, 126, 129, 135, 138, 143, 144, 193
Trinity University, 14, 38
Turner, Sue Ann, 86

UIW Eastside Center for Visual Science and Health Care, 208
University of Michigan–Flint, 3, 4
University of Monterrey, 183
University of Pittsburgh, 59
University of the Incarnate Word, as Incarnate Word College, xi-xii, 5, 7, 10, 110, 115–17; name origin, 37; name change, 115–19, 123; student demographics, 25, 34, 210–11; San Antonio off-campus degree programs, 71, 73, 99–104; foreign student exchange, 79, 93; doctoral programs, 129–30, 175, 195, 197, 198–99; rankings, xii, 85, 90, 126, 161
Ursuline Academy, 94–95

Van de Putte, Leticia, 179
Van Straten, Jim, 51, 57, 58–59, 76–77, 195
Vequist, David, 208
Veterinary, school, 181–82
Vichcales, Kevin, 185–86, 195, 207
Village of Avoca, 53–54
Virtual University, 143, 144, 152. 153–54
Vrla, Brooklyn Michaeline, 205
Vrla, Bryan, 205
Vrla, Nancy Agnese, 8, 18–19, 23, 38, 49, 78, 86—87, 105–06, 128, 169, 205

Walker, Joy Ann 109–10
Walker, Larry, 56
Wallace, Brian, 168
Waller, Jim, 178
Walsh, Annemarie, 130–31
Waterman, Bernard, 56
Watkins, Patricia A., 33, 67–68, 76–78, 96–97, 107, 118, 131–33, 136, 155–58, 173–74, 177, 179, 189, 191, 198, 207
Watson, Kathleen, 121, 122, 151
Watson, Mark, 151
Welkley, Sharon, 191, 207, 208, 210
Wesser, Patsy, 26
Wheeler, Sterling, 7
Whitehouse, Matthew, 198
Windcrest, 21
Women's Global Connections, 207
Wu, Meng Hsun, 176

Zehr, Maria Goretti, 121

ACKNOWLEDGMENTS

This book reflects the hard work of many people in and outside of the Incarnate Word community. It would have been impossible without their constant help and support.

Vince Rodriguez, Bill Moll and Dick McCracken have already been mentioned, but now Vince joins me in singling out several others for their extraordinary efforts.

Marisol Ramos Martinez and Mike Hood of the UIW graphic design office. They both endured a barrage of phone calls and emails for help with the photos—locating them, scanning them, creating contact sheets and adjusting the quality of several borderline photos. They took our man-tra—"This really is the last photo request"—in stride and with good hu-mor, as did Debra Del Toro and Margaret Garcia of the public relations office. We're also grateful to Debra and Margaret for securing permission from the San Antonio *Express-News* for the use of the cartoon and several archival photos.

Adela Gott of the instructional technology office. She provided equipment and assistance for the taped interviews with Lou. John Miller and Gino Segovia from convergent media services and Melvin Arnell of technical support services also answered frequent SOS calls during tech-nology crises.

Our critic readers—Lionel Sosa, Dr. Bob Connelly, Sister Audrey O'Mahony, Dick McCracken and Cindy Escamilla. Thanks for taking time out of your busy schedules to provide us with insightful comments.

Damita Fedor. As Lou's Executive Assistant she helped open many use-ful doors, answering endless questions and sharing contact information.

Dr. Roberto Montalvo. His technical support and research expertise saved many hours, as did the willing searches of Lorraine Ewers, Itza Ca-sanova, Annette Thompson and the archive staff of the Sisters of Charity of the Incarnate Word.

A final thank you goes to all those who shared their memories and photographs in order to bring the past twenty-five years back into focus.